A Relational Data Base
Management System

WILEY SERIES IN COMPUTING

Consulting Editor
Professor D. W. Barron, *Department of Mathematics, Southampton University*

Numerical Control – Mathematics and Applications

P. Bézier

Communication Networks for Computers

D. W. Davies and D. L. A. Barber

Macro Processors and Techniques for Portable Software

P. J. Brown

A Practical Guide to Algol 68

Frank G. Pagan

Programs and Machines

Richard Bird

The Codasyl Approach to Data Base Management

T. William Olle

Computer Networks and their Protocols

D. W. Davies, D. L. A. Barber, W. L. Price and C. M. Solomonides

Algorithms: Their Complexity and Efficiency

Lydia Kronsjö

Data Structures and Operating Systems

Teodor Rus

Writing Interactive Compilers and Interpreters

P. J. Brown

A Relational Data Base Management System

A. T. F. Hutt

Ronald C. Nelson
7/12/80

A Relational Data Base Management System

A. T. F. Hutt
International Computers Limited

A Wiley–Interscience Publication

JOHN WILEY & SONS
Chichester · New York · Brisbane · Toronto

British Library Cataloguing in Publication Data

Hutt, A. T. F.
A relational data base management system. – (Wiley series in computing).
1. Management information systems
2. File organization (Computer science)
I. Title
658.4′03 T58.6 79-40516

ISBN 0 471 27612 X

Typeset in Pacesetter Mark 4 Times by Pintail Studios Ltd., Ringwood, Hampshire and printed in Great Britain by Page Bros (Norwich) Ltd., Norwich, Norfolk

To

Anne, Betty,
and Frank Hutt

Contents

Preface

In 1973, the Television Service of the British Broadcasting Corporation, together with International Computers Limited and Southampton University, established a bursary at the University to investigate ways of using data base techniques to produce large management information systems. This work resulted in the design and partial implementation of the Relational Data Base Management System which is described in this book.

The origins of this work date back to 1969 when the Computer Department of the BBC's Television Service, under Mr. C. Lashmar, built the first release of the Television Management Information System. The purpose of the system was to maintain records of the costs incurred while producing television programmes, and to provide details of the costs to those involved in the work. Once this system was in service, user reaction led to the production of several subsequent versions which led to a point, in mid-1972, when further system developments were dependent on the use of better concepts and more advanced methods. Once this situation was recognized Mr Lashmar approached ICL and Southampton University with a proposal for a jointly sponsored bursary aimed at finding a practical solution to these problems. Such a bursary had advantages for all the parties involved: it offered the incumbent and Southampton University the opportunity to do research in a comparatively untouched field of study; and, if successful, it provided the BBC with a solution to its problems, and ICL with a contribution to its product line. It says much for the foresight of Professor Barron at Southampton and Mr T. J. Brooks of ICL that most of these hopes have been fulfilled.

At the present time, Autumn 1978, the Relational Data Base Management System (RDBMS) is a research vehicle which has been used to implement a number of trial information systems for a wide variety of organizations. It is expected that the system will be turned into a product, an operation which may involve large-scale changes and restructuring. The objective of this book is to report on the research work undertaken by the joint bursary and to record the design of the system in the form in which it was originally conceived.

As will become apparent, RDBMS is unlikely to be packaged as a single product aimed at a single group of users. It is more likely to form the basis of a spectrum of products aimed at meeting a wide variety of user needs. For example, it is possible to visualize a version of RDBMS aimed at satisfying the personal information needs of an individual user or a small group of co-workers. It is also possible to visualize a version of RDBMS capable of satisfying the corporate information needs of a large organization. Once it is remembered that a large number of people are also interested in the intellectual niceties of the relational data model, it is then apparent that this book may have a very wide readership, with wide-ranging computer skills. In order to match this wide appeal, the book contains all the basic material needed to understand a relational data base management system.

The material has been divided into four main parts. Part A briefly reminds the reader of the problems which need to be overcome when undertaking the design and implementation of an information system. It outlines the facilities supported by a relational data base management system and shows how such a system can be used to tackle information system problems. Part B describes a unified approach to the design and implementation of a large information system. This approach is presented as a recipe which separates the task into a number of steps, each with a well-defined objective, and clearly identifies the design decisions which are appropriate to each step. Part C describes a family of languages which allow users to interact with an Information System which takes the form of a relational data base. The final part, Part D, describes some of the techniques used in the implementation of the system and contains an appraisal of the system. The book is completed by a bibliography in which details of all the references cited in the text will also be found.

A Note on Terminology

The history of the relational data model has been bedevilled by problems with the relational terminology. Throughout this book the traditional relational data model terms: relation, tuple, attribute, and domain, have been replaced by the terms: entity set, entity, attribute and domain. The primary reason for this change is that it lets the term relation retain its usual mathematical meaning. A secondary reason for the change is that, as will become apparent in Part B, where necessary, it is possible to assign extra meaning to the term entity set.

Acknowledgements

There remains only the pleasant task of acknowledging the help I have received while carrying forward this work. I am firstly grateful to International Computers Limited, the Television Service of the British Broadcasting Corporation, Southampton University, the Science Research Council, and the National Research and Development Corporation for funding the work. I would also like to thank the staff drawn from these organizations who have acted as the project's steering committee; these include Mr C. Lashmar, Mr T. Smith, and Mr R. Pikett of the BBC Television Service, Mr T. J. Brooks, Mr G. C. A. Eyles, and Mr N. D. Hill of ICL, Mr K. Cunningham of the NRDC, and Professor D. W. Barron of Southampton University. I owe a special debt to Professor Barron who, together with Mr M. R. Must, provided me with a good deal of help, guidance, and encouragement in the course of my studentship. I would like to thank Mr T.

Gilham, Mr D. Waldridge, Mrs N. Stokes, and Mr P. Grave who have helped to produce parts of the system software. In addition to the above-mentioned who have had a direct hand in this work, many others have helped the project on its way. These include computer operators who have run the ICL 1906A computer at the Science Research Council's Rutherford Laboratory at Chilton, the users of the system who have struggled with its idiosyncracies, and a committee of senior managers within ICL who helped keep the project in being. To them all I offer my thanks.

The author wishes to thank International Computers Limited for agreeing to the publication of this book and for providing encouragement and assistance in order to bring it to completion.

Parts of two papers published in *Software Practice and Experience* (HUTT 4, HUTT 5) are reproduced in Chapter 20 by permission of John Wiley & Sons Ltd.

In preparing this book I would like to thank Professor Barron and Mr A. P. G. Brown who have read and commented on the earlier drafts. I would also like to give thanks to the typing pool under Mrs B. Jones who have undertaken the typing of the manuscripts.

Finally, I would like to thank my wife and family who have encouraged and supported me throughout the project.

ANDREW HUTT
Wokingham, Berkshire
December 1978

Part A

INTRODUCTION

1

Information and Its Users

Every organization, whether large or small, uses an Information System to maintain that kernel of information which is vital to its existence; these Informations Systems vary from the most primitive systems based on the backs of envelopes to systems which use vast complexes of computer hardware and software. Significant systems within this wide spectrum are:

1. *Pencil and Paper Systems*, which rely on pencil and paper techniques and the extensive use of filing cabinets.
2. *Batch Computer Systems*, which receive information on some input medium such as punched cards and output information on pre-defined listings and reports.
3. *Interactive Systems*, which rely on the extensive use of interactive terminals and allow users to interact directly with the information they require.
4. *Reactive Systems*, which are similar to Interactive Systems in so far as they rely on the extensive use of interactive terminals and allow users to interact directly with the information they require; however, they have the added property that they are sensitive to the needs of the organization and are thus capable of highlighting those situations where actions or decisions are necessary.

Given this spectrum of Information Systems, this book is primarily concerned with creating Interactive Information Systems; however, it is recognized that the techniques which are to be described could be used to produce Batch or Reactive Information Systems.

1.1 Information within an Organization

It is apparent that within any organization the totality of its information may be subdivided into a number of groups. Figure 1.1 illustrates that these groupings are typically:

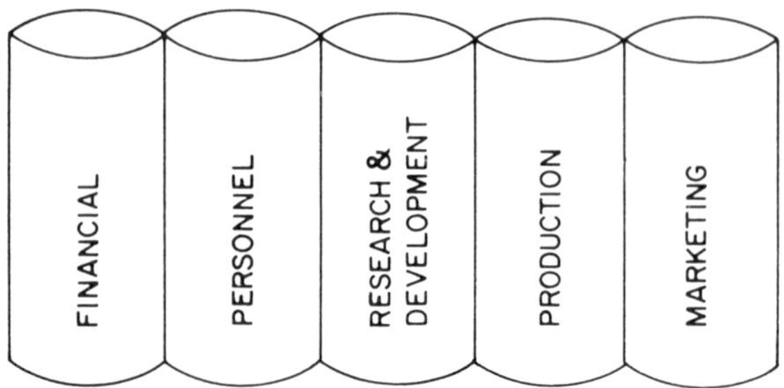

Figure 1.1 The information within an Organization

1. *Financial Information*, which defines the internal and external cash flow of the organization together with its external borrowings and loans.
2. *Personnel Information*, which describes the staff and related personnel.
3. *Research Development Information.*
4. *Production Information*, which is very much dependent on the type of business. For example, for a Television Company, this describes the programmes being produced and transmitted and the resources used in these activities.
5. *Marketing Information.*

1.2 Users of Information

In addition to identifying the information associated with an organization, it is also necessary to identify the users of that information. These users are the management of the organization, and they are traditionally represented as being separated into a number of levels depending on the significance of their decisions with respect to the overall progress of the organization. Typical levels of management, and thus potential system users, are:

1. *Senior Managers and Planners*, which encompasses the organization's leaders and long term planners.
2. *The Middle Management*, which encompasses all those leaders responsible for the year to year planning and leadership.
3. *The Operational Management*, which encompasses all those responsible for the month by month planning and leadership.
4. *The Supervisors*, which is concerned with the day to day leadership and management.

These levels are illustrated in Figure 1.2.

Note: The number of levels of user associated with a particular Information

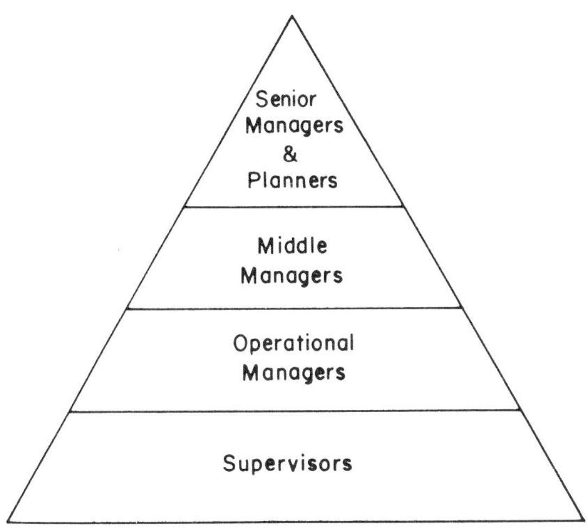

Figure 1.2 A typical hierarchy of Information users

System is dependent on the complexity and size of the organization, and there are many organizations which work happily using three or, sometimes, two levels of leadership, and thus levels of system user.

1.3 Building an Information System

With a fair idea of the overall shape of an organization, we are faced with the problem of defining an Information System which embodies part of the organization's information and serves a group of users. With this in mind, we are expecting to produce Information Systems which may:

1. Embody all or part of a particular set of information and serve all the users of that information.
2. Serve a complete level of users and give them access to all the information they need.
3. Serve a small group of users and give them access to some of the information they need.

Figure 1.3 illustrates the overall effectiveness of Information Systems which satisfy these objectives.

Given that the main objective is to create a computer-based Information System which contains a particular kernel of information and serves a particular group of users, then there are many ways of carrying out the job, the exact choice being dependent on the many user facilities which are needed. However, nobody should undertake this task without recognizing two important facts. Firstly, the information which is to be held in an Information System is one of the vital assets which must be exploited by the organization in order to survive, and consequently

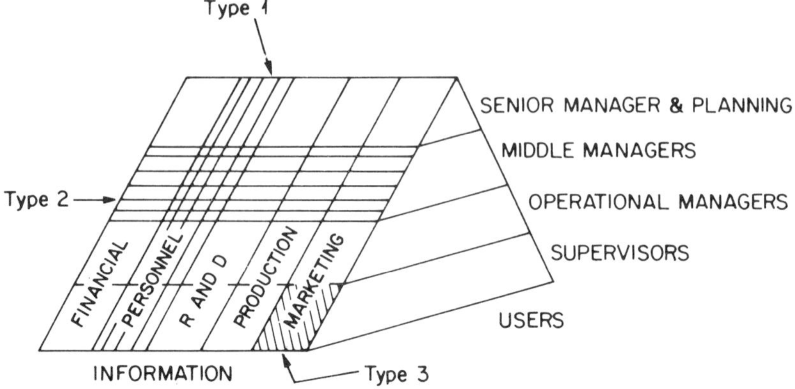

Figure 1.3 Information Systems serving Information to users

care must be taken to ensure that the information is not locked away merely because it cannot be accessed. Secondly, the storage, manipulation, and presentation of information is a costly business. Recognizing these two facts has led to a requirement for a system which satisfies four criteria.

1. It should embody a discipline to assist in the identification, definition, and control of information as an asset which can be exploited by the organization.
2. It should provide a user interface where an Information System is represented as a relational data base, and facilities to allow programs and users on terminals to interact with that data base.
3. It should embody control features to prevent users from abusing the system.
4. It should support monitoring facilities and simulation modelling features to enable the cost of using the system to be assessed.

These features, together with the many other facilities required to build Information Systems, have been integrated to form the nucleus of a system known as the Relational Data Base Management System (RDBMS) which is the subject of the rest of this book.

2

The Role of an Information System

An Information System provides an organization with a mechanism whereby users can assess information; it should also provide the organization with a discipline for identifying information. As an Information System can impinge directly on all those who use it, it is necessary to understand its relationship with both the real world which surrounds it and with its users who necessarily live in that real world.

2.1 The Field of Perception of an Information System

Abrial (see ABRIAL 1) showed that when designing or using an Information System, the designer or user has to distinguish between that part of the real world which is reflected in the system and that which is not. That part of the real world which is to be reflected in the system is said to lie within the *Field of Perception* of the system and may be called the *Perceived Field* of the system. This is illustrated in Figure 2.1.

When designing an Information System, the designer has to decide on the size of the Perceived Field, and there have been a number of cases where large corporations have set off to produce an Information System and decided on a Field of Perception which included the whole corporation. The result was two

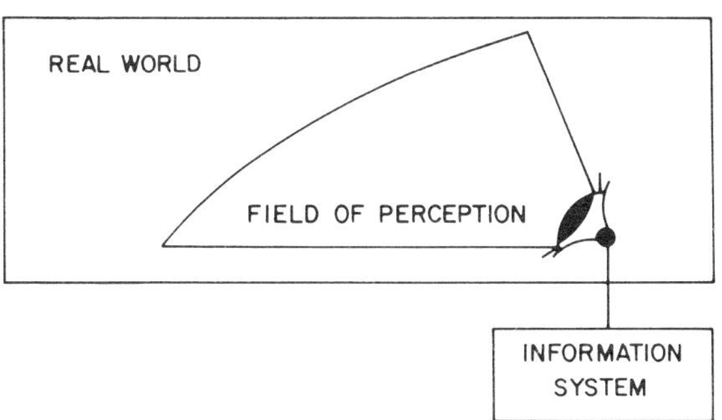

Figure 2.1 The Field of Perception of an Information System

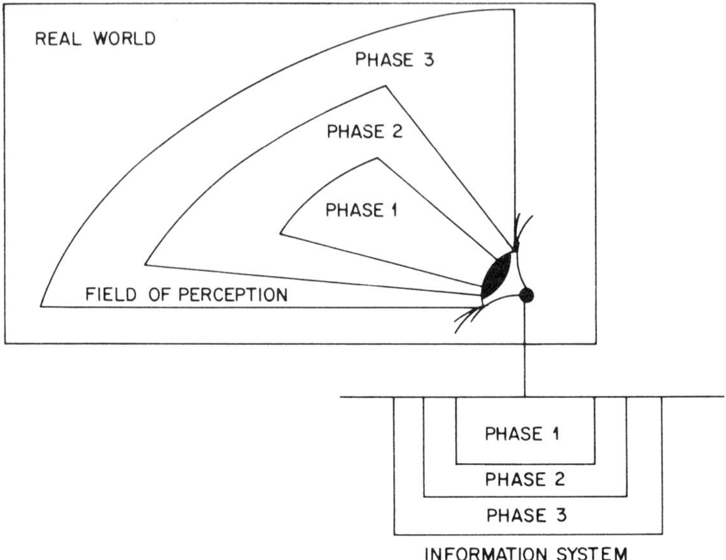

Figure 2.2 Phased expansions of a Field of Perception

years of design but no Information System and the single reason for this was that the Perceived Field was too big. Thus, a system designer should think of the Field of Perception growing via a number of phased expansions of the Information System. This approach is illustrated in Figure 2.2 and has a number of advantages. Firstly, it is more cost effective because it enables all users to gain experience slowly, and, secondly, it is more realistic because building enormous Information Systems takes a long time. However, this approach does demand that the underlying data base management system must permit piece-wise development.

2.2 The Users of an Information System

Having recognized that an Information System contains a distillation of the information from the real world surrounding it, it is now necessary to identify those users or user groups who have an interest in that information.

A quick look round an Information System shows that there are several classes of users associated with it. These are:

System Designers

These are users who are responsible for the actual design of the Information System and for the implementation of the data base management system used to support it. System designers are responsible for coordinating the formal definition of the Information System, for inputting this definition to the data base system and for creating the Information System.

Information System Operations Staff

This group of users must not be confused with computer operators, although they have a similar role. Whereas computer operators are responsible for the operation of the hardware and operating system, the Information System's operations staff are responsible for the Information System. They are responsible for maintaining consistent copies of the information and for the coordination of error checking and error recovery, which may involve the underlying hardware system, the data base management system, and, in extreme circumstances, the cooperation of end-users.

End-Users

These are users who actually use the information from the system. In the first instance, they have interests which lie outside the realms of the computer system. Codd (in papers CODD 6 and CODD 7) identified several categories of end-user depending on their involvement with the system. These groups in order of involvement are:

Casual Users These are users who only make intermittent use of an Information System and therefore cannot be expected to be able to use a formal system interface which requires the user to remember interface rules. Codd recognized that such users should be able to interact through a system interface which gives the impression of being similar to a natural language enquiry interface.

Parametric Users These are users who use the Information System to carry out routine tasks, such as inputting product details to a Stock Control System. These users make continual use of a standard system interface and thus need that interface to be tailor made to their specialist requirements.

Information Specialists These are users whose normal task is to use the system to generate information applicable to particular decisions. These users need to have a thorough understanding of the information held in the system, together with the mechanisms available to manipulate it.

RDBMS has been designed to directly support information system designers, the information system operations staff, parametric end-users, and information specialists. Furthermore, it has been designed to provide a platform for constructing systems to support casual users.

2.3 The Relationship between an Information System and RDBMS

Traditionally, an Information System consists of a suite of application programs using data supplied from a data base supported by a data base management system. This arrangement is illustrated in Figure 2.3.

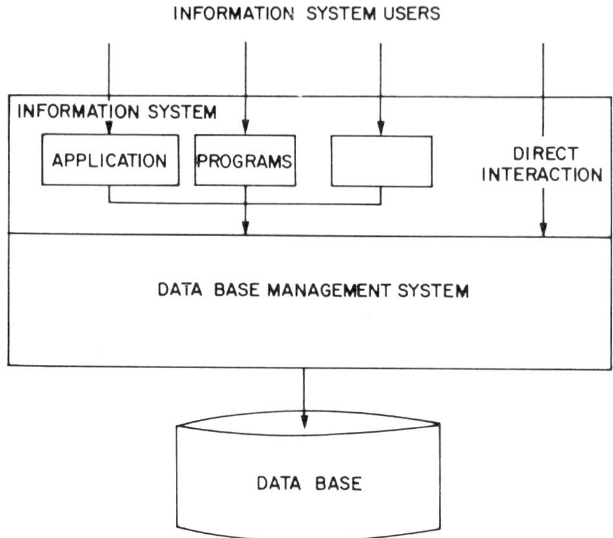

Figure 2.3 The traditional relationship between an Information System and a DBMS

The advent of the stand-alone data base management system has led to the development of Information Systems with no application programs; the whole of the Information System is generated from the data base management system. However, since it is not possible to generate the specialist algorithms required by the Information System, these data base management systems provide some means of adding these algorithms to their existing software.

RDBMS has been developed primarily as a stand-alone data base management system, but it does provide interfaces for application programs. As a stand-alone system it provides facilities whereby the designer of an Information System can incorporate his specialist algorithms within the RDBMS software. In the first instance these facilities are used to incorporate these algorithms required to perform integrity checks on the information to be held in the Information System. This ensures that information input, either directly via an interactive terminal, or via an application program, passes the same integrity checks. Given that application programs are no longer required to handle these integrity constraints, then it is apparent that most application programs are written either to perform specialist algorithms or to produce specialist outputs. RDBMS provides facilities whereby algorithms in these two classes can be incorporated in the system and invoked via a data manipulation language by end-users. Again, this approach attempts to ensure that algorithms necessary for the presentation of information are incorporated within the data base management system.

Obviously, there is a class of user written application programs which cannot be incorporated within the data base management system; such applications are treated using traditional methods. Figure 2.4 illustrates these facilities supported by RDBMS.

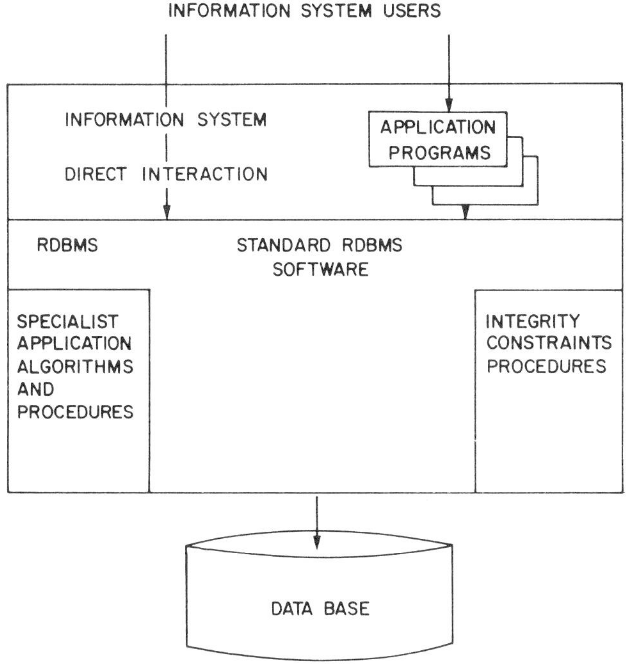

Figure 2.4 Relating an Information System to RDBMS

2.4 Help to System Users

Having briefly identified the users of the system it is vital to recognize that each group of users requires some help and assistance from their Information System. In practice this means that the data base management system used to support the Information System has to support these users too.

It is in this question of support to users that this system takes a different approach to some of those currently available. Basically, it has been recognized that the system must provide the following:

1. *Evidence that it is working correctly.* End-users need to know that any information they entrust to the system is validated according to the rules defined in the system description, and furthermore protected from felons and system malfunction. System designers need to know that their system descriptions are translated correctly and that the system has successfully found all the data base procedures and other own code it requires. Lastly, operation staff require statistics and other information to confirm or refute error reports produced by end-users and system designers.

2. *Facilities to subset information.* It is usually assumed that data base management systems provide comprehensive facilities for end-users to produce subsets of their information. It is also recognized that as system descriptions become

larger and more difficult to comprehend, so system designers need to be able to produce similar summaries and subsets of the system description. The data base management system must provide comprehensive facilities to manipulate the end-users' information, the system description, and the run-time statistics and reports.

3. *Facilities for costing system usage.* As end-users come to rely on the Information System and thus use it more regularly, it is necessary to provide some costing mechanism to prevent unruly use and wanton waste of the data base management system.

4. *Facilities for monitoring system usage.* As systems evolve, then from time to time bottlenecks will develop and system designers will need to detect and cure them before they can damage the end-user community. Such bottlenecks can be identified by monitoring system usage.

3

Describing an Information System

This chapter summarizes the Design Methodology associated with RDBMS and discusses the Multi-Level Schema.

3.1 Why Levels of Description?

One of the features of a large operational Information System is that the full description is both large and cumbersome. This affects the system's users in several ways. Firstly, while the system is being designed the system designer cannot produce the complete description in a single step, and needs some milestones to help him on his way. Chapter 2 introduced the concept of phased expansions of the Field of Perception as one possible solution to this problem, but within any single phased expansion the task is still too large for a single step, so there is still a need for milestones. Secondly, once the system is operational, end-users and operations staff (and systems designers) will require summaries of the description in order to investigate particular problems. Thirdly, during the operational life of a particular phase of a large system there is a need to be able to redesign parts of the system without affecting the rest. For example, when designing a data structure, the system designer may consider that a particular inverted file structure will meet the end-user's needs. However, if there is a change in these needs, then some other structure may be preferable. In this situation, the designers must be able to redesign the data structure without affecting the rest of the system.

Naturally, all these requirements lead to a demand for a System Description which embodies several different subdivisions of the total description. This now raises the problem of how to subdivide the Systems Description. The approach which has been adopted is firstly to subdivide the description of an Information System into a number of phased expansions of the Field of Perception, and secondly, within a particular phased expansion, to separate the description into six levels. These six levels of descriptions are ordered in such a way that it is possible to define a Design Methodology which provides an ordered progression through the design at each level. It is an important feature of the Design Methodology that any level of description can be redesigned, in which case this should not affect the design decisions made in an earlier level although it may invalidate those made at a later level.

3.2 The Design Methodology

The need to provide an iterative design process and to provide levels of the System Description has led to a multi-step Design Methodology where each step has a well-defined objective. These objectives are statements of the following:

1. *The Object Environment.* The designers start by identifying the perceived field of the new Information System and define the real world objects which exist within it. Having achieved this, the designers then identify the information which is associated with those objects. A formalization of the objects and information results in the Object Environment.
2. *The Information Environment.* Having completed the Object Environment, the designers define a number of entity sets, which are relations defined in Third Normal Form. These entity sets should be defined so as to model the Object Environment as closely as possible.
3. *The Encoded Environment.* Once they have defined the Information Environment, the systems designers are now in a position to consider the usage of that environment. In the first instance, this entails producing a statement of the most frequent requests for information, together with details of the amount of information to be processed. From this the system designer may either design a number of encoded entity sets which will satisfy the workload or use a data base monitor to simulate the effect on the system and thus identify the required encoded entity sets. This results in a definition of the first Encoded Environment. Once this has been used, the system will itself monitor the end-users' requests and thus produce statistics which will allow either automatic or system designer-assisted changes to be made to this environment which will thus improve the effectiveness of the system.
4. *The Stored Environment.* Once they have defined the Encoded Environment the system designers have defined the contents and rates of use of the encoded entity sets. They are now in a position to design the indexes, and identify the storage structures and the mappings required to support this level of activity. The result of this work is to define a number of stored entity sets which are to be maintained by the lowest levels of the system.
5. *The External Environment.* The Information Environment contains a number of entity sets which model the Object Environment as closely as possible. The External Environment contains a number of views of these entity sets which represent the data needs of particular groups of system users. These views are expressed using the normal languages supported by the system.
6. *The Software Environment.* All the other environments are concerned with the

definition of data and the identification of software which operates on this data. (This software may include algorithms for checking integrity constraints, for producing specialist outputs, and the application programs.) The Software Environment contains a model of all this software in the form of hierarchical trees and thus encourages the use of top-down design techniques and structured programming. The algorithms held in the Software Environment are in a form suitable for adding to the system as and when required.

Figure 3.1 illustrates the design process which leads to the specification of these various environments. It also shows that the process is iterative in so far as a change in the design at any level of the system only affects the design of the levels below it.

In addition to providing objectives in the design process, these Environments also provide the main interfaces to the system. Viewed in this light the Object Environment provides a high-level definition of the system which is available to all

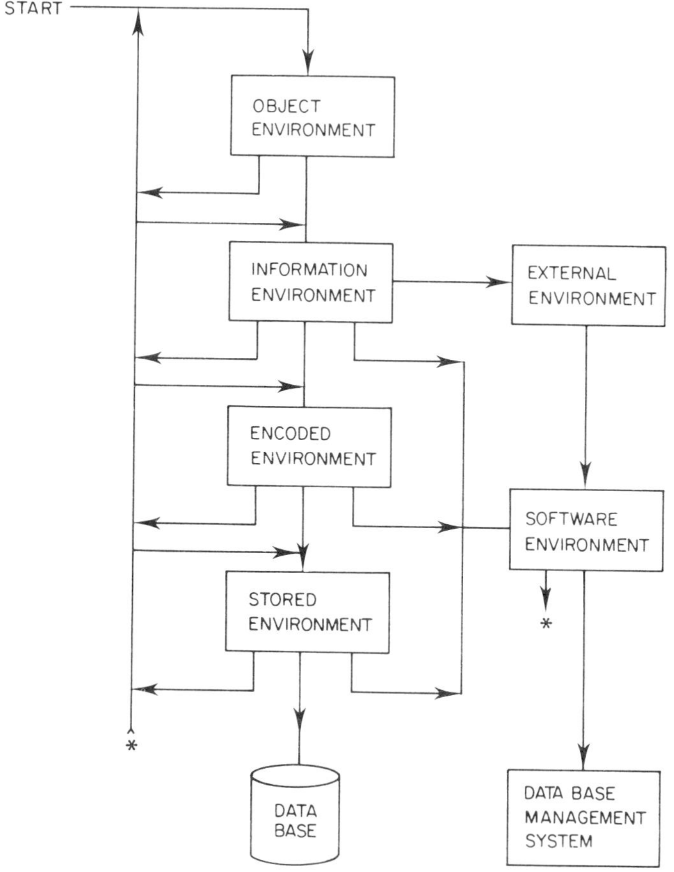

Figure 3.1 The design process

system users. The Information Environment not only provides a complete definition of the information maintained in the system but also provides a target for the languages which are used to manipulate that information. The External Environment provides means of producing alternative views of the Information Environment, while the Encoded, Stored, and Software Environments are only available to system designers and operation staff, and are used to design, monitor, and tune system performance.

3.3 Comparisons with other Data Base Systems

The previous section outlined how a system designer uses the six steps of the Design Methodology to design an Information System. However, it is perhaps important to stress that most data base systems exploit some sort of multi-level system description, and it is therefore worthwhile briefly discussing some of these systems.

The 1971 Codasyl DBTG Report (see CODASYL 1) recommends the use of three levels of description, one of which (the Schema Level) defines the data base, the second of which (the Sub-Schema Level) defines the view of a data base as seen by an application program, and the third (the Application Program Level) defines these application programs. The ANSI/X3/SPARC Study Group have published proposals (see ANSI SPARC 2) which separates the description into three main data base levels plus the Application Program Level. The three data base levels may be summarized as: the Conceptual Schema which defines all the information in the data base together with its integrity constraints, the External Schema which defines the end-user's view of that information, and the Internal Schema which defines the run-time model of the system. Another model, the DIAM model (see SENKO 3), defines four levels plus the Application Program Level. Two of these levels are comparable with the Conceptual and External Schemas identified by ANSI SPARC, and two of which provide a more detailed definition of the ANSI SPARC Internal Schema.

A more detailed appraisal of these various alternative approaches may be found in Chapter 21.

3.4 The Schemas

The previous section outlined how a system designer uses the six steps of the Design Methodology to design an Information System. As the designer completes a design of a particular environment he uses the appropriate level of schema to describe his design to RDBMS. All the schemas supported by RDBMS consist of a number of entity sets and thus take the same form as the Information Environment of an Information System. This choice has been made for three reasons:

1. The schemas can be designed using the same Design Methodology as that used to design an Information System. This gives both the designers of RDBMS and

prospective Information System designers experience with both the proposed Design Methodology and the Multi-Level Schema.

2. The entity sets of the Multi-Level Schema are very suitable for on-line interactive interrogation and manipulation using the normal system facilities.

3. The use of a Multi-Level Schema reduces the amount of software specifically required for Schema support, thus reducing the overall size of the system and its related costs and run-time efficiency.

3.5 The Translation of the Schemas

The previous sections outlined a hierarchy of schemas, each of which is realized in a number of entity sets. As yet there has been no formal statement of the actual information to be defined and manipulated in each schema; however, it is already apparent that, to be of use, they need to be related. This section briefly describes these relationships.

Given a hierarchy of schemas, there is inevitably some relationship between them. The first and vital relationship is that at each of the levels except the Software Environment level, the schema is used to describe data structures. The second relationship is that, given schemas at two successive levels in the hierarchy, then the upper schema defines a data structure and effectively commits the lower-level schema to supporting it. Thus the lower-level schema needs to contain all the parameters needed to carry out this task.

The schema for a particular environment is usually built up by defining it entity by entity, where each entity represents a single design decision. This information is then used to build up the necessary object schema. The approach to schema design outlined above has permitted a useful form of schema translation which allows a user to translate the whole schema for an environment by producing a default form of the schema for a lower level environment. Obviously such a schema is not optimum, because it only contains system defaults. However, this approach to schema translation allows for the inclusion of powerful defaults which, in some circumstances, may save the designer the task of exhaustively defining all the levels of his system.

3.6 Generations of the System

Throughout this chapter emphasis has been given to the fact that an Information System evolves through a number of phased extensions to its Field of Perception and, via a number of modifications, to tune a particular phased extension. Recognizing this naturally leads to a position where at any point in time there may be descriptions of several phased extensions of the system, and, within any phased extension, several generations of a particular part of the description. For example, there could be descriptions which define:

1. last year's phased extension.
2. the system which is currently running;
3. last week's generation of the phased extension of the system to be released next year;
4. this week's generation of the phased extension of the system to be released next year.

As this is a normal state of affairs it is necessary to provide facilities to identify the different phased extensions and generations of the system description. There are many solutions to this problem. For example, it is possible to keep the source for each generation of the Multi-Level Schema in separate text files, and thus generate separate instances of each system. Unfortunately, the problem of maintaining consistency between the generations of the system relies on mechanisms which are external to the data base management system, which is undesirable. RDBMS proposes to solve this problem within the data base management system by using the following mechanism.

From a user's point of view, each of the entity sets of the Multi-Level Schema contains descriptions of all the generations of the system in a single long display; each of the generations are then identified by two items of information, a Phased Release Number and a Generation Number. For example, given the entity set containing definitions of Functions, the user sees an entity set with the form of Figure 3.2. When accessing this entity set, the user can use a request of the form

– READ FUNCTION;

in which case he accesses the latest generation of all the functions in the latest phased release of the system, or

– READ FUNCTION SUCHTHAT FUNCTION.PHASED RELEASE = 1.46;

in which case he accesses the latest generations of all the functions in release 1.46, or

FUNCTIONS

NAME	DETAILS	PHASED RELEASE	GENERATION

Figure 3.2 Generations of functions

– READ FUNCTION SUCHTHAT FUNCTION.PHASED RELEASE = 1.46 AND FUNCTION.GENERATION < 10;

in which case he accesses the highest numbered generation prior to generation 10 of all the functions issued in release 1.46. This facility is available for all the entity sets of the Multi-Level Schema; it also carries over to the normal information in the system and is thus a fundamental feature that all users are expected to exploit.

4

Using an Information System

4.1 Introduction

RDBMS is designed to support an Information System and to allow end-users to access and control that system, either directly by using a terminal or indirectly via an application program. From the point of view of using an Information System, it is as well to recognize that these two methods of using the system are more or less equivalent. In the first case an end-user interacts directly with the system, while in the second case a programmer (who is a system designer) has to interact with the system. In both cases the facilities offered to each user group are more or less the same, and for this reason the system supports a family of languages, the Control Sub-Languages, which have the same power but are expressed in different forms (see Figure 4.1).

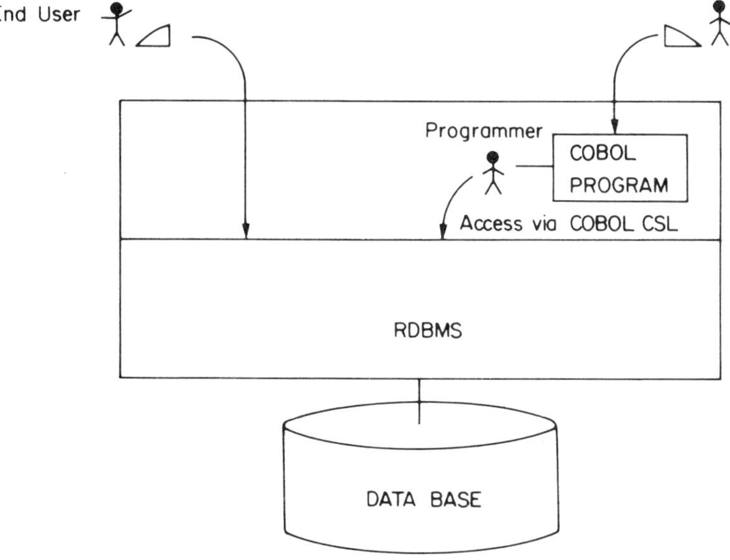

Figure 4.1 Using a Relational Data Base Management System

With this in mind, the rest of this chapter is concerned with the description of a Family of Languages; in particular it describes the principles which govern their design and their relationship with various high-level Languages such as COBOL, PASCAL, and CORAL 66.

4.2 A Family of Languages

The Control Sub-Languages have been provided to allow users to access and control an Information System. In their simplest form they allow users to create, read, update, and destroy information held in that system, and furthermore they can be used to read, create, update, and destroy the description of that system. In addition to these commonplace tasks, the language provides a set of powerful tools to allow users to identify the information that they require, thus ensuring that they do not have to bother with unnecessary details.

Given that all the member languages in the family permit users to carry out these tasks, then it is important to ensure that the languages are more or less similar, and achieving this similarity ensures that the languages are semantically equivalent. (This means each of the languages can be used to say the same thing although the way it is said may be different.) Although the languages are semantically equivalent, visually they are very different; this visual difference is due to the fact that the Control Sub-Languages are being used to extend existing traditional languages and in each of these cases it is aesthetically desirable that each of the extensions preserves the character of the existing language and is not an uncomfortable ad hoc addition.

The actual Control Sub-Languages are:

1. The Interactive Control Sub-Language, which is the main terminal-oriented language and is used by all system users.
2. The COBOL Control Sub Language, which has a syntactical form similar to COBOL.
3. The CORAL 66–ALGOL 60 Control Sub-Language, which has syntactical form suitable for inclusion in CORAL 66 and ALGOL 60.

4.3 The Control Sub-Language

It is virtually impossible to design a standard language which can be used successfully by all those who might wish to interact with an Information System. However, it is possible to design a basic language which satisfies the majority of users and to provide extensions to that basic language. This is the approach which has been adopted with the Control Sub-Language, and this section is devoted to a discussion of the design criteria which have influenced it.

At this stage in the development of Information Systems there are some features of these systems which have overriding influence on the design of data manipulation languages. These features include transparancy, privacy, and resilience, and without them it is not meaningful to discuss the existence of an Information System. In addition to incorporating these features, the language needs to meet a number of other objectives which can be identified as follows.

Special Purpose Data Manipulation Languages

A clear distinction must be made between general purpose data manipulation languages used by skilled programmers and information specialists, and more limited languages designed to incorporate the in-built assumptions of specialist users or to make direct computer access practical for the non-specialist user. This language belongs to the first category; languages in this class can be used as a basis for building specialist languages. Special purpose languages can therefore be implemented by using functions and macros.

Data Independence

The most important feature of the language is that it should permit data independence. One of the chief difficulties for users of a large Information System is that they cannot be expected to remember any facts about the system except the information they need to access; consequently, it is out of the question to expect these users to remember to manipulate files or other storage-dependent features of the system. Furthermore, as these features change during the life of the system, it is obviously very desirable for them to be kept out of sight.

Coherence

Each user of the Control Sub-Language should be given a coherent view of the system. The interface should not use different names or formats for essentially similar commands. The user should be able to use the same commands to read information about men from a Pay and Personnel system as he does to read information from the system description. However, the interface should not hide the distinction between things which are different.

The objective described above of providing a coherent interface for each user of the system should not be confused with the less reasonable objective of providing *one* single interface for all users of the system. It is recognized that different users will require different interfaces to the system, and this language provides a basis on which these specialist interfaces may be built.

Simplicity

Another requirement of the language is that it should be simple to use in so far as a user with a simple requirement is not required to handle lots of complexity. It must be recognized at this stage that a user undertaking a complex operation may need to use the full complexities of the language in order to achieve his goal, and that it is not a prime objective of the language to make complex operations appear simple.

Completeness

In a paper entitled 'Relational Completeness of Data Base Sub-Languages' (CODD 5), Codd described a method of assessing whether a data manipulation language was complete. It is true to say that a language which is relationally complete provides the user with a wealth of facilities for manipulating information in a relational data base. Consequently, it is desirable for all such languages to be assessed in this way.

4.4 The Control Sub-Language and a High-Level Language

In the previous sections, emphasis has been given to the Control Sub-Language as a stand-alone language. However, there are versions which are to be hosted within high-level languages, and for this reason it is vital to understand this 'hosting' relationship. This relationship has two parts, namely:

1. The mechanical problem of interfacing a high-level language Program to the Control Sub-Language.
2. The aesthetic and theoretical problems of extending the high-level language.

This section is devoted to the first of these problems, while the next section is devoted to the second.

The Sub-Schema Problem

Some data base management systems provide a sub-schema which defines the interface between the data base and a group of one or more application programs. The facilities associated with a sub-schema are:

1. Facilities to define that subset of the data base which is of direct interest to a group of application programs and to rename and redefine particular elements of information.
2. Facilities to implement privacy or access control checks.
3. Facilities to control the connectivity between the data base and the application programs.

In addition to these facilities, which are obviously oriented to the system designers and programmers, the sub-schema gives some assistance to the data base management system designer because the compilation of the sub-schema gives him an opportunity to compile a set of tables which can be linked to the application programs and data base management software at consolidation or run-time.

Finally, the sub-schema is also the target for the Data Manipulation Language which, in the case of the Codasyl DBTG Proposals, is very weak in data manipulation capabilities; consequently any shortcomings in the data manipulation language are usually compensated for in the facilities for mapping the sub-schema on to the data base schema.

The RDBMS Solution

Rather than provide a sub-schema which provides a single solution to all the problems identified above, the Relational Data Base Management System recognizes that these problems can be treated separately and that there are advantages in the adoption of the separate solutions. The solutions are:

1. *The data-independence problem.* This has been tackled by permitting all users of the Control Sub-Language to create entity sets which are linked to the permanent entity sets by powerful data manipulation facilities. The scope of these entity sets is such that they may be temporary, in which case their scope is dependent on the host language, or they may be permanent in which case they reside in the External Environment.
2. *Privacy checks.* These have been added as integral parts of the Information Environment and External Environments.
3. *The connectivity problem.* This is tackled in two ways. Firstly, the system encourages system designers to add application code to the Software Environment; such software is only loaded and connected as and when it is required. Secondly, the system holds the description of an Information System in an internal data base and provides facilities in the Control Sub-Language to give a system designer control over the binding.

The objective of providing these solutions is to exploit the system's powerful data handling facilities and to ensure that the question of when to bind the application code to the data management software is governed by the run-time considerations found within a particular Information System and not dictated by the design of the data base management system.

4.5 Extending a High-Level Language

To most system designers, hosting a language such as the Control Sub-Language into a high-level language is very much a question of finding a syntactic form of the high-level language which allows the user to write Control Sub-Language calls. This is without doubt a very important aspect of the hosting problem; however, there is another aspect of the problem, namely the effect that this new and powerful data base language has on the overall language.

In the past, hosting has been treated as an unequal partnership, with the hosting language being given some overriding superiority over the sub-languages. The

Control Sub-Language statements are so much more powerful than any existing high level statement that there is a need to review this partnership. (*Note:* Readers will find that the Interactive Control Sub-Languages provide facilities whereby a user can call functions which have been written in a high-level language, so in this situation the partnership has an additional difficulty of being recursive.) For the sake of discussion the partnership is treated as being that of equality, and all the following sections refer to the high-level language as an Algorithmic Sub-Language, a term which seems to be more honestly associated with its role.

The true nature of the hosting relationship is best discovered by considering the information which each of the Sub-Languages manipulates. On the one hand the Control Sub-Language allows access to all of the information within the data base, together with the descriptions of that information, and allows both information and descriptions to be passed to the Algorithmic Sub-Language. The Algorithmic Sub-Language gives access to a set of local variables including those shared by the Control Sub-Language. This relationship was first identified by Wilkes in his paper 'The Outer and Inner Syntax of a Programming Language' (see WILKES 1). However, Wilkes failed to draw a necessary conclusion. Throughout the life of an Algorithmic Sub-Language, extra bits and pieces have been added to the language which largely extend the Outer Syntax. Furthermore, in some languages the extensions have been so extensive that it is almost impossible to recognize the Inner Syntax which we now wish to exploit as the core of the Algorithmic Sub-Language.

Assuming that a user is going to use an Algorithmic Sub-Language to write procedures which can be called from the Interactive Control Sub-Language, most of the Outer Syntax becomes redundant. For this reason an extension to a high-level language seems to involve two steps:

1. Define a compatible Control Sub-Language which extends the Outer Syntax to incorporate a relational data base.
2. Remove all those features from the Algorithmic Sub-Language which are currently part of the existing Outer Syntax and which have been made redundant by the addition made in 1. above.

Most language designers achieve the first step in this process. However, very little attention has been given to the second step, which is unfortunate because such an approach could lead to new dialects of existing languages which are particularly well suited to writing code for Information Systems running in a data base environment.

Part B

DESIGNING AN INFORMATION SYSTEM

5

The Object Environment

5.1 Introduction

The first step in the Design Methodology outlined in Chapter 3 is to design an Object Environment. This Object Environment contains a conceptual model of the real world system that is to be supported by the proposed Information System. In order to achieve this objective it contains details of the objects which lie within the field of perception of the Information System, the relationships which exist between these objects, and the types of information which are associated with those objects. Such an environment is best conceived as a directed graph where each node identifies an object of a particular type, each arc identifies a dependency between two objects, and associated with each node is a collection of information types. A typical Object Environment is illustrated in Figure 5.1.

In many ways such an Object Environment has parallels in systems designed by several other groups of workers. For example it is similar to the Infological Model for Information Systems described by Sundgren (see SUNDGREN 1) and to the Entity Relationship Model described by Chen (see CHEN 1) and the so-called Trinity model identified at the IFIP TC-2 Working Conferences in 1976 and 1977 (see BENCI 1 and MOULIN 1). Each of these models uses different terminology to describe concepts which are basically similar.

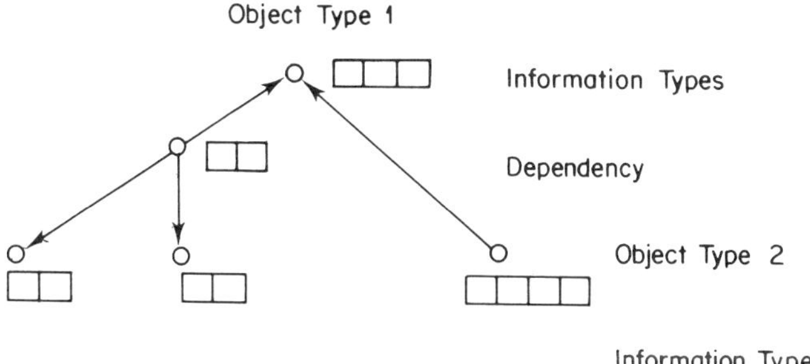

Figure 5.1 An Object Environment

5.2 Object Types

Atomic and Compound Object Types

As the designer looks at the perceived field of his prospective system he will identify a number of objects which he will choose to think of as being singular and indivisible. These are known as *Atomic Object Types.* Typical examples of atomic object types in the Object Environment of a Purchasing System would be a Product and a Supplier.

As shown in Figure 5.3, the identification of the atomic object types must be regarded as the first step towards completing the design of the Object Environment.

Once the designer has identified a number of atomic object types he will find that he wishes to describe relationships between them. For example, in developing the Purchasing System he will identify that the filing clerk running a manual implementation of such a system maintains a list of parts to be bought, a list of possible suppliers of each part, both of which are atomic object types, and an order ledger which notes when an order for a part is placed with a supplier. This order ledger realizes the relationship between part and supplier and, using this methodology, it is replaced by an object type Order which links two atomic objects, Product and Supplier. Any such object type which consists of a conglomeration of atomic object types is known as a *Compound Object Type.*

The distinction between an atomic object type and a compound object type is very similar to the distinction in mathematics between a set and a relation. In fact, a compound object may be defined in the form of a relation complete with a predicate. Thus an Order could be defined as:

$$\text{Order} = \{(\text{Product}, \text{Supplier}) : (p \in \text{Product}, s \in \text{Supplier}) \wedge R(p, s) = \text{true}\}$$

where

(*a*) Product and Supplier are two sets of values;

(*b*) p and s are two dummy variables representing members from the sets of Product and Suppliers respectively;

(*c*) $\wedge$ is read as AND;

(*d*) R is a two-place predicate which is defined as 'all those p which have been ordered from those s.' Such a predicate may be thought of as an integrity check which is to be imposed on the object type Order.

Other Object Types

The atomic and compound object types identified above are used to describe real world objects which are necessarily external to the system; the system merely maintains a description of the object. However, it has been found that in order to model all the aspects of an Information System it is necessary to introduce two new object types, namely:

1. *A data object*. This is an object which is used within the system to hold information. It includes not only the entity sets and attributes of the Information Environment, but the encoded entity sets and stored entity sets used to support the Information Environment.
2. *A software object*. This embodies the software which supports the system. This software includes not only end-user specialized algorithms such as Value Added Tax evaluation algorithms, but also the generalized mapping algorithms used within the system.

It should be stressed that data and software object types play no part in the description of the Object Environment; their use is restricted to the Information, Encoded, Stored, and Software Environments. Table 5.1 stresses this point by classifying a number of different object types.

Table 5.1

Object	Classification
A Product in a Purchasing System	Atomic
An Order in a Purchasing System	Compound
An Entity Set	Data
A File in a Purchasing System	Data
An algorithm to evaluate Value Added Tax	Software

5.3 Dependencies

As a designer identifies the atomic and compound object types in the system, he will recognize that there are dependencies between them. An example of such a dependency occurs in the definition of the Order Ledger, where it is defined that an Order can only be placed with a Supplier for a Product providing there are already atomic objects representing the Supplier and the Product. A dependency may be defined more formally as follows.

Given two object types A and B, where A is either an atomic or compound object type and B is a compound object type, then B is said to be dependent on A if at any given time each object of type B has no more than one object of type A associated with it. This relationship between A and B is denoted by:

$$A \rightarrow B$$

An implication of this relationship is that deleting an object from A may require the automatic deletion of the dependent objects in B in order to maintain the integrity of the system.

An example of dependence in the Object Environment for a Purchasing System is given below. This system contains three atomic object types:

1. *A Product*.

2. *A Customer.*

3. *A Supplier.*

and two compound objects:

4. *An Orderto*, which is defined as existing when an Order for a Product has been placed with a Supplier.

5. *An Orderfrom*, which is defined as existing when an Order has been received from a Customer for a Product.

In this environment, it is recognized that while it is possible to add Products, Customers, and Suppliers almost without restriction, the addition of an Orderto requires that the Supplier and the Product on which it depends already exists. Furthermore, the removal of a Product or a Supplier is only valid if there is no Orderto dependent on it.

Dependency Diagrams

Obviously, it is quite feasible to list the dependencies between objects in a given Object Environment; however, it is more convenient to illustrate these dependencies in some diagrammatic form. The form of which has been adopted is to create a directed graph where each of the nodes represents an object type, and each of the arcs represents a dependency. Thus, given two object types A and B where B is dependent of A, then this is illustrated as follows:

A B

To clarify this point further, Figure 5.2 illustrates the Object Environment for the Purchasing System defined earlier.

It is perhaps worthwhile noting that a dependency usually represents either a one to one or a one to many relationship between object types. For example in Figure 5.2 it is reasonable to expect many orders from a particular customer. Further to this, it is not usual to find loops in a dependency diagram because such loops would suggest that an object type is somehow dependent on itself, a situation which does not normally occur in the real world. These dependency diagrams are similar to the Data Structure Diagrams first identified by C. Bachman (see BACHMAN 1).

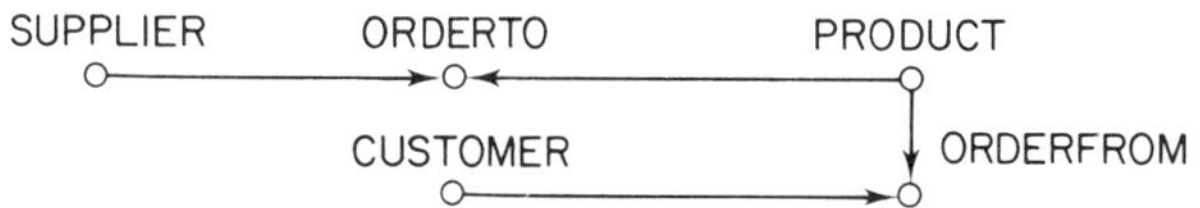

Figure 5.2 A dependency diagram for the Purchasing System

When the Object Environment is mapped into the Information Environment, these dependencies can only be represented by extending the Relational Data Mode. This is described in Chapter 6.

5.4 Stability with Respect to Time

Once a designer has produced a statement of an Object Environment he should try to ensure that it remains stable with respect to time.

An example of the problems of time arises in Section 5.3 where an Orderto is defined as: 'An Order placed with a given Supplier for a given Product.' Using an Object Environment which reflected this condition would result in users finding that they lose information as soon as the Order has been satisfied. In some cases this may be desirable; however, if this loss of information is not acceptable the definition of the compound object Orderto needs to be improved. In this case an Orderto could be defined as: 'an Order which was placed *in the last five years*, with a given Supplier for a given product.' The italic text highlights the strengthening required to the predicate governing Orderto. Using this definition, once the Orderto has been delivered, the information about that order will remain in the system because the object type Orderto is stable with respect to time, whereas the previous definition was unstable with respect to time. Whenever possible, designers should ensure that the object types of the Object Environment are stable with respect to time, as this is the only way of insuring against information loss in the system due to poorly defined predicates. One obvious implication of defining predicates in this way is that the designer has to ensure that it can be policed automatically by an Information System, which in turn requires that the necessary information types be added to the Object Environment.

For example, a review of the Object Environment for the Purchasing System shows that this can be achieved by:

(*a*) Defining for each product the time period during which it was in use.

(*b*) Defining for each Orderto and Orderfrom the date on which the order was completed.

There is no need to associate date information with a customer because, at least from a real world point of view, another organization is only a customer if it has actually bought something from you; if a former customer has not traded with you for five years then the organization is probably not a customer.

Defining an Object Environment which is stable with respect to time ensures that there is a minimum of information loss due to system definition. However, it does not prevent information loss which can arise from other happenings, such as malfunction of the underlying data base management system or hardware.

5.5 Information Types

Once the designers have completed the design of the object types they may now define the information types which are associated with them.

As the designers define the information types they need to do the following. Firstly, they define the relationship between the information types and the object types defined earlier, secondly they need to identify the relationships between information types, and thirdly they need to provide a definition of each information type. The next sections explain these tasks.

The Relationship with the Object Types

Given an atomic object type, the designer will identify a number of information types which are related to it either because they identify or describe an instance of the object type. Figure 5.2 illustrates that in the Purchasing System the atomic object type Supplier is identified by an information type Code and described by an information type Name.

Given a compound object type, then the designer will identify a number of information types which are related to it. Again, these information types will identify or describe an instance of the object type, but in addition some of the information types will describe the atomic object types which relate to the compound object type. For example, in the Purchasing System the compound object type Orderto is related to the atomic object type Product; consequently, associated with Orderto is an information type Product code which describes this relationship. In this situation the information type associated with the compound object type is said to be inherited from the related atomic object type.

Periodically, when defining the information types, it will be found that there is a need to hold information types which are directly related to an object type which is not as yet formally recognized. In this case it is wise to review the design and, if practicable, to introduce the necessary object type. This is particularly important when working on one stage of a multiphased expansion of the perceived field of the system, because this extra object type may not be particularly important in this phase but may appear in a succeeding phase; thus a fudge now may cause real trouble later. (See Figure 5.3.)

Object Types and their Associate Information Types

OBJECT TYPE	ASSOCIATED INFORMATION TYPE
SUPPLIER	<u>CODE</u>, NAME, ADDRESS, TERMS, AREACODE
CUSTOMER	<u>CODE</u>, NAME, ADDRESS, TRADE-GROUP
PRODUCT	<u>CODE</u>, NAME, DESCRIPTION, PRICE, DATEFROM, DATETO
ORDERTO	<u>PRODUCT CODE</u>, <u>SUPPLIER CODE</u>, ORDER NO. QUANTITY, ORDERDATE, DELIVERYDATE
ORDERFROM	<u>PRODUCT CODE</u>, <u>CUSTOMER ORDER</u>, ORDER NO., QUANTITY, ORDERDATE, DELIVERYDATE

Figure 5.3 The Information Types of the Purchasing System. The underlining denotes that the Information Type identifies the Object

Relationships between Information Types

All information types have a mode which describes their legible form as visible in the real world. Some information types are given this mode because they are defined to be fundamental, for example the customary form of a Product Code. Other information types inherit their mode from some intermediate information type. For example, in the Purchasing System, the information type Code associated with Supplier may have a mode which is defined as a 6 digit number. The Information Type Supplier Code in Orderto has a mode which is inherited from code in Customer. Each information type is therefore identified by two factors, namely its role and its mode, where the role defines the purpose of the information type and modes may be either fully defined or inherited from another information type. (See Figure 5.4.)

Defining the Information Types

Having identified each of the information types in terms of their association with object types, it is now necessary to provide each of them with a formal definition. The problem which arises at this point is to decide on the level of definition. It is obviously possible to define each information type in terms of its machine representation, but since this level of design is of use primarily to end-users and non-computer specialists, it is vital that information be defined in terms which are meaningful to them. Thus the description should contain the following.

1. A unique full name which is meaningful in the real world.
2. An English narrative describing it in terms of known concepts.
3. A unique coded name meaningful in the Information System.
4. A mode definition: which can take one of two forms, either

   (*a*) correspondence with another information type so that it inherits its mode,

   or

   (*b*) a primitive mode definition which incorporates the following:

      (i) An acknowledged legible form, for example string of 10 characters or signed integer 3 digits.

      (ii) A scale or cardinality, which describes the number of possible values which the type can take. For example, the information type 'sex' has a cardinality of two, i.e. male and female.

      (iii) A stated set of validity checks. This may be in terms of a range of possible values or an algorithm which calculates whether it is valid.

      (iv) A narrative explaining these values and their significance in the real world.

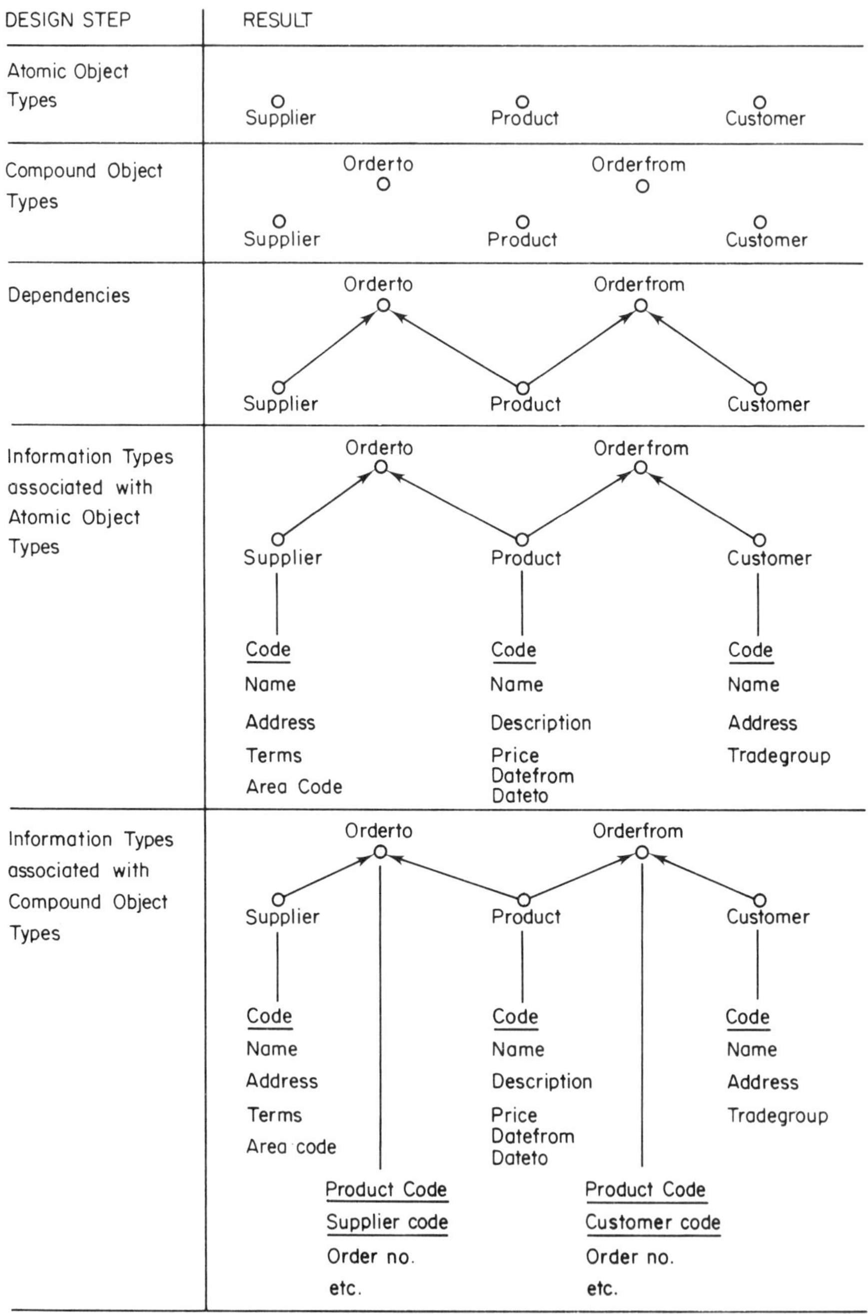

Figure 5.4 Designing an Object Environment

5.6 Changes to the Object Environment and Information Loss

Designing an Object Environment is not a task which, once completed, will last for ever. In Part A it was stressed that once a design has been completed there will always be pressures for a redesign. These pressures will naturally arise because once end-users have a better understanding of their Information System and their current information needs they will find they need new information.

In this situation these needs should be expressed in terms of changes to the Object Environment, and from this the system designers should be able to assess the cost of changing the system. However, in this position system designers should be particularly wary of changes which lead to information loss.

The most likely changes are:

1. An object type which was previously defined as being an atomic object type expands to become a compound object type.
2. A new atomic object type is introduced into the system.
3. A new compound object type is introduced into the system.
4. A compound object type is now defined as being an atomic object type.
5. An object type disappears.

Changes 1, 2, and 3 do not necessarily lead to any loss of information; consequently this type of change is quite acceptable. However, changes 4 and 5 above will have associated with them some loss of information, and in this situation it is vital to ensure that only the information associated with the atomic object types actually disappears.

5.7 An Example of an Object Environment

At the end of this chapter and each of the other chapters in this part is a worked example of the Purchasing System.

The Purchasing System–Object Types

The perceived field of the system contains seven object types as follows:

NAME	CLASS	DESCRIPTION
PRODUCT		An instance of this object identifies either a Product bought from a Supplier or a Product sold to a Customer in the last five years
SUPPLIER	Atomic	An instance of this object type identifies a Supplier who sold a Product in the last five years.

CUSTOMER	Atomic	An instance of this object identifies a Customer who bought goods in the last five years.
SALESMAN	Atomic	An instance of this object identifies a Salesman who served with the company in the last 20 years.
ORDERTO	Compound	An instance identifies an order for a Product from a Supplier in the last five years.
ORDERFROM	Compound	An instance identifies an order to supply a Product to a Customer, in the last five years.
SALESMAN TO CUSTOMER	Compound	An instance defines the relationship between a Salesman and a Customer, in the last five years.

Dependency Diagram

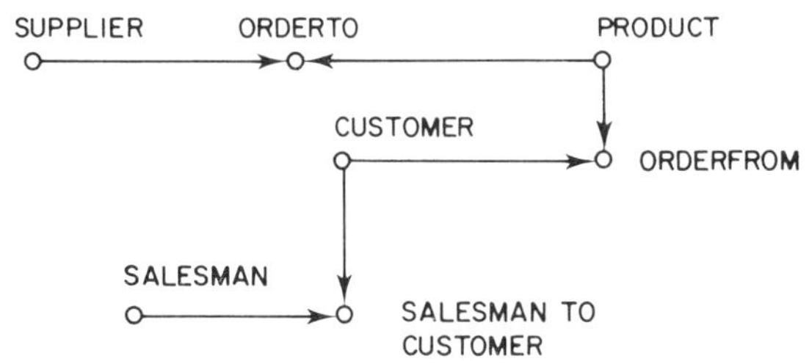

Object Types and their Associate Information Types

OBJECT TYPE	ASSOCIATED INFORMATION TYPES
PRODUCT	CODE, NAME, DESCRIPTION, PRICE, DATEFROM, DATETO.
SUPPLIER	CODE, NAME, ADDRESS, TERMS, AREACODE.
CUSTOMER	CODE, NAME, ADDRESS, TRADE-GROUP.
SALESMAN	CODE, NAME, COMMISSION, DATE.
ORDERTO	PRODUCTCODE, SUPPLIERCODE, ORDERNO, QUANTITY, ORDERDATE, DELIVERYDATE.
ORDERFROM	PRODUCTCODE, CUSTOMERCODE, ORDERNO, QUANTITY, ORDERDATE, DELIVERYDATE.
SALESMAN TO CUSTOMER	SALESMANCODE, CUSTOMERCODE, DATE.

The underline denotes that the information type identifies the object type.

Information Types

ADDRESS	Full name:	ADDRESS
	Narrative:	ADDRESS. in form: street, town, post code
	Mode:	String surrounded by quotes and containing commas
AREACODE	Full Name:	AREA-CODE
	Description:	Area Codes defined on a map
	Mode:	A single character.
CODE	Full Name:	CODE
	Description:	All Products, Customers, Suppliers and Salesmen each have a code taken from the range 9,999
	Mode:	Integer
COMMISSION	Full Name:	Salesman Commission.
	Description:	A single character code in the range A to F (see commission tables).
	Mode:	Character A to F.
CUSTOMERCODE	– see CODE	
DATE:	Full Name:	DATE
	Description:	A date for a Salesman to Customer relationship. Must be in the last five years.
	Mode:	Date
DATEFROM	Full Name:	Date-from
	Description:	Starting date for the period during which a Product is being either bought or sold. Must be in the last five years.
	Mode:	Date.
DATETO	Full Name:	Date-to
	Description:	End-date for the period during which a Product is being either bought or sold. Must be in the last five years.
	Mode:	Date
DELIVERYDATE	Full Name:	Delivery Date
	Description:	–
	Mode:	Date
DESCRIPTION	Full Name:	Product Description
	Description:	A short description, i.e. less than 100 characters
	Mode:	String of max. length 100 characters
NAME	Full Name:	Name
	Mode:	String of max length
ORDERDATE	Full Name:	Order Date
	Description:	–
	Mode:	Date
ORDERNO	Full Name:	Order number
	Description:	A six digit order number
	Mode:	Positive integer with maximum value 999,999

Information Types

PRICE	Full Name:	Price of Product
	Description:	A price in the form of decimal pounds and pence. Max price £1000,00
	Mode:	Real variable in the range £0.01 to £1000.00
PRODUCTCODE	See CODE	
QUANTITY	Full Name:	Quantity
	Description:	The quantity of a particular Product on an order.
	Mode:	A positive integer.
SALESMANCODE	See CODE	
SUPPLIERCODE	See CODE	
TERMS	Full Name:	Supplier Terms
	Description:	Suppliers give a percentage on orders over a particular value. This lists the values and the percentages.
	Mode:	String
TRADEGROUP	Full Name:	Customer Trade Group
	Description:	Customers have been divided into Trade Groups
	Mode:	A single character in the range A to P

6

The Information Environment

6.1 Introduction

The Information Environment, together with the Control Sub-Languages, defines the end-user's interface to the system. Subject to privacy constraints, all users see all the information held in the system as being contained in tabular structures known as entity sets which can be addressed by the Control Sub-Language. Figure 6.1 shows a typical example of an entity set containing details of products for a stationer's shop.

Each entity set is defined as being a rectangular array of data values with the following properties:

1. In any selected column the values are all of the same kind, whereas values in different columns need not be of the same kind.
2. Each value is a simple number or character string. Thus no row or column will contain a value represented as set of numbers or a repeating group.
3. All rows in an entity set must be distinct (duplicate rows are not allowed).
4. The ordering of rows within an entity set is not pre-defined by the system and may change without notice.
5. The columns of an entity set are assigned distinct names and the ordering of columns within an entity set is not pre-defined by the system.

Given an Information Environment in this form, the Control Sub-Languages provide a user with facilities to access and amend the contents of an entity set.

PRODUCT

CODE	NAME	DESCRIPTION	PRICE
1023	ADHESIVE	ADHESIVE IN JARS	0.19
1027	GLUE50	GLUE IN 50 GRAM POTS	0.11
1028	GLUE100	GLUE IN 100 GRAM POTS	0.15
1033	POLYCEL	POLYCELL PKTS	0.08

Figure 6.1 An entity set

These facilities allow a user to access an entity set by selecting values from particular columns and rows where the columns are identified by a list of column names and rows are identified by providing a list of predefined values for a particular column or columns. The facilities to amend the contents of an entity set allow a user to create new rows in and delete existing rows from an entity set; they also allow the user to modify the values in existing rows. In addition to these facilities which operate on a single entity set, the Control Sub-Language support operators which combine the contents of several entity sets to create new entity sets and thus provide the user with very powerful manipulation facilities.

More details about the Control Sub-Languages are provided in Part C. The present section is primarily concerned with the design of an Information Environment which may act as a target for the Control Sub-Languages, and consequently it is necessary to provide a clear statement of this work.

Given that the Information Environment is defined after the Object Environment, then the designer has already a complete high level definition of his Information System which acts as a reliable basis for this work. In general this work separates into a number of steps, as follows:

1. To define a number of entity sets which have the same form as relations.

2. For each entity set, to define its attributes and domains.

3. To confirm that each entity set is in third normal form and thus define functional dependencies between candidate key attributes and the other attributes.

4. To define the dependencies between the entity sets.

5. To specify the semantics or predicates which govern each entity set.

Note on terminology. Throughout this work, the terms entity set and entity are used instead of the Relational Data Model terms relation and tuple, respectively. The need for a change in terminology will become apparent in Chapters 7 and 8.

6.2 An Entity Set System

So far it has been proposed that the information which describes the objects of the Object Environment should be held in entity sets. It must also be recognized that these entity sets have properties which makes them particularly suitable for representing information. The following sections contain a brief résumé of the mathematical definition of set and relation and then show how these definitions form the basis for the definition of an entity set.

A Set

Each of the columns of an entity set consists of a set of values. The usual mathematical notation identifies sets by using upper case letters:

$$A, B, C.$$

However, it is often more practical to identify sets by using a single upper case letter followed by lower case letters:

Codes, Prices.

The elements of these sets are represented by lower case letters:

a, b, c, codes, prices.

The members of a set may be defined by either exhaustively listing the members or by defining the properties which an element must satisfy in order to join the set. The use of these two methods is best illustrated as follows:

- A set A which contains the numbers 1, 3, 5, and 10 is usually represented by $A = \{1, 3, 5, 10\}$
- A set B which contains all the even numbers is usually represented by $B = \{x : x \text{ is even}\}$

where x represents an arbitrary element of the set and : is read 'such that'.

In addition to denoting that a set contains members of a certain type, it is necessary to be able to say that an element is a member of a set. This is denoted by the symbol '$\in$' which is read as 'belongs to'. An example of the use of this symbol when discussing an element of b of a set B would be written:

$b \in B.$

A Relation

Using these definitions, it is possible to define a relation. In its simplest form a relation consists of three parts:

1. A set A.
2. A set B.
3. An open sentence or predicate $P(x, y)$ so that $P(a, b)$ is either true or false for any ordered pair (a, b) belonging to A and B.

The relation R from A and B is denoted by

$$R = \{(a, b) : (a \in A, b \in B) \wedge P(a, b) = \text{true}\}$$

where the sets A and B are known as the domains over which the relation is defined, and the symbol $\wedge$ is read as 'and'.

One example of this type of relation concerns the case where, if A is the set of all composers, B is the set of all symphonies, and

$P(x, y) =$ 'x wrote the y Symphony'

is an open statement on A, B, then

P(Beethoven, Eroica) = 'Beethoven wrote the Eroica Symphony'

is true thereby allowing the pair (Beethoven, Eroica) to belong to the relation R and

P(Britten, New World) = 'Britten wrote the New World Symphony'

is false thus preventing the pair (Britten, New World) from joining the relation R.

This example only considers a relation over two domains. However, it is possible to define a predicate in one variable, for example the sentence 'x is in the First Division', and in more than two variables, for example the sentence 'x times y equals z'.

A generalization of this leads to a definition of a relation with n domains which is called an n-ary relation. An n-ary relation R may be represented as follows:

$$R = \{(x_1, x_2, x_3, \ldots, x_n) : (x_1 \in X_1, x_2 \in X_2, x_3 \in X_3, \ldots, x_n \in X_n) \wedge P(x_1, x_2, x_3, \ldots, x_n) = \text{true}\}.$$

Finally it should be noted that any n-ary relation also takes the form of a mathematical set as defined earlier, and that the concepts of set and relation represent one of the cornerstones of the Relational Data Model which in turn forms the foundation of all relational data base management systems.

Entity Sets

The Information Environment contains entity sets which are used to contain information about real-world objects. For this reason each entity set which consists of a set of entries is said to take the form of an n-ary relation. Using this as a basis, the entity set PRODUCT represented in Fig. 6.1 would be defined by

$$\text{PRODUCT} = \{(\text{code, name, description, price}) : (\text{code} \in \text{Code, name} \in \text{Name, description} \in \text{Description, price} \in \text{Price}) \wedge P(\text{code, name, description, price}) = \text{true}\}$$

where the predicate P may be expressed as 'a product with a given code, name, description, and price marketed by a stationer'. Such a predicate obviously serves two purposes: firstly it describes the contents of the entity set, and secondly it may formally define the integrity checks which are to be performed on the entities in the set. Using such an entity set in a data base management system would result in users being faced with a tabular structure with the form of Figure 6.1, where each of the columns of the table represent a domain of the entity set.

Attributes

The above example defines an entity set PRODUCT which has domains of CODE, NAME, DESCRIPTION, and PRICE. However, it has been recognized that when defining entity sets it is necessary to allow domains to be repeated. For example, consider an entity set which is to be used to define for each product the time period during which it was in production. This entity set would be represented by

$$\text{PRODUCT PERIODS} = \{(\text{code, datefrom, dateto}) : (\text{code} \in \text{Code}, \text{datefrom} \in \text{Date}, \text{dateto} \in \text{Date}) \wedge R(\text{code, datefrom, dateto}) = \text{true}\}$$

where R is defined as 'product with a given code, which was produced during the time period from datefrom to dateto.'

The contents of such an entity set would normally be represented by:

PRODUCT PERIODS

CODE	DATE	DATE
1023	1/6/74	1/12/78
1027	9/8/75	1/12/78
1028	9/8/75	1/1/79
1033	1/10/76	1/11/79

From this definition it can be seen that while datefrom and dateto represent members of the set of Dates, in the predicate they serve different roles and, furthermore, an understanding of these roles is vital to anyone wishing to access or manipulate the entity set PRODUCT PERIODS. For this reason the term attribute is introduced to describe the role a particular domain will play in an entity set.

Figure 6.2 illustrates both the entity set PRODUCT and the entity set PRODUCT PERIODS using their full descriptions.

CODE/ PRODUCT CODE	NAME/ PRODUCT NAME	DESCRIPTION/ DESCRIPTION	PRICE/ POSITIVE STERLING VALUE
1023	ADHESIVE	ADHESIVE IN JARS	0.19
1027	GLUE50	GLUE IN 50 GRAM POTS	0.11
1028	GLUE100	GLUE IN 100 GRAM POTS	0.15
1033	POLYCELL	POLYCELL PKS	0.08

PRODUCT PERIODS

CODE/ PRODUCT CODE	DATEFROM/ DATE	DATETO/ DATE
1023	1/6/74	1/12/78
1027	9/8/75	1/12/78
1028	9/8/75	1/1/79
1033	1/10/76	1/11/79

Figure 6.2 Entity sets with their descriptions

In order to shorten the definition of attribute–name/domain–name this is called an *attribute*, and attributes will always be defined in terms of their role. The relationship between attribute and domain is almost implicit.

6.3 Normalization

The previous section described an entity set from the point of view of an entity set description which places few constraints on the choice of attributes for a particular entity set. This section describes a process known as normalization, which formalizes the relationships between the attributes of each entity set in a relational data base and leads to a relational data base which can be supported by a generalized relational data base management system.

The process was first identified by Codd and is now recognized as being fundamental to the analysis of data. For this reason it is worth setting up an example to demonstrate the process.

The example given in Figure 6.3 is based on a record typical of records found in a traditional purchasing system.

First Normal Form

The first step in the normalization process is to ensure that each of the attributes of an entity set is defined over a domain which is not itself an entity set. An entity set where no attribute/domain contains an entity set is said to be in *First Normal Form.*

Given the example of Figure 6.3, then there is little doubt that each of the attributes is described over simple domains and consequently it is already in First Normal Form.

<u>Attributes:</u> Customer Code
Customer Name
Customer Address
Salesman Commission Rate
Salesman Code
Salesman Name
Customer Trade Group
Product Code
Product Price
Quantity Ordered (by Customer)
Supplier Code
Supplier Terms
Supplier Name
Product Name
Product Datefrom
Product Dateto
Product Description
Quantity Ordered (from Supplier)

Figure 6.3 An example for normalization: the entity set DATA

Using entity sets in first normal form in a relational data base may cause a number of difficulties because they misbehave when accessed via a language such as the Control Sub-Language. The anomalies first identified by Heath (see HEATH 1) may occur whenever a user tries to create, delete, or update an entity in an entity set, and it arises because an entity set in first normal form may embody more than one fact. For example the entity set DATA maintains details of products, customers, suppliers, orders placed for products with suppliers, and orders placed for products by customers; and there is no doubt that certain users will wish to vary one or more of these facts independently from the rest. The following sections briefly describe the three anomalies identified above.

Update Anomalies

If the address of a particular customer is found to be in error and needs to be amended then recording the change in the entity set DATA will require changes to a number of entities. Furthermore the exact number of entities will vary with time, and the whole operation could be error prone and so lead to a position where a customer has more than one address.

Creation Anomalies

If it is necessary to add details of a new product to the entity set DATA, then this requires adding an entity with valid values for the attributes PRODUCT CODE, PRODUCT NAME, PRODUCT DESCRIPTION, and PRODUCT PRICE and unassigned values in all the other fields. This again may cause difficulties because other programs which use the entity set DATA may have to be aware of the significance of the unassigned values.

Deletion Anomalies

If it is necessary to delete information about a particular product then care has to be taken because deleting an entity which refers to a particular product may lead to the system losing details of suppliers, customers, and salesmen. Guarding against such losses may be costly.

Normalization is a process aimed at designing entity sets which do not suffer from these problems.

Functional Dependence

Functional dependence describes the relationship between two attributes in an entity set. Formally, this relationship is described by the following definition.

Given any entity set R with attributes A and B, then an attribute B is said to be functionally dependent on an attribute A if at every instance of time each value of

A has no more than one value of B associated with it. This dependency may be illustrated by the following example:

$$R.A \rightarrow R.B$$

which may be expressed as:

A determines B

where A is said to be a determinant of B.

Typical examples of functional dependency in the entity set DATA are:

Customer Code → Customer Name

Product Code → Product Name.

This demonstrates functional dependency between two attributes; very often in a real life situation, however, there is dependency not between single attributes but between groups of attributes. For this reason, given an entity set R which contains two groups of attributes, $G1$ and $G2$, where for each value of $G1$ there is only one value of $G2$, then $G2$ is functionally dependent on $G1$. This again may be denoted by:

$$R.G1 \rightarrow R.G2.$$

An example of a functional dependency involving more than attribute in the entity set DATA is illustrated by:

$$\left.\begin{matrix}\text{Customer Code}\\ \text{Product Code}\end{matrix}\right\} \rightarrow \text{Quantity Ordered (by Customer).}$$

In some cases the relationship between the groups $G1$ and $G2$ is such that there is a one to one correspondence between them, in which case this may be denoted by:

$$R.G1 \leftrightarrow R.G2.$$

Figure 6.4 illustrates functional dependencies in the entity set DATA.

Candidate Keys

When the system designer defines an entity set he will recognize that there is one or possibly more than one group of attributes on which all the other groups depend; such a group of attributes is known as the *Candidate Key* of the entity set. A group of attributes K is said to be a candidate key if it has the following properties:

1. In each entity of the entity set R, the value of K uniquely identifies that entity, e.g. $R.K \rightarrow R.M$, where M denotes the collection of all attributes of the entity set.

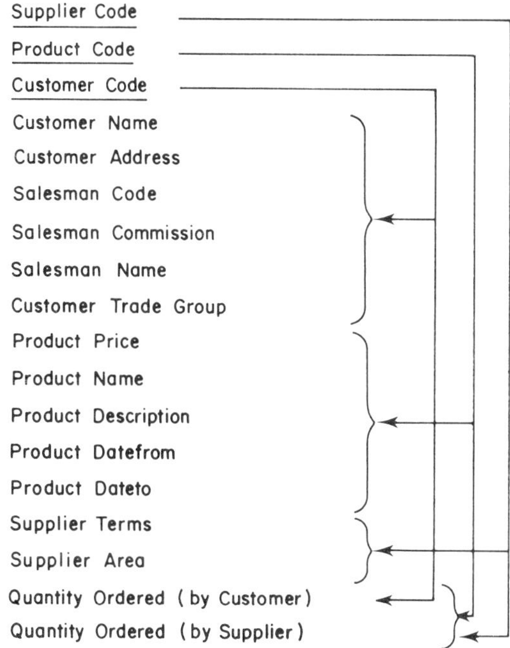

Figure 6.4 Functional dependencies in the entity set DATA

2. No attribute of the group K can be discarded without destroying the property above.

A group of attributes which forms the candidate key of the entity set DATA is: SUPPLIER CODE, PRODUCT CODE, and CUSTOMER CODE. In any given entity set it may be possible to identify more than one candidate key. For example the entity set DATA could also have a candidate key of SUPPLIER NAME, PRODUCT NAME, and CUSTOMER NAME, and in this situation it is necessary to choose one of these candidate keys and designate it the *Primary Candidate Key* or *Primary Key*.

In most cases where there is a choice of potential primary candidate keys, the actual key is chosen in such a way as to mirror accurately the design of the Object Environment.

Third Normal Form

Third normal form has been defined in several different ways. The first definition was by Codd (see CODD 3), while later definitions included those of Codd (see CODD 7) and Sharman (see SHARMAN 1). These later definitions are:

by Codd

An entity set R is in third normal form if it is in first normal form, and, for every attribute group C of R, if any attribute not in C is functionally dependent on C, then all attributes in R are functionally dependent on C.

by Sharman

An entity set is in third normal form if every determinant is a key.

These definitions are very similar, and both enshrine the simple idea that an entity set in third normal form should only embody a single fact. Consequently, an entity set such as the entity set DATA can only be reduced to third normal form by splitting it into a number of smaller entity sets. Figure 6.5 illustrates the entity sets which have been derived from the entity set DATA by the normalization process.

Entity Set:	SUPPLIER		
		Attributes:	Supplier Code
			Supplier Terms
			Supplier Area
Entity Set:	PRODUCT		
		Attributes:	Product Code
			Product Name
			Product Description
			Product Price
			Product Datefrom
			Product Dateto
Entity Set:	CUSTOMER		
		Attributes:	Customer Code
			Customer Name
			Customer Address
			Customer Trade Group
Entity Set:	SALESMAN		
		Attributes:	Salesman Code
			Salesman Name
			Salesman Commission
Entity Set:	ORDER FROM CUSTOMER		
		Attributes:	Customer Code
			Product Code
			Quantity Ordered (by Customer)
Entity Set:	ORDER TO SUPPLIER		
		Attributes:	Supplier Code
			Product Code
			Quantity Ordered (from Supplier)
Entity Set:	SALESMAN TO CUSTOMER		
		Attributes:	Salesman Code
			Customer Code

Figure 6.5 The entity set DATA when reduced to entity sets in third normal form

Entity Set: DATA2

Attributes: Customer Code
Customer Name
Customer Address
Customer Trade Group
Salesman Code
Salesman Name
Salesman Commission

Figure 6.6 An entity set in second normal form

Second Normal Form

The objective of the normalization process is to reduce entity sets to third normal form. *Second normal form* is a term used to describe an entity set defined when the condition 'every determinant is a key' is relaxed so as to allow a condition known as *transitive dependence*, which is best illustrated by an example. The entity set DATA2 shown in Figure 6.6 contains details of Customers and Salesmen. In this entity set, the attribute Salesman Name is directly dependent on Salesman Code and is transitively dependent on Customer Code.

Codd defined second normal form as follows. An entity set R is said to be in second normal form if it is in first normal form and every nonprime attribute is fully dependent on each Candidate Key of R.

Nowadays it is recognized that second normal form is something which designers should be aware of, but it plays no direct part in the normalization process. It is described here merely for completeness.

6.4 Relationships between Entity Sets: Dependencies, Predicates, and Triggers

So far an Information Environment has been defined as containing a number of separate entity sets, each of which is defined over a number of attribute/domain pairs. However, the Information Environment is to be used to represent the Object Environment which uses the concept of an inter-object dependency, so it is natural that the Information Environment should contain facilities for representing relationships between entity sets. There are three possible mechanisms for representing these relationships:

1. Dependencies.
2. Predicates.
3. Triggers and Events.

Dependencies

A dependency between two entity sets is defined as follows.

Given an Information Environment which contains two entity sets A and B,

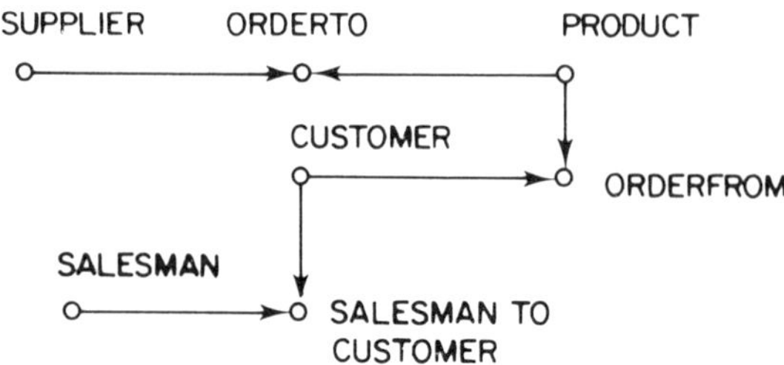

Figure 6.7 The dependency diagram for the Purchasing System

then entity set B is said to be dependent on entity set A if at any given time each entity in B has no more than one entity in A associated with it. This relationship is denoted by

$$A \twoheadrightarrow B.$$

As with Object Environment, dependencies in the Information Environment are best represented using a Dependency Diagram. An illustration of the dependency diagram for the Purchasing System is illustrated in Figure 6.7.

Describing Information Environment dependencies to RDBMS requires the system designer to identify the attribute or attributes in each entity set which are used to maintain the dependency. Assuming that the entity set PRODUCT identifies products by an attribute CODE, and ORDERTO identifies products by an attribute PRODUCTCODE, then the dependency between PRODUCT and ORDERTO is described by the expression

$$\text{PRODUCT . CODE} \twoheadrightarrow \text{ORDERTO . PRODUCTCODE}$$

where the '.' indicates the entity set to attribute relationship. Given a dependency in this form, then the information is used at run-time to police the creation of entities in the entity set ORDERTO by ensuring that the only permissible values of PRODUCTCODE are those that are defined in the set of values of PRODUCT . CODE. Converse rules apply when processing the deletion of entities from the entity set PRODUCT.

Predicates

It may happen that the relationship between two entity sets is too complicated to be represented by a dependency relationship. Such relationships are described using a predicate. This predicate, known as a static predicate, identifies for each of the permissible actions on an entity set (i.e. create an entity, destroy an entity, update an entity, and read an entity) the integrity constraints which must apply. Such integrity constraints may be expressed in the form of either a natural language statement or using the Control Sub-Languages.

If an integrity constraint is defined in terms of a natural language statement, then it is policed by software which is defined in the Software Environment. When at run-time, the system processes a Control Sub-Language statement which accesses an entity set guarded by this software, then the software is automatically called upon to carry out the required checks.

If an integrity constraint is defined in terms of the Control Sub-Language then it takes the form of a restricted Control Sub-Language predicate. When, at run-time, the system processes a Control Sub-Language statement which accesses an entity set guarded by a predicate, then the contents of the predicate are added to the Control Sub-Language statement and the result processed.

Chapter 12 describes the facilities provided by a Control Sub-Language predicate; the subset of the facilities available for use in static predicates are:

1. Comparison of an attribute value with a literal value.
2. Comparison of one attribute value within an entity with another attribute value within the same entity.
3. Comparison of an attribute value within an entity with the result of an arithmetic expression involving literals and other attribute values taken from the same entity.
4. Comparison of an attribute value within an entity with values of other attributes taken from other entity sets. This is effectively supported by the relational operators restriction and join.
5. Comparison of a set of attribute values with all the values of an attribute belonging to another entity set. This is supported by the relational operator division.

A predicate may embody two or more of these conditions where individual conditions are linked by the operators 'and', 'or', or ','. Further to this, any condition may have an error number associated with it so that data which fails the particular integrity check can be reported unambiguously to the user. Chapter 14 describes facilities for linking these error numbers to user-defined error messages. The effect of each of these facilities is fully described in Section 12.3.

Triggers and Events

Occasionally, when describing an Information System, it is necessary to incorporate side-effect-type mechanisms into the system. For example, the Information System may require all access to one entity set to lead to changes in another entity set; alternatively it may be that the addition of an entity to an entity set results in the production of a report. RDBMS can support these facilities by providing a trigger facility which is associated with an entity set and defines that when a particular condition involving information from that set occurs, then an event is caused. When an event is triggered then a unit of software is called to carry out the necessary processing. Parameters passed to the software unit via the event include a copy of the information which caused the event to trigger. In order to reduce the complexity of the system, RDBMS allows any number of triggers to be associated with an entity set, but imposes a restriction that only one event can be associated with each trigger.

6.5 Domains

Section 6.2 described the form of an entity set and the relationship between an attribute and a domain. This section describes the facilities for defining domains. In many languages and systems a domain definition encompasses several different aspects of a domain; for example it defines its legible form as seen by end-users, it defines its stored form, and it defines the effect of the operators of the Control Sub-Language. At this level in the system, a domain definition encompasses:

1. the legible form of the domain;
2. the effect of the Control Sub-Language on the domain;
3. the permissible values.

The stored form of the domain is defined at the Encoded Environment level of the system.

Standard Legible Forms

Within RDBMS the legible form of a domain is defined in terms of a mode such as integer or string and a length which defines the number of characters required to define a value. This information is used by RDBMS to handle the input/output of values. On input the system checks to ensure that the number of characters given by the user to represent a value does not exceed the number of characters given in the definition. On output the system uses the number of characters to format the value.

The permitted modes are:

1. *Integer:* which is written as a string of digits and preceded by an optional sign. On input a user must submit values with a plus or minus sign, while on output the system will suppress all plus signs. Typical values are: 6, 316, –74365, +75.

2. *Real:* which is written as a string of m digits preceding a decimal point which is followed by n digits, the whole of which may be preceded by an optional sign and followed by the exponential sign E (meaning 10 to the power of) which in turn is followed by an integer with an optional sign. Typical values are:

   +19.0, 0.82, –72.16,
   3.142E + 6 ($= 3.142 \times 10^6 = 3\ 142\ 000$)
   0.03E – 3 ($= 3.03 \times 10^{-3} = 0.00003$)

3. *Character String* (MINL, MAXL): a string of characters of minimum length MINL and maximum length MAXL surrounded by single or double quotes e.g. 'FRED', "JIM".
4. *Name* (MINL, MAXL): a string of characters of minimum length MINL and maximum length MAXL starting with a letter and containing letters and digits.
5. *Date:* a date of the form day/month/year, e.g. 10/10/74, 1/2/34.

Needless to say, each of these legible modes has associated with them a collating sequence and rules which govern the effect of the arithmetic operations.

In addition to these legible forms it has been found that it is convenient to provide a facility similar to the ALGOL 68 union-of-modes facility (see LINDSEY 1); this facility is known as an 'ANY'.

User-Defined Legible Forms

In addition to the standard legible forms described above, RDBMS provides facilities to allow system designers to define their own legible forms. Every such domain definition must have the following associated with it.

1. *A legible form*: which may be a list of legible forms, one for each value which can be assigned to the attribute. For example, the mode Product-Code could be defined as having a form :123 (e.g. a colon followed by three digits).
2. *An ordering*: which defines the effect of the comparison operators greater-than, less-than, and equals. In effect this order maps the attributes values defined above into the set of all integers. For example, given the attribute SEX, the comparison could be defined so that MALE > FEMALE.
3. *The effect of the arithmetic operators*: if it is sensible to do arithmetic with user-defined forms, then this should be defined. For example, the attribute COLOUR has values YELLOW, BLUE, and GREEN and YELLOW + BLUE = GREEN is thus defined.

System designers implement user-defined forms by writing software to recognize the new form and adding it to RDBMS by using the own-code facilities of the Software Environment (see Chapter 9). They implement the ordering and the effect of the arithmetic operators by using the domain encoding features of the Encoded Environment (see Chapter 7).

The implementation of the RDBMS Multi-Level Schema has led to the system supporting a domain of mode 'CSL string' which is used to implement the predicates described in Section 6.4. This must be regarded as an RDBMS Defined Mode, as it is only required to implement one Information System (i.e. the Multi-Level Schema).

The Domain Values

No matter whether the system designer gives a domain a standard or user-defined legible form, he is allowed to define its values. Basically, each domain has the following associated with it.

1. *An unassigned value*: which is the value to be given to the domain if no other value is assigned to it.
2. *A default value*: which is the value to be given to the domain in response to the user using the default value facilities of the Control Sub-Language.
3. *A number of valid values*: which may be described by defining the validation rules governing them.

Again the system provides a number of standard facilities for validating domain values which are:

1. *Validation by range*: the domain value is defined as lying within one or more ranges of domain values.
2. *Validation by set*: the domain value is defined as being equal/not equal to a member of a given set.
3. A combination of 1 and 2 above.

Should the system designer find that he cannot use these mechanisms to validate a set of domain values, then the system allows a set of domain values to be validated by a user-written own-code procedure. Such a procedure is added to the system by using the Software Environment facilities described in Chapter 9.

6.6 Mapping Objects to Entity Sets

So far this chapter has described the facilities supported by the Information Environment; this section describes how these are used to support the Object Environment identified in Chapter 5.

Given an Object Environment which defines a number of object types, each with its associate information types, then it is fairly natural to map each object type and its associated information types into an entity set with its associated attributes and domains. In practice it has been found that while there is often a one to one correspondence between the objects and entity sets, the operational needs of the Information System often leads to a situation where it is not necessary to support all the objects. For example, if the proposed Purchasing System is used in such a way that nobody uses the entity set PRODUCT, then there is little or no point in implementing it until it is to be used. It should however be recognized that the system designer is merely deferring the implementation of the entity set rather than cancelling it from his design.

Having identified the necessary entity sets, attributes, and domains, then the system designer has to fill in the rest of the design. For each domain he needs to define the rules governing the domain values and their use. For each entity set he has to identify the functional dependencies between the attributes and confirm that they are in third normal form. Finally, he has to define the relationships between the entity sets and produce narrative descriptions of the predicates governing each set.

Given this information, then the design of the Information Environment is complete. All that remains is to identify the privacy restrictions governing that environment.

6.7 Users, Ownership, and Privacy

The Information Environment defines the main end-user interface to the system; consequently it also provides the mechanisms needed to identify and to handle data ownership and privacy.

Associated with each data base is a user known as the Data Base Controller who is responsible for the data base and for registering data base users. Depending on the budgets assigned him by the Data Base Controller a user may be able to define new entity sets. A user who defines a new entity set is said to be the owner of that set and is responsible for the values held in it. The owner of an entity set can use the privacy facilities to control other users' access to it. The following briefly provides a more detailed description of these facilities.

The Data Base Controller

The Data Base Controller is identified by the fact that he was the user who initially set up the data base.

The Users

The Data Base Controller describes those users who are able to access his data base by identifying the user's name and associate budgets.

These budgets define the user's overall use of the system (defined by an absolute limit/unit time and an increment), the maximum cost for an individual user request, and whether the user is allowed to own entity sets.

Ownership

If a user is allowed to own entity sets then he is allowed to create new entity sets or views of entity sets. Once a user defines an entity set or view then he is said to be the owner and is responsible for allowing users access to it.

Assigning Access Rights to Other Users

The owner of an entity set may assign rights to access the values in that entity set to some other user. When assigning such rights the owner of an entity set has to identify the subject of the rights, the rights, and the user being assigned the rights. An owner may assign rights by identifying one of the following:

1. A complete entity set which is identified by the entity set name.
2. Specific attributes in an entity set which are identified by entity set and attribute names.
3. Specific attribute values in an entity set which are identified by a Control Sub-Language predicate which uniquely identifies the values in the entity set.

The access rights assigned to a user may take the form of one or more of the following:

> NO ACCESS, READ ACCESS, UPDATE ACCESS, CREATE ACCESS, DESTROY ACCESS, and ALL ACCESS.

Once a user has been assigned rights to access information in an Information System then he may assign those rights to other users.

6.8 An Example of an Information Environment

This section takes the example of the Object Environment for the Purchasing System described in the previous chapter and defines the related Information Environment.

The Entity Set Descriptions

The system supports the following entity sets:

Entity-set Name	Attributes	Domains
PRODUCT	<u>CODE</u>	DOMCODE
	NAME	DOMNAME
	DESCRIPTION	DOMDESC
	PRICE	DOMPRICE
	DATEFROM	DOMDATE
	DATETO	DOMDATE
Predicate:	An entity can belong to the set providing the company has bought or sold the product with the given code in the last five calendar years.	
SUPPLIER	<u>CODE</u>	DOMCODE
	NAME	DOMNAME
	ADDRESS	DOMADDRESS
	TERMS	DOMTERMS
	AREACODE	DOMAREACODE
Predicate:	An entity can belong to the set providing the company has bought a product from the supplier in the last five calendar years.	

Entity-set Name	Attribute	Domains
CUSTOMER	CODE	DOMCODE
	NAME	DOMNAME
	ADDRESS	DOMADDRESS
	TRADEGROUP	DOMTRADEGROUP
Predicate:	An entity can belong to the set providing the company has sold products to the customer in the last five calendar years.	
SALESMAN	CODE	DOMCODE
	NAME	DOMNAME
	COMMISSION	DOMCOMMISSION
	DATE	DOMDATE
Predicate:	An entity can belong to the set providing the salesman has worked for the company in the last 20 years.	
ORDERTO	PRODUCTCODE	DOMCODE
	SUPPLIERCODE	DOMCODE
	ORDERNO	DOMORDERNO
	ORDERDATE	DOMDATE
	DELIVERYDATE	DOMDATE
	QUANTITY	DOMQUANTITY
Predicate:	An entity can belong to the set providing the dependencies PRODUCTCODE and PRODUCT. CODE and SUPPLIERCODE and SUPPLIER.CODE are satisfied.	
ORDERFROM	PRODUCTCODE	DOMCODE
	CUSTOMERCODE	DOMCODE
	ORDERNO	DOMORDERNO
	ORDERDATE	DOMDATE
	DELIVERYDATE	DOMDATE
	QUANTITY	DOMQUANTITY
Predicate:	An entity can belong to the set providing the dependencies PRODUCTCODE ∈ PRODUCT.CODE and CUSTOMERCODE ∈ CUSTOMER.CODE are satisfied.	
SALESMAN TO CUSTOMER	CUSTOMERCODE	DOMCODE
	SALESMANCODE	DOMCODE
	DATE	
Predicate:	Dependencies CUSTOMERCODE ∈ CUSTOMER.CODE and SALESMANCODE ∈ SALESMAN.CODE must be satisfied.	

Note: underlines indicate candidate key attributes.

Dependencies

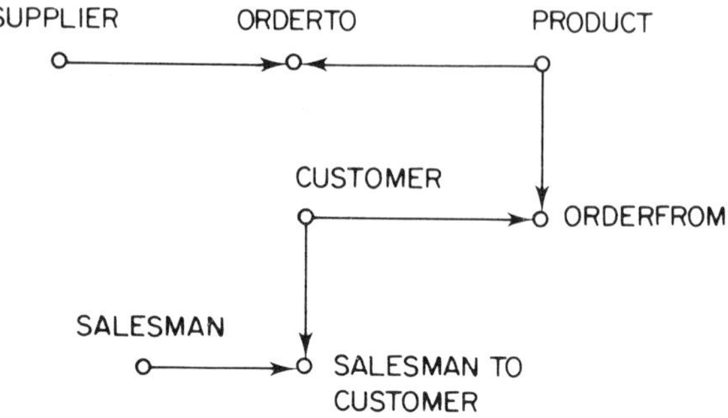

Domain Definitions

Domain name	Mode	Length	Checks
DOMADDRESS	string	1–200	none
DOMAREACODE	string	1–1	set A, B, C, F, G, H, J.
DOMCODE	integer	4	range 0 to 9,999
DOMCOMMISSION	string	1–1	set A to F
DOMDATE	date	8	none
DOMDESCRIPTION	string (100)	1–100	none
DOMORDER NO	integer	5	range 0 to 10,000
DOMPRICE	real	4, 2	range 0.01 to 9999.99
DOMQUANTITY	integer	5	limits +ve
DOMTERMS	string	1–1	set A to M, P. R
DOMTRADEGROUP	string	1–1	range A to P

where the length values have the following meaning

for integer : *m* legible integer characters
for string : LMIN – LMAX legible characters
for real : *m*, *n*, e.g. *m* integer before the decimal point and *n* after
for date : 8 characters

7

The Encoded Environment

7.1 Introduction

Given an Information Environment which contains a number of entity sets and an estimate of the types and frequency of accesses made by users to those entity sets, then the Encoded Environment provides mechanisms which allows system designers to tune an Information System so as to increase its efficiency and thus make it more cost effective.

In this situation, the efficiency of an Information System is dependent on three factors:

1. The usage of the Information Environment, as reflected in the pattern of requests submitted via the Control Sub-Language.
2. The choice of access paths used to support that Information Environment.
3. The choice of the storage structures and mapping algorithms used to maintain the access paths.

The design of the Encoded Environment is concerned with the first two of these factors; consideration of the third factor is deferred to the design of the Stored Environment. The rest of this section describes the mechanisms which may be used to map the Information Environment to the Encoded Environment and describes how the designer should use them.

7.2 Mapping the Information Environment into an Encoded Environment

In defining an Encoded Environment, the system designer has two mechanisms at his disposal. These are:

1. The encoded entity set.
2. The information-dependent mappings which map entity sets into encoded entity sets.

The Encoded Entity Set

In the Encoded Environment each access path is represented by an encoded entity set which is a tabular structure with the following properties.

1. Each encoded entity set contains a number of encoded entities, each of which is defined over one or more encoded attributes.
2. Each encoded attribute is defined over an encoded domain. Furthermore, within an encoded entity set, one or more of the encoded attributes may be defined as candidate key and/or access key attributes. As with the Information Environment, the identification of candidate key attributes clarifies the functional dependencies within the encoded entity set. The identification of access key attributes defines the encoded attributes which are to be used to provide access to the entities in the set. Obviously, in those cases where a non-candidate key attribute is chosen as an access key, a particular value of an access key will define several different encoded entities, the entities being distinguished by the values of the candidate key attributes.
3. Each encoded domain has a clearly defined machine representation such as integer, real, string, or date. These, in fact, define an internal canonical form of the domains.
4. Access to an encoded entity set involves either accessing each of the encoded entities in turn or subsetting the encoded entities by providing some suitable selection criteria and then accessing each of the encoded entities in the subset. The subset of an encoded entity set may be defined by providing selection criteria involving encoded attribute values. If such a criterion identifies an access key attribute then the system will exploit the index structures identified in the underlying Stored Environment, otherwise processing the selection criteria will involve testing each encoded entity in turn. Naturally, such a subset may contain none, one, or more encoded entities.

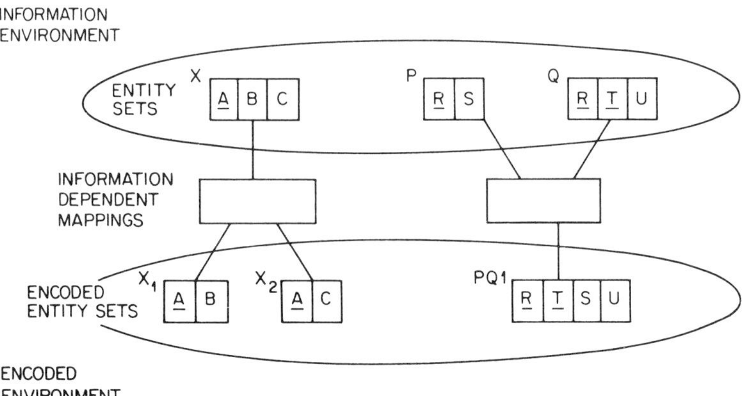

Figure 7.1 Information-dependent mappings

An Information-Dependent Mapping

The term *Information-Dependent Mapping* is used to describe the collection of algorithms which are used to support the entity sets of the Information Environment by using the encoded entity sets of the Encoded Environment.

The interaction between the two Environments and the information-dependent mapping is illustrated in Figure 7.1. A basic feature of the information-dependent mappings is that they support the predicates which are associated with each entity set and described in the Information Environment Schema. They also define how entity sets are mapped into encoded entity sets and how domains are mapped into encoded domains. Thus, given an Information Environment, the system designer defines:

1. *The static predicates*: these embody the local and global conditions an entity must satisfy in order to belong to an entity set. Each predicate consists of a unit of software which is generated by the system designer from the Information Environment predicate, and validates an entity in terms of its content, thus allowing for checks between attribute values. It also uses the dependency and privacy information to validate an entity against information in other entity sets. This static predicate is in force for the whole time that an entity set is in existence. As described in Chapter 6, most of this software is generated by adding parameters in the form of Control Sub-Languages clauses to the standard system; however, the Software Environment does provide facilities for a user to provide his own code.
2. *Rules for encoding entity sets*: these define how an entity set is mapped into the encoded entity sets of the Encoded Environment. These rules incorporate the relational operators, permutation, projection, join, restriction, selection, union, intersection, and difference, together with the non-relational operator order.
3. *Rules for encoding domains*: these define how a domain is mapped into an encoded domain.

System designers should recognize that the execution of the static predicates will affect the choice of access key attributes within the Encoded Environment; however, no special attention needs to be paid to this matter because the software responsible for adding static predicate information to CSL statements operates at a higher level than the data base monitor which will advise a system designer on optimal mappings for entity sets and domains. The next two sections of this chapter discuss the rules for encoding entity sets and encoding domains, while the last section discusses the data base monitor in more detail.

7.3 Encoding Entity Sets

Given an entity set in the Information Environment then this may be mapped directly to an encoded entity set and all access to that entity set will be supported by making the appropriate use of the underlying encoded entity set. However, given an Information Environment containing many entity sets, and a usage profile which records the anticipated and/or actual use of those entity sets, then it becomes apparent that mapping each entity set into a single encoded entity set may produce a very inefficient system. Such a system may be made more effective by using operators to map entity sets into encoded entity sets, the choice of these operators being directly related to the capabilities of the end-user interface, in this case the Control Sub-Languages.

As explained in Chapter 4, the Control Sub-Languages are relationally complete, and consequently an end-user may use any of the relational operators: permutation, projection, join, restriction, selection, union, intersection, and difference; together with the non-relational operator: order.

Figure 7.2 shows how an end-user may, via the Control Sub-Languages, exploit these operators to produce temporary entity sets in the External Environment. From the diagram it is apparent that the cheapest way of providing these facilities is to maintain encoded entity sets which are a mirror image of those in the External Environment. For this reason, it is appropriate to consider the use of relational operators to map entity sets into encoded entity sets.

From the point of view of encoding entity sets there is some ambiguity about the use of the relational operators. For example, a projection could be interpreted as either taking one entity set and producing two or more encoded entity sets, or taking one encoded entity set and producing two or more entity sets. As the Control Sub-Language supported by this system also permits the use of these operators, the rule has been established that the Information Environment forms the basis for all relational operators. Thus a projection always takes an entity set and produces two or more encoded entity sets. Figure 7.3 illustrates the effect of

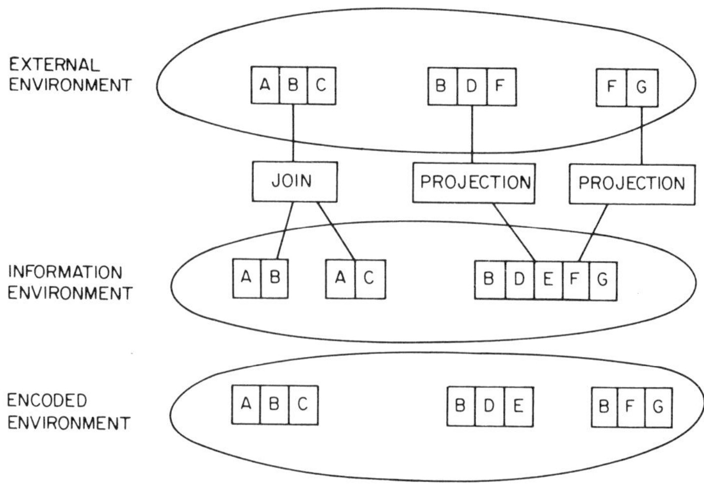

Figure 7.2 Mapping from the external to encoded Environment

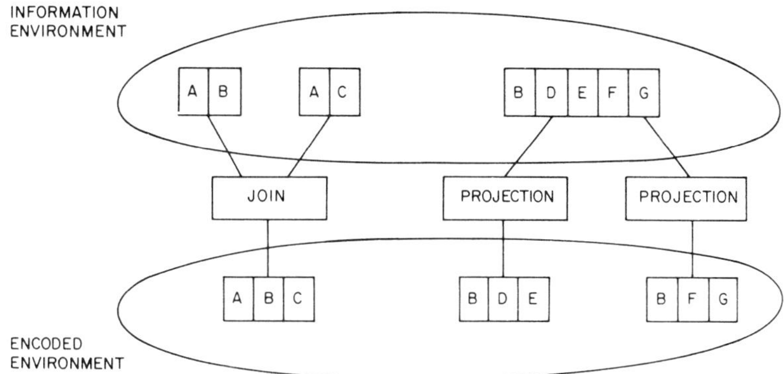

Figure 7.3 Using the relational operators to encode entity sets

these relational operators, while the following sections provide a further description of their use.

In describing the use of these operators it is necessary to ensure that operations which the end-user performs at the level of the Information Environment can be transformed without loss of information into operations at the level of the Encoded Environment. The following sections discuss each of the permitted operations in order to assess the potential for information loss.

Projection

Given an entity set S with three attributes A, B, and C, where A is a candidate key attribute and the others are functionally dependent on it, then the projection operator can be used to define any of the following encoded entity sets:

EES1 ($\underline{A}$, B, C)
EES2 ($\underline{A}$, B)
EES3 ($\underline{A}$, C)
EES4 (B, C).

When holding either EES1 or EES2 and EES3, the system designer knows that he is maintaining all the information in the original set S because the join of EES2 and EES3 over A is the same as EES1. However, if he maintains EES2 and EES4, then he introduces some inconsistency into the system because the join of EES2 and EES4 is not necessarily equivalent to EES1; this is known as the so called 'Connection Trap'. In this case the system designer can get round the problem by maintaining EES4 in addition to EES1 or (EES2 and EES3).

Join

Using the join operator to encode entity sets, the system designer identifies two or more entity sets and maps them into a single encoded set. However, the system designer must recognize that in the general case he is reintroducing into his system the creation and deletion anomalies which he removed by the normalization process. There are a number of solutions to this problem.

One general solution which may be used is to encode two entity sets by using the so called 'Joined Normal Form' operator. This operator, which was first identified by Babb (see BABB 1), maintains an encoded entity set containing the join of two or more entity sets and uses flags to distinguish between the attribute values related to each of the individual entity sets. Values of the entities of the individual entity sets are recovered by making the necessary projections conditional on these flags Other general solutions involve the use of techniques to distinguish between entities drawn from the individual entity sets and involve the user of either pointer chains as used in System R (see ASTRAHAN 2) or record type flags.

The join operator itself may only be used safely in restricted circumstances, such as the case where there is a one to one dependency between two entity sets. It is also safe to use it if the resulting encoded set may only be read.

Selection, Restriction, Intersection, and Difference

Given an entity set which may contain several thousand entities, then it may be convenient to split these entities into groups and hold the groups in separate encoded entity sets, the groups being defined by some common criteria such as NAMES with initials A to M, and N to Z. This is achieved by defining some selection criteria to govern the encoding. The original set can be recreated using the relational operator union on the two encoded entity sets.

Other criteria for subsetting the entities of an entity set, such as 'all entities which are not in the encoded entity set *Y*' may be defined using the relational operators restriction and difference.

7.4 Encoding Domains

In the Encoded Environment, the system designer describes an encoded domain by its internal form which may be defined as being one of the following:

1. a binary integer,
2. a real,
3. a string,
4. a date.

Chapter 6 described how for each domain in the Information Environment the system designer defines its legible form, an ordering of the possible domain values, and the effect of the arithmetic operators on the domain values. However, the ordering and effect of arithmetic operators can only be supported by exploiting the facilities for domain encoding. Domain encoding is achieved by providing for each domain a unit of software which maps that domain into an encoded domain. Much of this software is an integral part of the system. For example, the system provides facilities to directly encode integers, reals, strings, and dates. It also provides facilities for encoding strings to integers, strings to reals, strings to strings. Without a doubt the most useful of these is string to integer, and, using it, a system designer can map a set of names or characters into a set of integers. The ordering of the names and the effect of the arithmetic operators is then defined by the order of the integers and the effect of the arithmetic operators on those integers. In those cases, where a system designer needs domain encoding over and above that provided in the system, he can use the facilities of the Software Environment to extend the system by writing his own algorithms.

7.5 Deciding on an Encoded Environment: the Data Base Monitor

Given an Information Environment and the Control Sub-Language statements which represent the requests for information for a given period of time, then the system designers need to define an Encoded Environment which processes the requests at a minimal cost of computer resources. One way of achieving this objective is to consider the usage of the Information Environment in terms of:

1. *Within-Set Attribute Usage:* which analyses the usage of particular groups of attributes.
2. *Within-Set Entity Usage:* which analyses the usage of particular groups of entities.
3. *Between-Set Attribute Usage:* which analyses the usage of more than one set, the sets being related by the frequent use of Control Sub-Language statements involving join and restriction.

Once this information has been gathered, then it is a fairly straightforward task to use one or more of the relational operators to map the entity sets to the required encoded entity sets. However, this raises the question of how best to collect this information. Pragmatically, there are only two solutions to this problem: either the end-users provide an estimate of their system usage, or the system itself provides a statement of the actual usage. In fact, the system designers should use both methods and balance the estimates against the actuals.

The RDBMS monitor output is presented to the system designers in the form of entity sets. For example, the Within-Set Attribute Usage is defined in an entity set which consists of

$$\text{WSA USAGE} = \{\text{Entity Set, Start Attribute, End Attribute, Access Rate, } P(w, x, y, z) = \text{true}\}$$

where P is defined as: 'Entity Set identifies the entity set under consideration, Start Attribute and End Attribute identify two attributes within Entity Set, and Access Rate identifies the frequency with which the system has used values of Start

Attribute to identify value of the End Attribute.' (Access Rate may be thought of as identifying the frequency of use of the 'Access Path' from Start Attribute to End Attribute.) Given an entity set SUPPLIER with attributes SCODE, SAREA, and STERMS, then WSA USAGE could contain details of six possible access paths:

SCODE → STERMS
→ SAREA
STERMS → SCODE
→ SAREA
SAREA → SCODE
→ STERMS.

Obviously, within this entity set all these access paths could be provided by using a serial search of the third normal form. However, this may be inefficient and more effective structures are available.

If in this set all the access paths are used to the same extent, then the set can only be supported using a totally inverted structure:

SCODE → STERMS
→ SAREA
STERMS → SCODE
SAREA → SCODE.

However, if some paths are heavily used and others are never used, then the set may be better supported by a partially inverted structure. One such partially inverted structure is:

SCODE → STERMS
STERMS → SCODE
SCODE → SAREA.

This illustrates the use of system monitoring in the case of Within-Set Attribute Usage; the Within-Set Entity Usage and Between-Set Attribute Usage are defined and used in a similar way.

7.6 An Example of an Encoded Environment

This section describes a possible encoding of the example Information Environment described at the end of Section 7.3. In doing this work, it has been decided that an optimal encoding of the Information Environment is to use 6 encoded entity sets, as follows:

Encoded entity-set name	Encoded attributes	Mapping
EESSUPPLIER	CODE NAME ADDRESS TERMS AREA	SUPPLIER is mapped to EESSUPPLIER
EESORDERFROM	PRODUCTCODE SUPPLIERCODE ORDERNO ORDERDATE DELIVERYDATE QUANTITY	ORDERFROM is mapped directly to EESORDERFROM
EESPRODUCT	CODE NAME DESCRIPTION PRICE	PRODUCT is mapped directly to ESSPRODUCT
EESORDERFROM	PRODUCTCODE CUSTOMERCODE ORDERNO QUANTITY	ORDERTO is mapped partially into EESORDERTO and partially into EESORDERFROMDATES. This separation relies on the fact that there is a one to one relationship between (PRODUCTCODE, CUSTOMERCODE) and ORDERNO.
EESORDERFROMDATES	ORDERNO ORDERDATE DELIVERDATE	
EESCUSTOMERS	CUSTOMERCODE SALESMANCODE CUSTNAME CUSTADDRESS TRADEGROUP SALESMANCODE SALESMANAME SALEMANDATE	the entity sets CUSTOMER, SALESMAN and SALESMAN TO CUSTOMER are joined to form a single entity set. (Allowable only if there is a one to one relationship between Customer and Salesman.)

These encodings are illustrated in Figure 7.4, and the underlines indicate access key attributes.

INFORMATION ENVIRONMENT
MAPPING
ENCODED ENVIRONMENT
SUPPLIER
ORDERTO
PRODUCT
ORDERFROM
CUSTOMER
SALESMAN TO CUSTOMER
SALESMAN
DIRECT
DIRECT
DIRECT
PROJECTION
JOIN
EES SUPPLIER
EES ORDERTO
EES PRODUCT
EES ORDER FROM
EES ORDER FROM DATES
EES CUSTOMERS

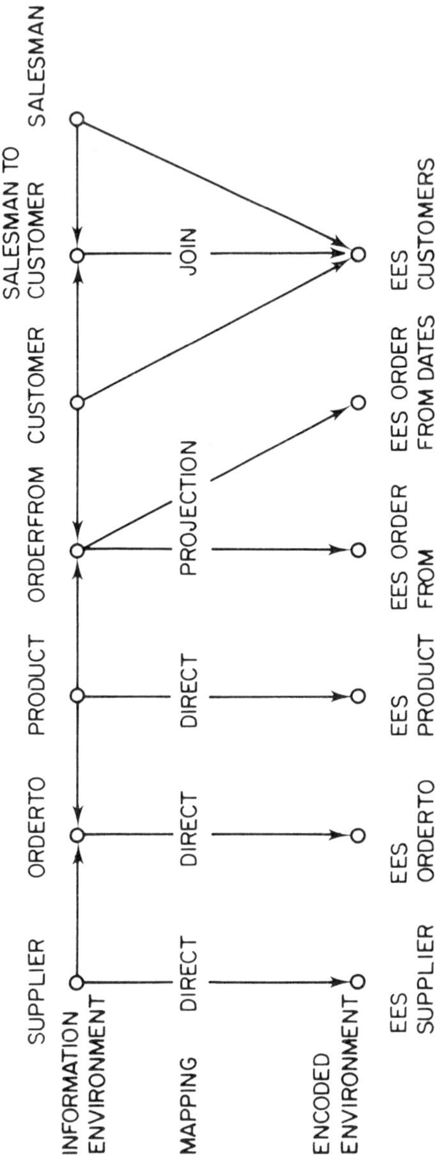

Figure 7.4

8

The Stored Environment

8.1 Introduction

When the designer has completed the design of an Encoded Environment, he has defined a set of encoded entity sets with encoded attributes, some of which are designated access key attributes, and thus provide access to the non-access key attributes. He has also defined for each access key attribute some weighting which reflects its frequency of use. Given this as a starting position, then designing a Stored Environment is very much a question of designing storage structures to meet these performance objectives.

At this level in the system, the designer has two mechanisms at his disposal. These are:

1. The stored entity set.
2. The data-dependent mapping.

8.2 The Stored Entity Set

A stored entity set is similar to an entity set in so far as it is a tabular structure with the following properties:

1. Each stored entity set is defined over one or more stored attributes.
2. Each stored attribute is defined over a stored domain and may be defined as being an access key attribute or a non-access key attribute.
3. Each stored domain has a clearly defined hardware representation such as integer, real, string, or date. It may also take the form of a container which has the property that it consists of a string of characters which has a maximum and minimum length. The only permissible operations on a container are the read and write operations which are used to make its contents accessible to the mappings higher in the system.

In addition to these fixed properties, a stored entity set has the following optional properties:

4. *Attribute ordered*: a stored entity set is said to be attribute ordered because it has an explicit ordering for the attributes.
5. *Entity ordered*: a stored entity set is said to be entity ordered because it has an explicit ordering for the entities.
6. *Insertable*: a stored entity set is said to have the property of insertability if extra entities may be added to it and deleted from it at any point.
7. *Expandable*: a stored entity set is said to be expandable if extra entities can only be added to it or deleted from it at the end of the set.

8.3 The Data-dependent Mapping

A data-dependent mapping is a mapping algorithm which supports a stored entity set by mapping it into one or more lower level stored entity sets. One example of a data-dependent mapping is an index sequential access method which supports a file of records consisting of keys and data and maps it into a set of blocks by using an index which maintains details of the highest keyed record in each block. Such a mapping supports a stored entity set defined as

stored entity set A is (string KEY, container DATA)

and maps it into two stored entity sets

stored entity set INDEXA is (string KEY, integer BLOCK NUMBER)
stored entity set BLOCKSA is (integer BLOCK NUMBER, container RECORDS).

In fact, data-dependent mapping is a term which has been used to cover a wide variety of the conventional access methods. It is used to describe simple access methods such as index sequential, the various varieties of B-Tree, and Chaining and Tagging algorithms. It is also used to describe more complex access methods such as the chained lattice structures supported by the basic data handler of an IDMS system (see ICL 7) and the hierarchical record structures of IMS (see IBM 3). Naturally, some of these more complex structures may only be represented by using a succession of stored entity sets and mappings.

The point which is vital is that many of the conventional access methods fall into this general category of data-dependent mappings because they can only be used successfully at this level of the system.

8.4 Backup, Lock Management, and Error Recovery

In addition to the basic tasks of maintaining data in stored entity sets, the Stored

Environment may support three other facilities which are fundamental to the successful implementation of an Information System, namely:

1. Backup
2. Lock management
3. Error recovery.

Some of these facilities are supported by the algorithms built into the data-dependent mappings identified in the previous section, while others are supported by the underlying operating system. This split of responsibility between the operating system and the data base management system can cause a lot of difficulty because of the seemingly illogical interactions which occur between them.

Most operating systems support a *Primitive File System* which is responsible for mapping data sets or primitive files (i.e. files seen as a collection of blocks), on to the storage hierarchy of the machine, and for making blocks from those files available to the data base management system. In turn, the Stored Environment level of the data management system maps stored entities into these blocks, maintains pointers and other similar data used to link entities to form stored entity sets, and makes the stored entities available to the higher levels of the system.

Backup

System designers need to ensure that the mapping of stored entity set to primitive file does not make unnecessary demands on the primitive file system. For example, the system designers could define a primitive file which occupies 6 volumes and is sparsely used. Now, if the primitive file system demands that all these volumes be on-line, then it would be advisable to redesign the encoded and stored entity sets so that the heavily used information occupies a single primitive file which is always on-line, and the rest occupies one or more primitive files which are kept on a lower level of storage until they are required.

The primitive file system will provide an Information System with backup by maintaining dumps of its primitive files. Such dumps form a basis for the backup facilities to be built into the data base management system which may itself choose to maintain journals containing before-looks or after-looks of stored entities.

As the cost, efficiency, and availability of an Information System is directly related to the backup facilities used to support the system, it is important to ensure that the level of backup for such a system is appropriate to the needs of the end-user. For example, designing an Information System with a 95% availability requires a lot of design to ensure that the recovery time for a particular stored entity set is as short as possible. An Information System which can afford half a day to recover from a system failure does not require this design as it may rely entirely on the underlying operating system facilities.

Lock Management

The current state of technology requires that locking in the system is activated at the level of individual data objects which may take the form of either a stored entity, or a stored entity set supported by the Stored Environment, or a block or primitive file supported by the primitive file system. System designers should be wary of restrictions involving the number of users tasks which can access a primitive file or the number of primitive files available to a user task because they can ruin the effectiveness of an Information System. Obviously, not all these problems can be solved by amending or changing the data-dependent mappings, and there are occasions when the problem can only be overcome by changing the Encoded Environment.

Error Recovery

Recovering from a systems failure is, conceptually at least, a three-stage operation. The first stage is concerned with containing the error so as to prevent it from propagating further; the second stage is concerned with assessing the damage; while the third stage is concerned with recovering from the damage. Again, the relationship between the data base management system and the operating system can cause a lot of difficulties, and the system designer needs to spend some time making sure that the two do not react in such a way as to jeopardize the integrity of the Information System. For example, the operating system may abandon the data management system before it has completed containing an error, and, worse still, may pre-empt recovery by automatically abandoning files and seemingly corrupt blocks. Such actions may necessarily leave the data management system with the unenviable task of taking the best available copy of a data base and validating its contents to ensure that the integrity constraints described in the Information Environment still apply.

8.5 Defining a Stored Environment

The First-Level Stored Entity Sets

Given an Encoded Environment, each encoded entity set is defined over a set of encoded attributes, some of which are access key attributes. From this level, the designer of the Stored Environment can create the *first level* of stored entity set by taking each of the access key attributes in the encoded entity set and mapping it into an access key attribute in the stored entity set, and mapping all the other encoded attributes into an associated container. Obviously, if the designer wishes to use any compression or conversion techniques to provide a packing between the entities of the two environments, then this is defined at this stage in the design.

Lower-Level Stored Entity Sets

Having defined this first level of stored entity set, then the designer needs to choose a data-dependent mapping to map it to a lower level set. The choice of data-dependent mapping is governed by the efficiency constraints imposed by:

(*a*) the design decisions of the Encoded Environment,

(*b*) the efficiency of the data-dependent mappings.

Obviously, to make this choice meaningful, the efficiency of each of the data-dependent mapping algorithms needs to be quantified. This usage may be quantified under four headings:

1. *Currency usage*: a call on a mapping (a currency call) may result in a call on other lower level mapping. Such calls are known as currency calls (the reasoning for this is presented in the paper HUTT 1 and in Chapter 18), and it is possible to quantify the effective call rate on a particular mapping. This call rate defines its currency usage.

2. *Lower container space utilization*: a mapping which is concerned with mapping an upper level set into a lower level set must allow for insertions and deletions in that set, and thus automatically leads to problems of garbage collection and space utilization.

3. *Lower container working set*: in certain circumstances a mapping may need to access one, two, or more lower level containers in order to process a particular request. Given a sequence of typical requests, this defines the working set of the mapping.

4. *The CPU utilization*: a mapping is called to carry out a number of different operations on a stored entity set. For example, to read an entity, to write an entity, and to destroy an entity. There is necessarily a trade-off between the amount of CPU time used to achieve these various operations, and the system designer needs to be able to quantify and exploit that trade-off.

Figure 8.1 identifies the data-dependent mappings currently supported by the system and gives estimates as to their performance when judged against the first three of the above factors. Given this information and the overall space–time efficiency objectives of the Information System, then the system designer has some guidelines for helping him to select the most cost-effective mappings.

Figure 8.1 The characteristics of some data-dependent mappings

	Characteristics of entities		Characteristics of mappings			Effectiveness	
Mapping name	Upper set	Lower set	Space usage	Address mechanism	Currency usage upper—lower	Lower set space utilization	Working set size
SERIAL	(container data1)	(container data2)	Each lower level entity contains 1 or more upper level entities placed contiguously	serial no random access by key	N—1 depending on comparative size of data1 & data2	minimal (½ length data1 per data2)	1 or 2 lower level entities
KEYED SEQUENTIAL	(string key, container data1)	(integer no container data2)	Each lower level entity contains 1 or more upper level entities placed contiguously depending on address algorithm	serial random access by key calc.	serial N—1 depending on sizes, random 1—1	wastage depends on address con-vertion algorithm	1 lower level entity
INDEX SEQUENTIAL	(string key, container data1)	(string key integer cont no) (integer cont no string key container data2)	Set1 full of indexes Set2 packed to % full	serial random via index	serial N—1 random access 1—2 or 3 de-pending on buffering strategy and index sizes	index wastage ½ lower set entity data wastage ½ lower set entity per indexed set	2 or more depending on usage and buffering strategy
RANDOM	(string key container data1)	(integer entity, container data2)	Each lower level entity contains none one or more upper level entities depending on address algorithm	serial — all set members but not in order random access via algorithm	serial N—1 random 1—M depending on overflow to handle double hits in address algorithm	dependent on address algorithm	1 or 2 lower level entities.
IN-CORE BINARY TREE	(string key container data1)	(container data2) a single entity	upper level entities mapped into lower level entity by a tree	binary tree	1—1	amount of core dependent on overall size of upper level set	size of lower set depends on total data size

9

The Software Environment

9.1 Introduction

All through the definitions of the Information Environment, the Encoded Environment, and the Stored Environment, there have been continual references to mappings of one type or another, and building a mapping into the system implies that somewhere or other there is some run-time software to support it. Obviously, much of this run-time software can be generated from algorithms provided with the basic system; however, it is an important feature of RDBMS that designers can replace the system software with their own code. The Software Environment is used to maintain this software.

When a release of RDBMS is made, the release includes a copy of a Software Environment which contains a useful summary of all the system components provided in that release. In addition to summarizing the system components, this Software Environment highlights those components which may be altered in order to make modifications to the system. These modifications provide facilities for adding and altering the following:

1. *CSL output functions*, which provide a means of producing specially formatted outputs. An example of this is the software required to produce a special screen format on a video.

2. *CSL inline functions*, which provide a means of producing capabilities which operate on all the members of an entity set. An example of this would be a function MAXMIN which produced the maximum and minimum of an entity set attribute.

3. *Information-dependent mappings*, which provide a means of writing software to support the predicate governing an entity set.

4. *Data-dependent mappings*, which provide a means of using own-code software to support a stored entity set. A user would use this facility in order to add a Binary Tree algorithm to the System.

5. *Domain scanning facilities*, which provide a means of handling a domain with a different syntactic form to those currently supported by the System. An example of this would be used to include a Project Number of the type: ":XYE".

6. *Domain encoding facilities*, which provide a means of using own-code software to encode domain values. An example of the use of this facility is providing an encoding from the values R, O, Y, G, B, I, V to values 1, 2, 3, 4, 5, 6, 7.

7. *Domain validation facilities*, which provide a means of using own-code software to validate the values of a domain.

8. *Encoded domain processing facilities*, which provide a means of handling an encoded domain which has a form different to those currently supported by RDBMS. An example of the use of this facility would be to incorporate ODC strings into RDBMS and thus enable it to be used for bibliographic retrieval purposes.

As well as keeping account of the RDBMS software, the Software Environment may be used by the designer of an Information System to model and support those application programs which merely use RDBMS as a source of data.

These facilities are fairly comprehensive, and furthermore not all the facilities are necessary to produce a normal Information System. For this reason the facilities are divided into two groups. The first group contains those which are intended for regular use and thus are automatically available to the designers of an Information System. The facilities in this group include those for adding new CSL output functions, CSL inline functions, information-dependent mappings, domain encoding and validation procedures, and for handling application programs. The second group contains those facilities which tend to be difficult to use. The facilities in this group include those for adding new data-dependent mappings, new domain scanning, and new encoded domain processing facilities.

This wide applicability leads to a Software Environment which is capable of modelling complex software, and embodies the mechanisms necessary to bind this software together and thus generate the data base management system required to support an Information System. The rest of this chapter identifies a model which may be used to represent complex software structures, and describes the own-code facilities supported by RDBMS.

9.2 An Analysis of Software

When designing a mapping, or any other algorithm, the designer starts by adopting a top-down approach, and in order to achieve this he has to think of his software as having three facets or functional parts. These are:

1. The Data Objects associated with it;
2. the Functions it supports;

3. its Units.

A data object is defined as any data used within the system. The term may be applied to any entity set, attribute, encoded entity set, or stored entity set; it may also be applied to any item of data such as an integer which is used within an algorithm and is thus local to it. Given a particular algorithm, then the data objects associated with it are dependent on its position in the system and the functions it supports.

A unit is the name given to a unit of design in a mapping. At the higher levels of the design process this relates to conceptual rather than actual software, but, at the lower levels of the design, a unit relates to a procedure or a macro.

An interface to a mapping can be divided into a number of functional parts where a function has the same significance as an action in a Data Manipulation Language. A Unit which takes the form of a procedure or macro has a function which takes the form of a formal procedure or macro declaration.

Relationships between Data Objects, Functions, and Units

If a system is to be described by giving separate descriptions for the three functional parts outlined above, then there has to be a description of the relationships between these parts. Basically, each function provides an interface which allows a user to manipulate a data object type which is represented by a function parameter; furthermore, each function is supported by a single unit. In general, each unit supports its function by making calls on one or more lower level units, by accessing data objects, and by calling other functions. In fact a unit can make several different types of use of a data object; for example it may read it, or assign a value to it. For this reason it is necessary to describe the relationship between a unit and the data objects it accesses. Figure 9.1 illustrates the relationship identified in this section.

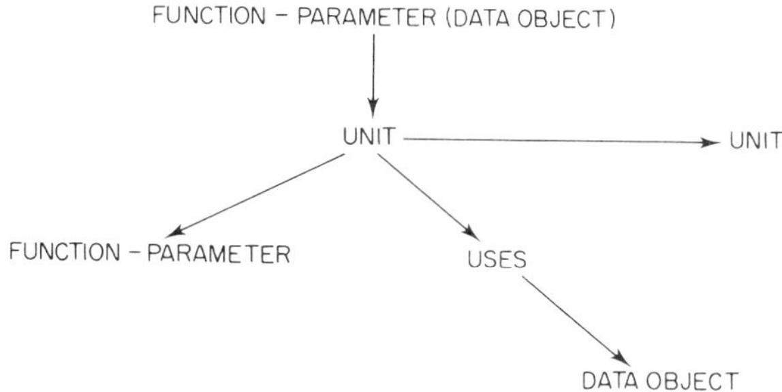

Figure 9.1 Relationships between data objects, functions, and units

9.3 Maintaining Descriptions of Software

Having recognized that a mapping or algorithm has three functional parts, and described how these parts are interrelated, it is now necessary to outline the facilities supported by the Software Environment. These facilities may be separated into facilities for maintaining the descriptions of data objects, units, functions, and the relationships between them (these are described in this section), and facilities for generating software from these descriptions (these are described in a later section).

In fact the facilities supported by the Software Environment not only recognize the relationships described above but need to recognize two other relationships. One relationship is concerned with identifying that each unit of software is written and maintained by a programmer who is treated as a system user. The other relationship is concerned with the problem of binding software and the fact that certain unit names need to be available to such software as the linkage editor or loader. These relationships are supported by introducing three new concepts, namely Responsibility, User, and Calls.

Within RDBMS, the Software Environment is represented by adding a further level to the Multi-Level Schema. The dependency diagram governing this level is illustrated in Figure 9.2.

When using the Software Environment Schema, the user only uses the entity set Data Object to describe the data which is local to a unit. Descriptions of a data object such as an entity set which has already been defined in one of the other Environments are always available to this level of the system; the user merely refers to them, and the full description is accessed by the code generators described later.

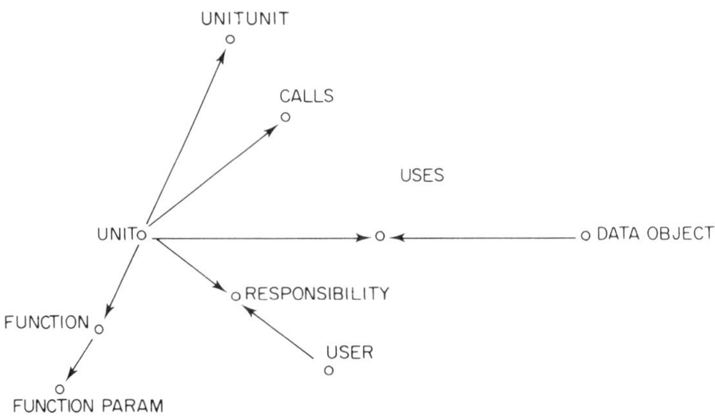

Figure 9.2 Dependency diagram for the Software Environment

Descriptions of Units

Each unit in the system has the following information associated with it:

1. A Name.
2. A Group Number: the software is separated into groups such that a group number identifies a logical unit of design. For example, typical groups of software in a compiler could be the Lexical Analyser and the Syntax Analyser.
3. An Identifier: which is a reference for the software and is unique within a group.
4. Details of when it was produced and who was responsible.
5. A Natural Language narrative describing its operation.
6. A code body, written in an Algorithmic Language such as COBOL, ALGOL, or PASCAL.

This information is maintained in an entity set UNIT.

Hierarchies of Units

Devotees of Structured Programming or Structured Modelling have already identified that software can be represented using hierarchical tree structures, and there is no doubt that a tree structure is useful for representing the connectivity of a system. This connectivity occurs because either:

1. a unit decomposes into one or more lower level units, or
2. a unit calls one or more other units.

Obviously, within any large software system there are units which are related by both factors. Furthermore, a unit may be called by more than one other unit, and a unit may call itself recursively; for this reason a representation of the connectivity of such a system results in a lattice structure. Within the Software Environment, this lattice structure is maintained by using an entity set UNITUNIT.

With any large system representing decomposition, using this mechanism can become rather cumbersome, and for this reason a second method has been found useful. Given the entity set UNIT, the senior system designer can make a judicial choice of identifiers in UNIT.IDENTIFIER, so that the designer can produce a hierarchical representation by using the Control Sub -Language Output Function TREES. This function will interpret values of UNIT.GROUP and UNIT.IDENTIFIER in order to produce a hierarchical representation of the system. Figure 9.3 illustrates the entity set UNIT and the effect of the function TREES.

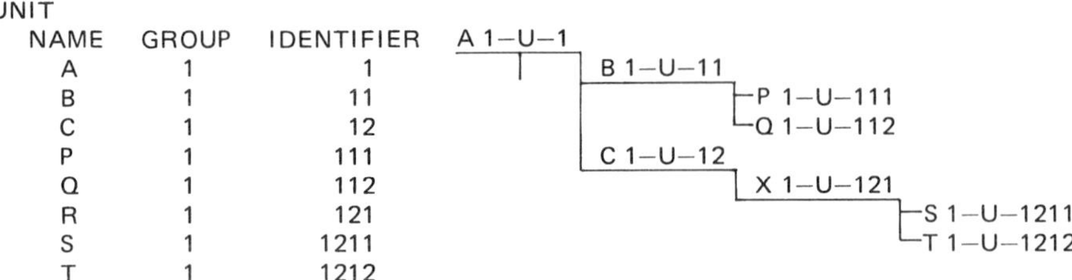

UNIT

NAME	GROUP	IDENTIFIER
A	1	1
B	1	11
C	1	12
P	1	111
Q	1	112
R	1	121
S	1	1211
T	1	1212

Figure 9.3 The entity set UNIT and the Control Sub-Language function TREES

Functions

Each of the functions held in this system are maintained in an entity set FUNCTION, where each entity describes a particular function. The majority of functions are either procedure or macro declarations, and in these cases the system merely maintains details of the form of the declaration as written in an Algorithmic Language and details of its parameters; some functions however are available to system users via the Control Sub-Language interface, in which case the function may have more than one representation, e.g. its Algorithmic Language form and its Control Sub-Language form.

9.4 Generating Code from the Software Environment

Adding new software to RDBMS requires the designer of an Information System to undertake two tasks which may be summarized as follows:

1. Design an algorithm which supports the required capabilities and satisfies the design criteria appropriate to its level in the system, and add its description to the Software Environment.

2. Generate the algorithm as an object code module and bind it to the rest of the RDBMS code.

In order to gain more insight into this process it is worthwhile considering an example, and with this in mind we will consider the case of adding a new CSL Inline Function MAXMIN to the system.

The Inline Function MAXMIN

Briefly stated, the purpose of MAXMIN is to take as input any entity set containing a single integer attribute and produce a new entity set containing two single-valued attributes containing the maximum and minimum values of the set.

The Design

In order to achieve this the designer has to design a new mapping which, by following the design rules for this level of the system, must contain four parts. Three of these parts are responsible for the initialization, execution, and deinitialization of the function, while the fourth is responsible for its overall control.

Given these rules, then the designer would produce a specification of the units and data to be used by the function MAXMIN which could lead to the two tree structures illustrated in Figure 9.4 together with further information to connect them together.

Generating the Code

Once this step has been completed, the designer will use the code generators and compilers to produce an object code version of MAXMIN.

RDBMS itself provides no facility for generating object code: at best the Software Environment acts as a combined file system and macro processor which will create a source of code segment which may then be presented to a compiler. Figure 9.5 illustrates the relationship between the information maintained in the system and an algorithmic language compiler.

Briefly, in order to compile the source code for a particular unit, the code generator has to bring together the following:

(a) the code body for the unit

(*b*) the definition of the function it supports

(*c*) the definitions of the functions it calls

(*d*) the definitions of the data objects it supports and uses.

From this information the system is able to generate the relevant source code segment, which may be presented to a compiler in the normal way.

Binding Code in RDBMS

The technique used to bind user-generated object code to the rest of RDBMS is

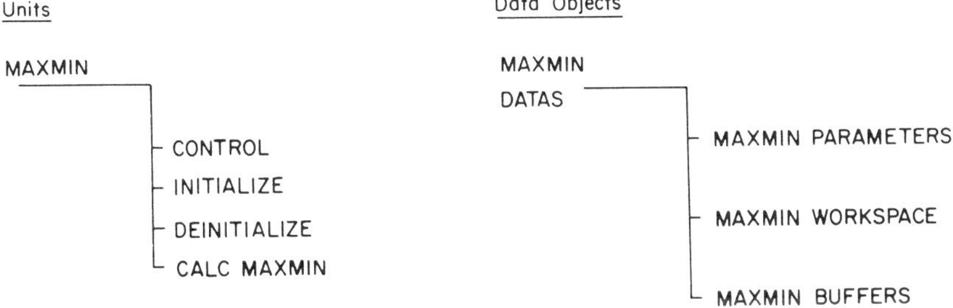

Figure 9.4 A model of the function MAXMIN

undoubtedly dependent on the underlying operating system. If the underlying operating system relies on a traditional linkage editor then the whole business may involve a system designer in a fair amount of work. With an operating system which supports run-time binding of object code, this problem may be hidden from view.

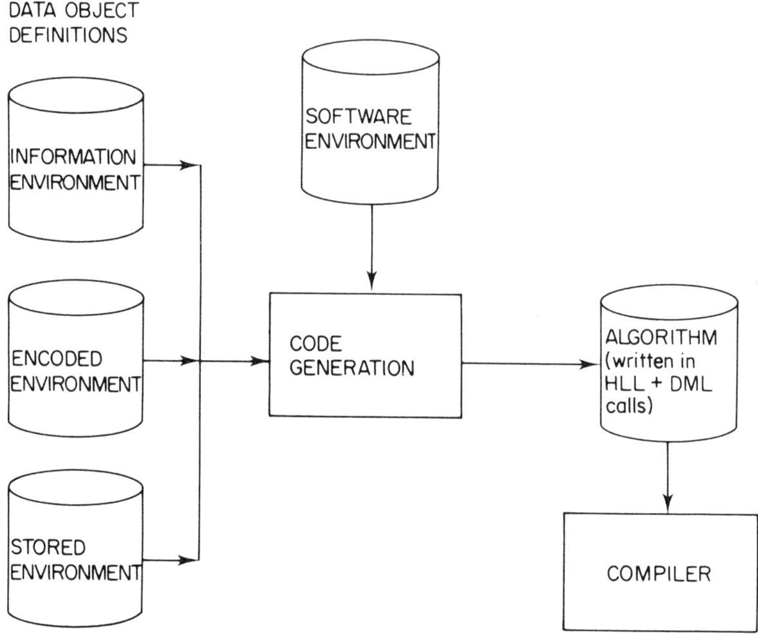

Figure 9.5 The relationship between the DBMS and an Algorithmic Language Compiler

Part C

INTERACTING WITH AN INFORMATION SYSTEM

10

A Family of Languages

As described in the System Overview in Part A, end-users can interact with an Information System based on RDBMS by using one of the family of languages known as the Control Sub-Languages. The relationship between these languages and the Job Control and Algorithmic Languages in which they are embedded has already been discussed in Chapter 4.

The system supports a number of Control Sub-Languages as follows:

1. *The Interactive Control Sub-Language*; which is used by all end-users to interact with the system.
2. *The CORAL 66–ALGOL 60 Control Sub-Language*; which provides an extension of CORAL 66 and ALGOL 60 to allow algorithms written in these languages to access information supported by RDBMS.
3. *The COBOL Control Sub-Language*; which provides COBOL with a sub-schema and data manipulation language similar to those provided by a CODASYL system.
4. *The Algorithmic Control Sub-Language*; which is an interface supported by RDBMS to act as a target for the CORAL 66–ALGOL 60 and COBOL Control Sub-Languages identified above.

The wealth of material required to describe all these languages is obviously beyond the scope of this book. For this reason this Part of the book provides a detailed description of one language: the Interactive Control Sub-Language, hereafter known as CSL, and follows it with a brief description of the Algorithmic Control Sub-Language and the COBOL Control Sub-Language. The rest of this Introduction describes the syntax of the Interactive and Algorithmic Control Sub-Languages.

10.1 An Approach to Language Specification

The widespread use of syntax driven compilation almost dictates that all the language descriptions should be based on some syntactic notation. This section defines the notation used to express the forms the CSL constructs may assume. The notation is a modified version of that used to express ALGOL 60 (see ALGOL 1) and is described here for completeness.

The Basic Notation

In each syntax rule, the name of the construct is written on the left-hand side of a right pointing arrow. Each of the forms or alternatives which the construct may take is written on the right-hand side separated by a vertical rule. For example:

primary-colour → red | blue | yellow

which means 'in this system a primary-colour is any one of red, blue, or yellow and no other alternatives are allowed.'

Note that construct names are in lower case, and when a name is made up of two or more words they are connected by hyphens. The name of consecutive constructs can therefore be written consecutively without connecting hyphens.

Actual CSL text will occur in the description of constructs. This can always be distinguished from the constructs because CSL constructs consist of:

1. Key-words: which are not used for construct names and which are underlined.
2. Special symbols such as '='. The only special symbols used in the syntax notation are ' →', '[', ']', '*' and ' | '.

Bracketing

The symbols '[' and ']' are used as brackets within the syntax rules. Thus the rule

condition → [<u>while</u> | <u>until</u>] boolean-serial-clause

means the same as

condition → <u>while</u> boolean-serial-clause | <u>until</u> boolean-serial-clause.

Notice that [*a* |] means *a* or nothing. For example

a → [*b* |] [*c* |]

means the same as

a → *b* | *bc* | *c* | nothing.

Repetition

A construct may be repeated an indefinite number of times; the symbol * is used to express this.

An asterisk may appear once within a pair of brackets and denotes that:

1. the contents of the brackets may be repeated any number of times; but
2. the last repetition ends at the point where the asterisk appears.

Thus

$$a \rightarrow b[c * d]e$$

means

$$a \rightarrow bce \mid bcdce \mid bcdcdce \mid \text{etc.}$$

The following flowchart outlines the sequence of repetition:

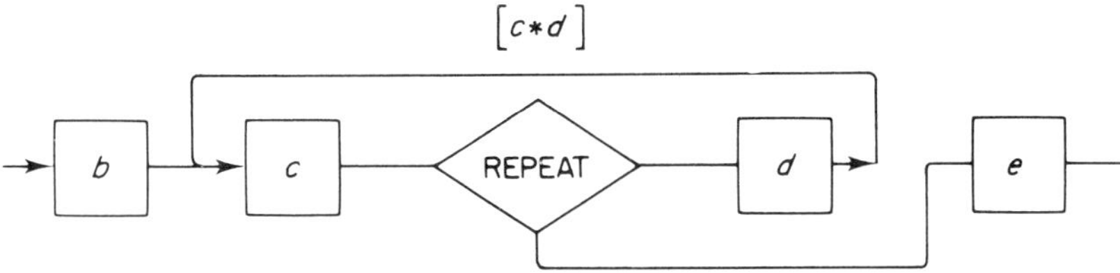

Notice that

$a \rightarrow [*b]z$ means $a \rightarrow z \mid bz \mid bbz \mid$ etc.

while

$a \rightarrow [b*]z$ means $a \rightarrow bz \mid bbz \mid bbbz \mid$ etc.

Upper Case Letters

In many syntax rules upper case lettering appears as part of the construct names. This is a shorthand notation for writing down a number of similar rules. Each rule using upper case names stands for all those rules which can be derived from it by replacing each occurrence of an upper case name with one of the alternatives which are given for the upper case name in the meta-syntax, with the restriction that where the same upper case name appears more than once in a rule it must be replaced by the same alternative on each occasion. (This mechanism defines a Two-Level Grammar, similar to that used in the Original Report on ALGOL 68 (see WIJNGAARDEN 1).) Thus if

$$X \rightarrow x \mid y \mid z$$

is a meta-syntactic rule,

$$Xa \rightarrow bXb \mid Xc$$

is equivalent to the three rules

$$xa \rightarrow bxb \mid xc$$

$$ya \rightarrow byb \mid yc$$

$$za \rightarrow bzb \mid zc.$$

10.2 The Syntax of the Interactive Control Sub-Language

1.	Interaction	→	command end
2.	command	→	read-statement | ACTION1-statement | login-statement | logout-statement | set-statement | deset-statement | select-statement | ACTION2-statement | copy-statement
3.	ACTION1	→	update | destroy | create | write
4.	ACTION 2	→	select&read | select&update | select&create | select&update | select&write
5.	read-statement	→	read target-list [multi-set-predicate |] [order-expression-list |]
6.	ACTION1-statement	→	ACTION1 single-set-target-list [single-set-predicate |] [order-expression-list |]
7.	login-statement	→	login user-name, work-space-name
8.	logout-statement	→	logout
9.	set-statement	→	set currency-name [access-rights-list |] to target-list [predicate |] [order-expression-list |]
10.	deset-statement	→	deset currency-name
11.	select-statement	→	select count from currency-name-*a* starting position [ref currency-name-*b* |]
12.	ACTION2-statement	→	ACTION2 count from currency-name-*a* starting position
13.	copy-statement	→	copy target-list-1 [for copy-access-right |] from target-list-2 [predicate |]
14.	target-list	→	single-set-target-list | multi-set-target-list
15.	target-list-1	→	single-set-target-list

16.	target-list-2	→	multi-set-target-list
17.	multi-set-target-list	→	[single-set-target-list *,]
18.	single-set-target-list	→	[target-list-part *,]
19.	target-list-part	→	function | set-attribute-list | simple-expression | result-name
20.	predicate	→	multi-set-predicate | single-set-predicate
21.	multi-set-predicate	→	such that [msp-member, *]
22.	single-set-predicate	→	suchthat [ssp-member, *]
23.	msp-member	→	assignment | quantifier-list (msp-part) | msp-part
24.	msp-part	→	join-expression | selection-expression
25.	ssp-member	→	assignment | quantifier-list (selection-expression) | selection-expression
26.	assignment	→	[result-name | set-attribute] := [function | simple-expression]
27.	quantifier-list	→	[quantifier *,] | not
28.	quantifier	→	[quant |] currency-name from set-name
29.	quant	→	all | some
30.	join-expression	→	[join-clause * and]
31.	join-clause	→	selection-expression | join-part | (join-part)
32.	join-part	→	[join * logical-oper]
33.	join	→	set-attribute join-compare set-attribute
34.	selection-expression	→	(selection-clause) | selection-clause
35.	selection-clause	→	[selection-part * logical-oper]
36.	selection-part	→	selection | (selection)
37.	selection	→	[comparison * logical-oper]
38.	logical-oper	→	and | or
39.	comparison	→	simple-expression compare simple-expression
40.	join-compare	→	*< | *≤ | *= | *≥ | *> | *<>
41.	compare	→	< | ≤ | = | ≥ | > | <>
42.	simple-expression	→	term | add-operator term | simple-expression add-operator term
43.	term	→	factor | term multiply-operator factor
44.	add-operator	→	+ | –
45.	multiply-operator	→	* | /
46.	factor	→	set-attribute | text | number | date
47.	order-expression-list	→	withorder [order-expression *,]
48.	order-expression	→	[set-attribute | attribute] [up | down]
49.	set-attribute	→	set-name . attribute-name
50.	set-name	→	name | currency-name | view-name
51.	currency-name	→	name

52.	attribute-name	→ name
53.	result-name	→ name
54.	view-name	→ name
55.	date	→ digit digit / digit digit / digit digit
56.	name	→ letter-string [digit-string ǀ]
57.	letter-string	→ [letter *]
58.	digit-string	→ [digit *]
59.	number	→ N ǀ N . N ǀ . N
60.	count	→ N
61.	position	→ N
62.	N	→ [digit *]
63.	text	→ quote [character *] quote
64.	access-rights-list	→ for [access-right *,]
65.	access-right	→ readaccess ǀ updateaccess ǀ createaccess ǀ destroyaccess ǀ writeaccess
66.	copy-access-right	→ updateaccess ǀ createaccess ǀ writeaccess
67.	character	→ letter ǀ digit ǀ other-char
68.	letter	→ A ǀ B ǀ — — ǀ Y ǀ Z
69.	digit	→ 0 ǀ 1 ǀ 2 ǀ 3 ǀ 4 ǀ 5 ǀ 6 ǀ 7 ǀ 8 ǀ 9
70.	quote	→ ' ǀ "
71.	end	→ ;

10.3 The Syntax of the Algorithmic Control Sub-Language

This language is described in Chapter 16; in this definition of its syntax the numbering of the statements is the same as that used in the definition of the Interactive Control Sub-Language. This numbering has been retained in order to make easy comparisons between the two.

1.	Interaction	→ command : response
2.	command	→ set-statement ǀ deset-statement ǀ select-statement ǀ ACTION2-statement ǀ binding-statement
4.	ACTION 2	→ select&read ǀ select&update ǀ select&create ǀ select&update ǀ select&write
9.	set-statement	→ set currency-name [access-rights-list ǀ] to target-list [predicate ǀ] [order-expression-list ǀ]
10.	deset-statement	→ deset currency-name
11.	select-statement	→ select count from currency-name-*a* starting position [ref currency-name-*b* ǀ]

12. ACTION2-statement → ACTION2 count from currency-name-*a* starting position
14. target-list → single-set-target-list | multi-set-target-list
17. multi-set-target-list → [single-set-target-list *,]
18. single-set-target-list → [target-list-part *,]
19. target-list-part → function | set-attribute-list | simple-expression | result-name
20. predicate → multi-set-predicate | single-set-predicate
21. multi-set-predicate → such that [msp-member, *]
22. single-set-predicate → suchthat [ssp-member, *]
23. msp-member → assignment | quantifier-list (msp-part) | msp-part
24. msp-part → join-expression | selection-expression
25. ssp-member → assignment | quantifier-list (selection-expression) | selection-expression
26. assignment → [result-name | set-attribute] := [function | simple-expression]
27. quantifier-list → [quantifier *,] | not
28. quantifier → [quant |] currency-name from set-name
29. quant → all | some
30. join-expression → [join-clause * and]
31. join-clause → selection-expression | join-part | (join-part)
32. join-part → [join * logical-oper]
33. join → set-attribute join-compare set-attribute
34. selection-expression → (selection-clause) | selection-clause
35. selection-clause → [selection-part * logical-oper]
36. selection-part → selection | (selection)
37. selection → [comparison * logical-oper]
38. logical-oper → and | or
39. comparison → simple-expression compare simple-expression
40. join-compare → *< | *≤ | *= | *≥ | *> | *<>
41. compare → < | ≤ | = | > | ≥ | <>
42. simple-expression → term | add-operator term | simple-expression add-operator term
43. term → factor | term multiply-operator factor
44. add-operator → + | –
45. multiply-operator → * | /
46. factor → set-attribute | text | number | date
47. order-expression-list → withorder [order-expression *,]
48. order-expression → [set-attribute | attribute] [up | down]

49.	set-attribute	→	set-name . attribute-name
50.	set-name	→	name | currency-name | view-name
51.	currency-name	→	name
52.	attribute-name	→	name
53.	result-name	→	name
54.	view-name	→	name
55.	date	→	digit digit / digit digit / digit digit
56.	name	→	letter-string [digit-string |]
57.	letter-string	→	[letter *]
58.	digit-string	→	[digit *]
59.	number	→	N | N . N | . N
60.	count	→	N
61.	position	→	N
62.	N	→	[digit *]
63.	text	→	quote [character *] quote
64.	access-rights-list	→	<u>for</u> [access-right *,]
65.	access-right	→	<u>readaccess</u> | <u>updateaccess</u> | <u>createaccess</u> | <u>destroyaccess</u> | <u>writeaccess</u>
66.	copy-access-right	→	<u>updateaccess</u> | <u>createaccess</u> | <u>writeaccess</u>
67.	character	→	letter | digit | other-char
68.	letter	→	A | B | — — | Y | Z
69.	digit	→	0 | 1 | 2 | 3 | 4 | 5 | 6 | 7 | 8 | 9
70.	quote	→	' | "
72.	binding-statement	→	<u>binding</u> currency-name as [attribute name (location)*,]
73.	response	→	address
74.	location	→	mode address
75.	mode	→	integer | real | text | date
76.	address	→	byte-start byte-length
77.	byte-start	→	integer
78.	byte-length	→	integer

11

Using the Information Environment

11.1 Introduction

An Overview of the Language

The user accesses the Information Environment by using CSL. The language provides the user with the following capabilities:

1. It allows him to create and destroy the whole or part of an entity set. It also allows him to transfer the contents of an entity set between the Information Environment and his terminal or work space.
2. It allows him to set up pointers or currencies such that the name of the currency can be used as a convenient shorthand for the entity set at which it points. The entity set pointed at by a currency may be thought of as the value of the currency.
3. It allows the user to describe new entity sets which exist solely within the User Work Space and which are related to existing entity sets by powerful mathematical operators and predicates.

The User Work Space

The user first addresses the system by issuing a LOGIN statement and providing a password and other credentials. The system checks this information and, providing the user is accredited, sets up a work space. This work space will remain in existence and associated with that user/terminal until the user breaks that association by using a LOGOUT statement. The whole interactive session which is delimited by LOGIN and LOGOUT is hereafter known as a Job.

The work space is best thought of as a repository used by the system to support the user's requests. However, as users develop their ability to use the system, the work space may be used to hold temporary entity sets which the user can create more or less at will.

The Interaction

Once the user has created a work space he can begin to use the system. The user operates the system via a sequence of interactions. Each interaction consists of a command which may identify some information followed by the information in question. Thus a typical interaction would consist of:

```
– READ PRODUCT
> PRODUCT
> CODE NAME  DESCRIPTION     PRICE
> 59   INK   INK IN POTS     0.20
> 73   PEN   IN PACKS OF 10  1.00
> 84   NIB   IN PACKS OF 5   0.20
```

The above example illustrates an important feature of the system, namely the clear distinction between the command part of the interaction and the information part. This distinction needs to be maintained in the user terminal, and for this reason the terminal operates in three modes:

1. *Command Mode:* which allows the user to submit a new CSL statement.
2. *Information Mode:* which allows the user to submit new information.
3. *Error Mode:* which is the mode the system resorts to whenever there has been an error. The system provides mechanisms whereby a user can move from error mode to either command or information mode.

The system supports a variety of different types of terminals, for example videos and teletypes, and the exact mechanism used to distinguish between these modes is very much terminal dependent. The text of this book uses three distinctive characters to maintain this distinction: '–' is used to indicate command mode, '>' is used to indicate information mode, and '$' is used to indicate error mode. It also uses the character ';' to move from command mode to information or error mode and back again. The RDBMS Reference Manual (see HUTT 2) defines the exact mechanisms used to represent these modes on the different types of terminal.

11.2 Accessing Information

The language statements can be divided into a number of groups. This section describes the statements which are used to access entities from an entity set; the following sections describe those used to create and destroy entities and set and deset currencies.

A Simple Read

Given the Purchasing System outlined in Chapter 6, then the user can retrieve information about Products by using a READ statement. The complete interaction would look like this:

```
– READ PRODUCT;
> PRODUCT
> CODE NAME DESCRIPTION     PRICE
> 59     INK     INK IN POTS        0.20
> 73     PEN     IN PACKS OF 10  1.00
> 84     NIB     IN PACKS OF 5    0.20.
```

In terms of the languages, the command may be divided into READ which is called an *Action*, and PRODUCT which is called the *Target* of that action. The information output by the system consists of all the entities currently in the entity set. This information is presented in a tabular form which consists of a two-part heading or proforma, the first part of which contains the entity set name, the second part of which contains the attribute names. In the example above, these names have been fixed by the system designers and are merely provided to enable end-users to keep track of their information. Once the heading has been produced the information is output. When using this basic READ statement, the order of the attributes values and the format of the individual values is dictated by the Information Environment Schema submitted by the system designers. Chapter 12 describes those facilities which are available to end-users to vary this output.

A Simple Update

In addition to reading information from the system, users must be able to add new information to the system and to correct and alter existing information. The ability to add new information is provided by the CREATE statement, while the ability to alter existing information is provided by the UPDATE statement. This section describes the UPDATE statement while the CREATE statement is described in the next section.

The UPDATE statement can be used to alter an entity or group of entities providing that alteration does not affect the values of candidate key attributes. If the user wishes to alter the candidate key attributes this is considered to be altering the existence of the entity and the user uses either a CREATE or WRITE statement.

When processing an UPDATE interaction, the system accepts the command and outputs the definition of the entity set in the form of a Proforma. For example:

```
– UPDATE PRODUCT;
> PRODUCT
>CODE   NAME  DESCRIPTION  PRICE.
```

This is followed by an invitation for the user to submit his data in lines, each of which defines an entity for the entity set identified by the proforma. The diagram below illustrates the complete interaction once the user has submitted an entity.

```
– UPDATE PRODUCT;
> PRODUCT
> CODE  NAME   DESCRIPTION          PRICE
> 59    "INK"  "INK IN 10CC POTS"   0.25
> ;
```

where each entity must contain the attribute values in the order defined by the proforma although those values need not be aligned under attribute headings. The attribute values for a particular entity are accepted by the system, providing *the attribute values are individually valid and the system already contains a valid value for the attributes which make up the candidate key.*

A Simple READ and UPDATE (Videos Only)

In addition to the simple READ and UPDATE statements, the use of video terminals with a facility to amend information on the terminal screen has resulted in the following use of a combination of READ and UPDATE statements.

The user starts by typing a conventional READ statement which results in the required information being shown on the screen in the usual way. Having done this, the user edits the information on the screen and then issues an UPDATE statement with no target list to signify that he has no further edits to perform and that the information can be returned to the system. The key to this facility is the complete separation of the command mode area of the video screen from the information mode area.

11.3 Creating and Destroying Information

The READ and UPDATE statements described in the previous section allow the user to amend the entities in the entity set identified in the target list, but does not allow him to create and destroy these entities. The CREATE and DESTROY statements are designed to permit this.

The CREATE Statement

The CREATE statement allows the user to add new entities to an existing entity set. Thus the interaction below illustrates the interaction necessary to add a new entity to the set PRODUCT illustrated above.

```
– CREATE PRODUCT;
> PRODUCT
> CODE  NAME         DESCRIPTION      PRICE
> 60    "INK BLUE"   "IN 10CC POTS"   0.25
> ;
```

The CREATE statement will fail if the system finds an existing entity with the given candidate key. It will also fail if the user fails to give a complete candidate key. For example, when creating entities for an entity set which has a candidate key with more than one attribute, then the user must supply values for all the candidate attributes. The use of this facility is shown in the following example which creates new entities in the entity set ORDERFROM.

```
– CREATE ORDERFROM;
> ORDERFROM
> PRODUCTCODE CUSTOMERCODE ORDERNO ORDERDATE DELIVERYDATE QUANTITY
– 60         1793         1007    10/3/74   30/6/74      2
– 64         1793         1005    10/3/74   30/6/74      5
$ ERROR TYPE 600 : DEPENDENCY ON PRODUCTCODE NOT
  SATISFIED
– ;
```

In this example, the first entity is valid because it passes the validity checks. The second entity fails the validity checks because comparison with the contents of the entity set PRODUCT shows that the system does not contain a product with candidate key (64).

The DESTROY Statement

The user can destroy entities in an entity set by using the DESTROY statement; the interaction below illustrates the interaction necessary to remove an entity from an entity set.

```
– DESTROY PRODUCT;
> PRODUCT
> CODE NAME  DESCRIPTION         PRICE
> 59   "INK" "INK IN 10CC POTS"  0.25
> ;
```

The DESTROY statement will fail if the system cannot find an entity the exact contents of which match the entity submitted by the user.

The WRITE Statement

The user of the system may often wish to submit information to an entity set without concerning himself as to whether he is creating a new entity or updating an existing entity. This facility is provided by a WRITE statement.

When processing a WRITE statement, the system first attempts an UPDATE action; however, if the user has submitted a new candidate key value it is processed as a CREATE action.

11.4 Currencies

In the previous sections all the interactions addressed the information in the system by its entity set name, which is fine for the user who wishes to access the set once and then deal with information from another set. The user who intends to make extensive use of an entity set, however, can make more effective use of the system by establishing a conceptual pointer to refer to that set. Such a conceptual pointer is called a *currency*. For users with little experience of data base systems a currency serves the same purpose as putting your finger into one part of a book when referring to another: it serves to mark the place. The rest of this section discusses how the user sets up currencies and the advantages of using them.

Creating a Currency

The user establishes a currency by means of a SET statement, which takes the following form:

```
– SET P TO PRODUCT;
```

The effect of this statement is to create a named currency P which points at the entity set PRODUCT. Having established this currency the user can use the currency name as a convenient shorthand for the entity set name. For example, the statements

```
– SET P TO PRODUCT;
– READ P;
```

have exactly the same effect as the statement

```
– READ PRODUCT;
```

However, in the first case the user has established a relationship between P and PRODUCT; furthermore, this relationship is preserved by the system until such time as the user either specifically breaks the relationship by using a DESET statement or destroys his work space by using a LOGOUT statement.

Description Inheritance

When a user creates a currency to point to an entity set, the system establishes a correspondence between the currency and the description of the entity set at which it points. In fact, the currency is said to *inherit* the description of the set.

One important result of description inheritance is that the currency inherits the names of the attributes. Thus the command:

```
– SET P TO PRODUCT;
```

not only creates a pointer P to point to PRODUCT but also allows the user to refer to the attributes of P. Thus the user can address

P. CODE, P. NAME and P. PRICE

and these address

PRODUCT. CODE PRODUCT. NAME and PRODUCT. PRICE

respectively. This important feature of the system is known as *name inheritance.* Should the user find that he requires to change the name of an attribute, this can be achieved by using an assignment clause, which is discussed in Chapter 13.

Interlocks

It is an important feature of any Information System that it should allow many users concurrent access to the information held in the Information Environment, but it is well understood that this is only safe and practicable providing that the users are not allowed to corrupt each other's work. For this reason the system allows the users to lay claim to an entity set or part of an entity set by creating a currency which restricts others' access to that set. This is done by submitting a currency in the normal way and submitting additional parameters: a set of access rights, which informs the system of the users interlock requirements. The interaction below shows a user's request to gain read access to the entity set PRODUCT.

```
– SET P FOR READACCESS TO PRODUCT;
```

The access rights are introduced by the FOR clause and allow the user to state his needs in terms of one or more of the following: READACCESS, UPDATEACCESS, CREATEACCESS, DESTROYACCESS, and WRITEACCESS. Once a currency has been established with the given access rights then the user can use the relevant action in a command which names the currency in its target list. Given this information, the system is able to deduce the access rights which are permissible to other users and thus schedule the use of the Information Environment.

Strengthening Interlocks

Once the user has created a currency to point to an entity set, then that currency can only be removed by either using the DESET statement or destroying the work space. However, the case can arise where the user may wish to increase the strength of the locks on a currency. This can be done by submitting a new SET statement identifying the necessary new interlocks. This is demonstrated in the following example:

```
– SET P FOR READACCESS TO PRODUCT;
– SET P FOR READACCESS, CREATEACCESS TO P;
```

The first of these interactions establishes a currency P to allow read access to the entity set PRODUCT, while the second interaction is used to strengthen the interlocks associated with P so as to allow the use of the CREATE statement.

The DESET Statement

Once the user has created a currency to point to an entity set, then the currency will remain in existence until either it is specifically removed by a DESET statement or the user's work space is destroyed by a LOGOUT statement.

In normal circumstances, the existence of many currencies is not too restricting for the system; however, if the user has established access rights which effectively lock-out large sections of the Information Environment, then this can cause other users a large amount of disruption. For this reason users are encouraged to DESET currencies as soon as possible.

11.5 Copying Information

So far all the data manipulation statements READ, UPDATE, CREATE, DESTROY, and WRITE have been concerned with the transfer of information between a users' terminal and the entity sets of the Information Environment; the COPY statement is concerned with the transfer of information from one entity set to another. The example below shows the use of the COPY statement to copy information into an entity set PRODUCT1 from an existing entity set PRODUCT:

```
–COPY PRODUCT1 FROM PRODUCT;
```

The system requires that both the entity sets identified in a COPY statement exist in the Information Environment. The effect of the statement is merely to copy information from one to the other.

As described above, the effect of the COPY statement is exactly the same as if the user had read the information from the entity set PRODUCT on to his terminal and then resubmitted it to the entity set PRODUCT1 by means of a WRITE statement. A user may qualify the effect of the COPY statement by using a FOR clause. Thus, for example, a user wishing to update the entity set PRODUCT1 by taking information from the entity set PRODUCT can achieve this by using a COPY statement of the form:

```
–COPY PRODUCT1 FOR UPDATEACCESS FROM PRODUCT;
```

Needless to say, the only permissible access right which can be used in a COPY statement are writeaccess which is the default, CREATEACCESS, and UPDATEACCESS.

11.6 The Cost of an Interaction

Whenever a user submits a request to RDBMS, the system carries out calculations in order to estimate the cost of processing the request and the length of time the user is likely to have to wait in order to get his results. Naturally, if the cost of processing a request is low and the timescales reasonably short then the system carries out the work as quickly as possible. However, if the request demands more resources than the user is allowed in his budget, or if the time scales are longer than some default, then the system asks the user for further instructions. In either of these cases the user has the choice of either cancelling the request or submitting it for processing on the Background System, which is considerably cheaper but results in a delay. In the case when the system notes that the request may take some time, the user can signify that he intends to wait for the results, whereupon the system will carry out the work.

12

Manipulating Entity Sets

Chapter 11 described how CSL provides facilities for a user to transfer information between a given entity set and his terminal. This works well providing the user wishes to access the whole of a single set; however, if the user wishes to do more than this, then he has, implicitly or explicitly, to create a new temporary set. This temporary set exists within the user's work space and is linked to the entity sets of the Information Environment by the successive use of the relational operators. These operators are:–

1. Permutation
2. Projection
3. Selection
4. Restriction
5. Join
6. Division
7. Union
8. Intersection
9. Difference

and a definition of them may be found in Appendix A. Needless to say, this is not a minimum list of operators in so far as it is possible to manage the system with fewer operators (for example many systems do not support a restriction operator), but it does define those operators which are supported by RDBMS.

12.1 Relational Algebra and Relational Calculus

Given that the relational operators provide the basic mechanisms for manipulating entity sets, then there are basically two ways of representing these facilities within CSL. One approach is to allow the user to state in some algebraic form the rules which relate a new temporary set to the existing sets, while the other approach requires a user to state the conditions which need to be met for an entity from an existing set to belong to the new set. Languages based on these approaches are said to be based on Relational Algebra and Relational Calculus respectively. In order to stress the differences between these two approaches, the next two sections contain an outline description of the relational algebra language ISBL which is supported by the Peterlee Relational Test Vehicle (PRTV) (see NOTLEY 1, TODD 2, and HALL 1), and an overview of CSL which is a relational calculus language.

A Relational Algebra: ISBL

ISBL provides a user with an interface where each of the relational operators is represented by a special symbol or symbols. The following examples, which are based on the Purchasing System described in Chapter 6, demonstrate the use of this type of interface.

EXAMPLE	MEANING
PRODUCT % NAME, CODE	% implies a permutation and projection of the attributes NAME and CODE from the entity set PRODUCT
PRODUCT ; CODE > 100	; implies a selection of all entities from the entity set PRODUCT which have a CODE greater than 100
PRODUCT * ORDERFROM	* implies a join of the entity sets PRODUCT and ORDERFROM

The operators union, intersection, difference, and division are represented by the use of (+), (.), (–), and (÷ ÷) respectively. As the use of any of these operators always produces an entity set, they can be combined together to form longer expressions. For example a user wishing to select all entities from the entity set PRODUCT where CODE is greater than 100 and wishing to project out the attributes CODE and NAME would achieve this by writing:

PRODUCT ; CODE > 100 % CODE, NAME.

A Relational Calculus: CSL

Within CSL each temporary entity set exists within the user's work space and is linked by a predicate and target-list to the permanent sets of the Information

Environment. All CSL statements which subset or manipulate entity sets and thus define a temporary set have the following form:

Action Target–List Predicate Order–Expression–List

where action is any of the six basic actions: SET, CREATE, DESTROY, UPDATE, WRITE, and READ described in Chapter 11 and the three parts target-list, predicate, and order-expression-list allow the user to define a new set with its predicate and state how he wishes to view it. The effect of these various parts are:

1. *Target-list:* this defines the attributes of an entity set which the user wishes to access in the order he wishes to see them.
2. *Predicate:* this is used to define the conditions an entity must satisfy in order to belong to the set and to describe how the set is derived from the other sets in both the user's work space and the Information Environment.
3. *Order-expression-list:* this is used to control the order of entities in the entity set.

The fact that CSL is based on the relational calculus does not mean that the user of CSL should not be aware of the relational operations which underline the system. Some of these operators are explicitly available within CSL, while the use of the others is implied within CSL. The target-list gives the user explicit control over the permutation and projection operators, while the predicate gives explicit control over the selection, join, restriction, and division operators. The use of the other operators is implied from a combination of both the action, the target-list and the predicate.

The remaining sections in this Chapter describe the target-list, the predicate, and the order-expression-list.

12.2 The Target-List

All the basic statements, READ, UPDATE, WRITE, CREATE, DESTROY and SET expect the user to submit a target-list. In all cases this target-list defines the entity set which the user wishes to access. It defines the attributes of the entity set and it defines their order. It thus implies the use of the permutation and projection operators.

In the language there are two classes of target-list:

1. *A single-set-target-list:* which allows the user to identify attributes drawn from a single entity set. Typical forms for a single-set-target-list are:

PRODUCT
PRODUCT.CODE
PRODUCT. (CODE. NAME)
PRODUCT. CODE, PRODUCT. NAME

2. *A multi-set-target-list:* which allows the user to identify attributes drawn from one or more entity sets. Typical forms for a multi-set-target-list are:

PRODUCT. CODE, CUSTOMER. NAME
PRODUCT. (CODE, NAME), CUSTOMER. (CODE, NAME)

The following examples illustrate the use of these target-lists.

Example 1

– READ PRODUCT. (NAME, CODE, PRICE);
– READ PRODUCT. NAME, PRODUCT. CODE, PRODUCT. PRICE;

These two statements have the effect of reading all the entities from PRODUCT and permuting the attributes to the order NAME, CODE, and PRICE.

Example 2

– READ PRODUCT. (NAME, PRICE);

This statement has the effect of reading entities which consist of a projection of NAME and PRICE from PRODUCT.

12.3 The Predicate

Each entity set of the Information Environment may be governed by a predicate, which states the conditions an entity must satisfy in order to belong to the set. These predicates, called static predicates, are defined by either using natural language, in which case they are supported by software which is part of the Software Environment, or by CSL-style predicates. In either case the static predicate is incorporated into the run time system (see Chapter 20). When a user of CSL defines a temporary entity set, he needs to define a predicate which defines how the entities in this temporary set are derived from the entities of the existing sets. These predicates, called dynamic predicates, are directly interpreted by the system software.

CSL predicates take the form of a series of propositions in either the Propositional Calculus or First Order Predicate Calculus.

Propositions

Propositional Calculus (often mistakenly described as Boolean Algebra) is a method of calculating with sentences or declarations each of which produces a value 'true' or 'false'. In CSL, such a sentence is called a comparison, and examples of comparisons are:

```
PRODUCT. CODE = 4
PRODUCT. NAME < 'INK'
PRODUCT. CODE > ORDERTO. PRODUCTCODE
```

where the entity set name used on the left-hand side of the comparison must appear in either the target-list or on the right-hand side of a preceding comparison or join, and the attribute-name must identify an attribute which exists within that entity set. The comparisons which are provided are: less-than, less-than-equal, equal, greater-than-equal, greater-than, and not-equal defined by $<$, $\leqslant$, $=$, $\geqslant$, $>$, and $<>$, respectively. The evaluation of a comparison is a two-stage operation. The first stage, type checking, is concerned with checking to ensure that either the operands identified on the left- and right-hand side are defined over the same domain and are thus directly comparable, or that the domain on the right-hand side can be coerced into the same form as that on the left-hand side, in which case they are coerced to the common form and then compared. If this check succeeds, the coercion and comparison result in a value of either 'true' or 'false'.

In many cases a user may wish to access entities which are constrained by more than one comparison. In this case the user may provide a list of comparisons linked by the logical operators AND and OR.

For example, using the Purchasing System, the interaction to read all ORDERFROM from customer with code 1997 which are to be delivered after 1/6/74 would be written:

```
– READ ORDERFROM SUCHTHAT ORDERFROM.
  CUSTOMERCODE = 1977 AND ORDERFROM.
  DELIVERYDATE = 1/6/74;
```

The operators AND and OR can be used to link together any number of comparisons. The value of a sentence containing the operators AND and OR is determined by evaluating each comparison to produce a value of 'true' or 'false' and then applying the usual AND and OR operators to these values.

Well-Formed Formulae

Given a Proposition with several comparisons, for example,

```
PRODUCT.CODE = 4 AND PRODUCT.NAME = 5 OR PRODUCT.
PRICE = 0.25
```

it may be interpreted as either

(PRODUCT. CODE = 4 AND PRODUCT. NAME = 5)
OR PRODUCT. PRICE = 0.25

or

PRODUCT. CODE = 4 AND(PRODUCT. NAME = 5
OR PRODUCT. PRICE = 0.25)

and there needs to be some convention to distinguish between the two meanings. The result of using this convention is to produce what are called *Well-formed formulae*. Within CSL, the convention has been adopted that propositions are evaluated from left to right with AND taking precedence over OR (i.e. AND is evaluated before OR). A user wishing to resolve ambiguities may do so by using brackets.

Joins

A multi-set-target-list allows a user to access a temporary set, the attributes of which are drawn from the attributes of more than one of the permanent sets in the Information Environment, the temporary set being constructed by means of the relational operator: join. The conditions governing a join may be defined either explicitly or implicitly.

A user defines a join explicitly by identifying the entity sets to be joined together in the target-list and then using the predicate to state explicitly the conditions used to drive the join. Such a condition is signified by an operator of the form '* compare' where the '*' indicates that a join is to be performed and 'compare' indicates the conditions governing the join. Given two sets PRODUCT and ORDERFROM, then the user may find all orders of Products from Customers by performing the following:

– READ PRODUCT. (CODE, NAME, PRICE), ORDERFROM. (CUSTOMERCODE, ORDERNO) SUCHTHAT PRODUCT.CODE *= ORDERFROM.PRODUCTCODE;

In this example, the target-list identifies 5 attributes, three from PRODUCT and two from ORDERFROM. The predicate shows that a join is to be governed by the values of PRODUCT.CODE and ORDERFROM.PRODUCTCODE.

A user defines a join implicitly by merely identifying the entity sets to be joined in the target-list. In this case the system will use information from the dependency diagrams to establish the join conditions. Thus, for example, providing there is a dependency between PRODUCT.CODE and ORDERFROM. PRODUCTCODE, then the effect achieved by the above example could be achieved by an interaction of the form:

```
– READ PRODUCT. (CODE,NAME,PRICE), ORDERFROM.
  (CUSTOMERCODE, ORDERNO);
```

The system will fail a user's attempt to join implicitly entity sets which are not linked by a dependency.

Row Variables, Universal and Existential Quantifiers

From time to time a user will find a need to join an entity set to itself or to confirm that all the entities in an entity set satisfy a given condition. In order to solve these requirements it is necessary to enhance CSL by providing

1. *A variable:* which identifies an entity in a given set and which is local to a CSL statement.
2. *A quantifier:* which may take the form of either the universal quantifier ALL or the existential quantifier SOME.

Within CSL, a variable is defined within the predicate of a CSL statement by giving it a name which is not currently being used for anything else, and then relating it by using a FROM clause to either a permanent or temporary entity set. Once a variable has been defined and related to an entity set, it inherits the names of the attributes of that set. In the example below:

```
– READ PRODUCT SUCHTHAT P FROM PRODUCT (P.CODE > 4);
```

which reads all entities from PRODUCT with CODE greater than 4, P FROM PRODUCT defines a variable which is related to PRODUCT and P.CODE may be used as a convenient shorthand for PRODUCT.CODE.

Within CSL, a quantifier is represented by adding either the universal or the existential quantifier to a variable definition. The universal quantifier is represented by ALL, while the existential quantifier is represented by SOME. The examples below illustrate the use of these quantifiers.

```
– READ PRODUCT SUCHTHAT ALL P FROM PRODUCT
      (P.CODE > 4);
```

which has the effect of producing the whole of the entity set if all the entities satisfy the condition CODE > 4 and nothing if the condition is not met.

```
– READ PRODUCT SUCHTHAT SOME P FROM PRODUCT
      (P.CODE > 4);
```

which has the effect of selecting all those entities from the entity set which satisfy the condition. In both these examples, the brackets are used to define the scope of the quantifier.

The use of variables within a CSL statement changes the predicate from a Proposition which has a well-defined truth value into a Propositional Form which need not have a well-defined truth value because it is not always possible to evaluate it. This lack leads to a system of logic which can produce three possible results: 'true', 'false', and 'not assessable'. In fact, the position is not as bad as this because the use of the universal and existential quantifiers goes some way to reducing the chances of a predicate producing a 'not assessable' result. Consider the three statements:

- 'Products are supplied from London'
- 'All Products are supplied from London'
- 'Some Products are supplied from London'

The first of these is a propositional form because we do not know to which particular Products it refers, and, as such, it has a 'not assessable' result. The other two are in fact propositions and have truth values which can be determined by looking at the products in question, i.e. those listed in the entity set PRODUCT. The second statement is true if there is no product represented in PRODUCT which is not supplied from London, while the third statement is true if there is a product represented in PRODUCT which is supplied from London. Thus on the face of it quantifiers transform Propositional Forms into Propositions with truth values which can be determined.

Given a predicate containing one or more variable declarations, then these variables may be either bound or free. A variable is said to be bound if it exists within the scope of a quantifier, and it is said to be free if it is not governed by a quantifier. CSL has followed the definition of Codd's Alpha Sub-Language in effectively banning all free variables by insisting that all variables which appear as if they are free are governed by the existential quantifier 'SOME'.

In general a variable has a scope which is delimited by the CSL statement; however, it may happen that a user may need to restrict the scope of the variable to only part of the predicate. This is achieved by using brackets. For example, the statement to read all the details of products which have product.code greater than 4, and product.name equal to ink; and the assumption that all products have a price greater than £0.25, could be written as follows:

- READ PRODUCT SUCHTHAT SOME P FROM PRODUCT (P.CODE < 4 AND P.NAME = 'INK' AND ALL Q FROM PRODUCT (Q.CODE = P.CODE AND Q.PRICE > 0.25));

The first variable P has a scope which governs the whole predicate while the second variable Q has a scope which only governs the clause (Q.CODE = P.CODE AND Q.PRICE > 0.25)

Prenex Normal Form

A predicate is said to be in Prenex Normal Form if it has a form where the quantifier and variable declarations precede all the comparison statements; while CSL formulae need not be in Prenex Normal Form, the system will always transform them into Prenex Normal Form prior to processing them. Transforming the previous example into Prenex Normal Form results in the following:

– READ PRODUCT SUCHTHAT ALL Q FROM PRODUCT (SOME P FROM PRODUCT (Q.CODE = P.CODE AND Q PRICE > 0.25 AND P.CODE < 4 AND P.NAME = INK));

12.4 The Order-Expression-List

Given an entity set defined by a target list and a predicate, then the user may require that the entities are presented to him in a particular order. This is achieved by adding an order-expression-list to the command. An example of the use of an order-expression-list is:

– READ PRODUCT WITHORDER PRODUCT.PRICE UP;

The order-expression-list is introduced by *withorder* and contains one or more order-expressions separated by commas. Each order-expression names an attribute and states whether it is to be ordered in ascending or descending order defined by *up* and *down* respectively.

When defining an order-expression the attribute names must be either named in the target-list or exist in the set named in the target list. CSL allows a user to submit an ordering on more than one attribute, the most significant ordering being written first. Thus in the example below, PRODUCT is ordered by PRICE and then within each value of PRICE it is ordered by NAME:

– READ PRODUCT WITHORDER PRODUCT.PRICE UP PRODUCT.NAME DOWN;

12.5 Within an Entity Set

The previous section defined the major facilities for manipulating entity sets; however, there are occasions when it is inconvenient to manipulate a whole entity set. Examples of this arise in the following cases:

1. The user has issued a Read statement which identifies a set of 500 entities. As a terminal can only display 20 entities at a time, the system has to feed them to the terminal in batches of 20.
2. The user wishes to read and update entities one at a time.

In order to solve these problems CSL provides a set of statements which can be used to address entities within an entity set. These statements are:

SELECT, SELECT&READ, SELECT&UPDATE, SELECT&CREATE, SELECT&DESTROY, and SELECT&WRITE. The rest of this section is concerned with discussing these statements.

The SELECT Statement

Given that a user has a SET statement to establish a currency *P* to point to a given entity set, then he may wish to define a new set which consists of a number of adjacent entities from this set. This is achieved by using the SELECT statement, which has the following form:

> SELECT count FROM currency-name-*a* STARTING position REF currency-name-*b*.

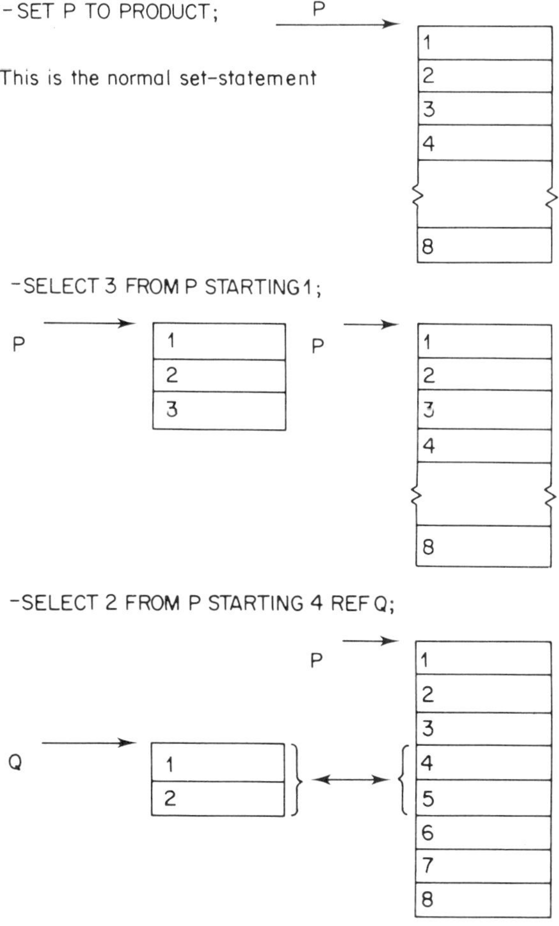

Figure 12.1 Creating a small entity set

The effect of the SELECT statement is to establish either an explicit or implicit ordering on the entities defined within the set referenced by currency-name-*a*. Once this ordering has been established, the system creates a new small set which is referenced by currency-name-*b*. (See Figure 12.1). The contents of the new small set are defined by count and position, where count defines the number of entities in the set, and position is a positive integer which defines the entity in the existing set which is to be first in the new small set. (The first entity in any set is assigned the number 1.)

In addition to using the SELECT statement to define a new small set it is possible to use it in a way which defines a succession of small sets, illustrated in the example below:

```
– SET P TO PRODUCT;
– SELECT 3 FROM P STARTING 1;
– SELECT 4 FROM P STARTING 1;
```

In this example, the SET statement establishes a currency P which references the set PRODUCT. The first SELECT statement then re-uses the currency P to define a set which consists of 3 entities from Product while the second SELECT statement has the effect of desetting P and setting the currency P to define a small set which consists of 4 entities drawn from entities 4, 5, 6, and 7 from Product. This is illustrated in Figure 12.2.

Using the Basic Statements within an Entity Set

The basic statements READ, UPDATE, CREATE, DESTROY, and WRITE will all operate on a currency which identifies a small entity set, which has been identified by a previous SELECT statement. These statements will work in the usual way providing they contain a target-list which only contains the currency-name. For example, the CSL statements:

```
– SET P TO PRODUCT;
– SELECT 10 FROM P STARTING 1;
– READ P;
```

allows the user to read the first 10 entities in Product.

The Select-& Statement

In addition to the basic statements which can be used in conjunction with the SELECT statement to provide access to a set, the system provides a number of statements, the Select-& statements, which provide a combination of a SELECT statement and a basic statement. The effect of these statements is best illustrated as follows:

– SET P TO PRODUCT;
– SELECT&READ 10 FROM P STARTING 1;
– SELECT&READ 10 FROM P STARTING 1;

In this example the SET statement establishes a currency P to refer to PRODUCT and the currency points to the complete set. Statement 2 has the effect of selecting the first 10 entities from Product and transferring them to the user's terminal. Statement 3 has the effect of selecting the next 10 entities from Product (e.g. entities 10–19) and transferring them to the user's terminal. The successive use of Statement 3 will gradually transfer all the entities in the set to the user's terminal.

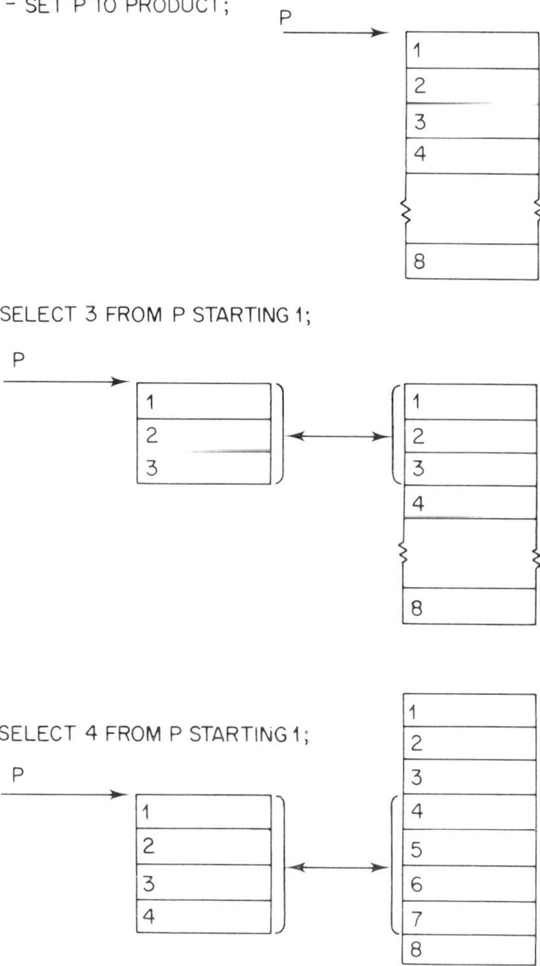

Figure 12.2 Creating a succession of small sets

12.6 The Default Currency

The default currency is a language device provided by the system to allow users to access the contents of an entity set which is too large to display on the user terminal. When the user first accesses a set by using one of the basic statements, the system processes the first terminal screen full and establishes a default currency to the rest. These can then be accessed by naming the default currency in the target list of another basic statement. For example:

```
– READ PRODUCT;
> PRODUCT
> CODE NAME PRICE
  {
  { 20 entities
  {
> DEFAULT ESTABLISHED
```

The user can then access these entities by issuing the following statement:

```
– READ;
```

The effect of this statement is to execute implicitly a SELECT statement of the form

```
– SELECT 20 FROM DEFAULT STARTING 1;
– READ DEFAULT;
```

which naturally provides the next 20 entities.

In those cases where a user issues a basic statement, the target-list of which names an entity set, then the default currency remains in existence until the user issues another basic statement. In those cases where a user issues a basic statement the target-list of which names a currency, then desetting the currency automatically desets the default currency.

12.7 The Scope of Names

The previous sections in this chapter have all been written in such a way that all references to entity set attributes take their full form (e.g. PRODUCT.CODE). In fact the early versions of RDBMS were built using this as the only mechanism for addressing attributes; later releases provided more flexibility. It is the purpose of this section to discuss the rules governing the scope of system objects and thus to identify the scope of their names.

In RDBMS an object is said to be global if it is defined by using the facilities of the Multi-Level Schema. Thus global objects include users, entity sets, attributes, macros, views, units, and all the other objects identified in Part B. An object is said to be local to a job if it is defined implicitly or explicitly by the use of CSL. The important local objects are:

1. *The default currency:* which is a system currency which is used to refer to any set which has been partially accessed.
2. *The statement currency:* which is a system currency which is local to a CSL statement.
3. *User-defined currencies:* which the user defines by means of a SET statement.
4. *Variables:* which the user defines by using a FROM clause in a predicate.

The following sections provide a more detailed explanation of these objects.

The Default Currency

This is a system currency, the operation of which has been described in Section 12.6.

The Statement Currency

When processing a CSL statement, the statement currency is initially void, and thereafter is set to each entity set name found in the statement. Once the statement currency has been set then a user may refer to attributes by merely giving the attribute name. Using this device, the statement

```
– READ PRODUCT.CODE SUCHTHAT PRODUCT.CODE > 10;
```

which reads all product codes greater than 10 could be rewritten as

```
– READ PRODUCT.CODE SUCHTHAT CODE > 10;
```

Within a CSL statement a user can reset the statement currency as many times as he likes. In the interaction

```
– READ PRODUCT.CODE, PRICE, ORDERFROM.QUANTITY
SUCHTHAT PRODUCT.CODE *= ORDERFROM.PRODUCTCODE
      AND CUSTOMERCODE = 10;
```

which reads details of product codes, prices and quantities ordered by the customer with customer code = 10, PRICE and CUSTOMERCODE are interpreted as PRODUCT.PRICE and ORDERFROM.CUSTOMERCODE respectively.

User-defined Currencies

User-defined currencies are explicitly set and deset by the user using the SET and DESET statements.

Variables

Variables only have the scope of the CSL statement in which they are first identified.

13

Arithmetic Expressions and Functions

The previous chapter completes the discussion of the basic manipulation features of the language. This chapter describes the facilities for computing values within entity sets and for building specialist user interfaces. These features may be subdivided into:

1. *Arithmetic expressions:* which allow a user to carry out arithmetic operations on the attributes within an entity set.
2. *Built-in functions:* which allow users to carry out operations such as 'total all the values of a particular attribute'.
3. *Input/output functions:* which provide users with non-relational representations of entity sets.

The chief distinction between arithmetic expressions and functions is that whereas an arithmetic expression is evaluated for each entity in an entity set, a function operates on all the entities in the set. Input/output functions may also be used to handle computed outputs; their primary use, however, is to support non-relational views of entity sets. The following sections describe these facilities.

13.1 Arithmetic Expressions

An arithmetic expression is a grouping of identifiers, numeric constants, and operators. The identifiers represent the names of attributes in an entity set, and the operators the unary operators plus and minus which are represented by '+' and '–', and the binary operators add, subtract, multiply, and divide which are represented by '+', '–', '*', and '/', respectively. Given any entity set, then the user may define arithmetic expressions involving the attributes of each of the entities in that set. One method of achieving this is to write a procedure (see Figure 13.1) which reads each entity and then evaluates the required arithmetic expression and prints out the result.

```
PROCEDURE VALUE OF PRODUCTS
   BEGIN
   CURRENCY P;
   SET P TO PRODUCT;
   SELECT & READ (1 FROM P, RESPONSE); COMMENT TO INITIALISE P;
   WHILE RESPONSE ≠ END OF SET DO
      BEGIN
      WRITE TEXT (P.NAME);
      PRINT (P.PRICE * P.QUANTITY,4,0);
      SELECT & READ (1 FROM P, RESPONSE);
      COMMENT TO SELECT NEXT ENTITY FROM P AND READ IT;
      END;
   END; (PROCEDURE VALUE OF PRODUCTS)
```

Figure 13.1 Procedure to calculate value of products written in an Algol-like language

A more convenient approach to this problem is to use a CSL arithmetic interaction of the form:

```
– READ PRODUCT. (NAME, PRICE * QUANTITY);
> PRODUCT
> NAME RESULT1
```

These two examples produce exactly the same result and serve to illustrate how an arithmetic expression performs.

Assignment

In writing arithmetic expressions it is often useful and necessary to assign the result to a named variable. Such an assignment is represented by the symbol ': =' and takes the form of:

VALUE : = PRODUCT.PRICE * PRODUCT.QUANTITY

where the value on the left-hand side is assigned the results of the expression on the right-hand side.

Arithmetic Expressions in the Target-List

The system will allow the user to provide arithmetic expressions in the target-list of the READ and SET statements only: arithmetic expressions written in the target-lists of other statements are invalid.

In writing an arithmetic expression, the user can write an expression of the form:

– READ PRODUCT.PRICE * PRODUCT.QUANTITY;

which produces an entity set with an attribute which the system will designate as

RESULT1. It is possible to issue statements containing more than one arithmetic expression as demonstrated in the following example where using an entity set X with attributes A, B, C, and D the user could write expressions of the form

– READ X.A + X.B, X.C + X.A.;

or alternatively

– READ X. (A+B,C+A);

The attributes in such sets are designated names of RESULT1, RESULT2, . . . , RESULTN where N identifies the number of the expression in the target-list.

This facility may also be used in the target-list of a SET statement. For example

– SET P TO X. (A+B,C+A);

has the effect of creating an entity set P with two attributes RESULT1 and RESULT2.

Arithmetic Expressions in Predicates

Within any predicate an arithmetic expression may be used as part of a comparison. For example:

– READ PRODUCT SUCHTHAT PRODUCT.PRICE * PRODUCT.-QUANTITY < 100;

or

– CREATE PRODUCT SUCHTHAT PRODUCT.PRICE * PRODUCT.-QUANTITY < 100;

However, an arithmetic expression may also be used in a predicate to define the value of a variable expressed in a target-list. Using this facility the first example in the previous section could be expressed:

– READ VALUE SUCHTHAT VALUE := PRODUCT.PRICE * PRODUCT.QUANTITY;

where VALUE is assigned the result of the arithmetic expression. This assignment mechanism may also be used with CREATE, DESTROY, UPDATE, and WRITE statements. For example:

– CREATE PRODUCT.CODE, VALUE SUCHTHAT PRODUCT.-QUANTITY: = VALUE/100;

allows the user to submit integer values which are used to update Quantity on the basis of the above expression.

Rules Governing the Use of Arithmetic Expressions

These rules are:

1. An expression can only operate within a single entity set.

2. When evaluating an expression, the usual rules of precedence are applied to the operators. Ambiguity over the precedence of operators is resolved by using brackets.

3. In writing an arithmetic expression, the user has to ensure firstly that the modes of the attributes can be used in an arithmetic expression, and, secondly, that the modes are compatible. An attribute can only be used in an arithmetic expression providing it is defined over a domain which is mapped into an encoded domain which has the form of integer or real. Given that all the attributes satisfy this condition, then the arithmetic expression can be evaluated. In general, the result of an arithmetic expression is a real if one of the attributes is defined over a domain of real, otherwise it is an integer. A user can determine the mode of the attribute/domain produced by an arithmetic expression by using the operators INTEGER and REAL which ensures that the expression produces the necessary result. The use of this facility is demonstrated as follows:

   – READ PRODUCT. (CODE, INTEGER PRICE * QUANTITY);

13.2 Built-In Functions

Given any entity set then the user may need to carry out a simple operation such as total all the values of a particular attribute. One method of achieving this is to read all the values of the attributes and sit down with a calculator; however, as this is a fairly simple task, the system contains a built-in function which the user may call.

From the user's point of view, a built-in function is an algorithm which the user calls passing an entity set as a parameter. The algorithm is executed and the result is either left in another entity set which the user can access, or displayed on the user's terminal. Obviously, the built-in function is a very powerful facility, but most algorithms used within a particular Information System will satisfy specialist needs and consequently the system itself only contains a few simple functions. There are facilities in the Software Environment to allow a system designer to define new functions and thus extend the system to meet the needs of his Information System.

The following functions are provided:

Function Name	Parameters	Effect
TOTAL	An entity set with one integer or real attribute	This function adds all the integer or real values together; the result is the total left in an entity set containing one integer or real.
COUNT	Any entity set	This function counts the entities in the set. The result is left in an entity set containing the count as an integer.
MAX	An entity set with one attribute	This function searches the whole set for the entity with the maximum value. The result is left in an entity set with an entity containing the maximum value.
MIN	An entity set with one attribute	This searches the whole set for the entity with the minimum value. The result is left in an entity set with one entity containing the minimum value.

Calling Functions as part of the Target-List

Functions can be called from the target-list of either READ or SET statements. When it is used, the function call must be written as part of the target-list in the form:

FUNCTION (FUNCTION-PARAMS)

where FUNCTION represents the function name and the brackets contain parameters which may take one of the following forms:

1. An entity-set-name, in which case the entity set must contain the necessary number of attributes and no more. Thus TOTAL expects an entity set with only one integer attribute.
2. A single-set-target-list.

3. A currency-name.

4. An arithmetic expression.

The following examples demonstrate typical function calls:

Example 1

```
– READ MAX (PRODUCT.PRICE);
```

Example 2

```
– SET P TO PRODUCT.PRICE;
– READ MAX (P);
```

Example 3

```
– READ MAX (PRODUCT.PRICE * PRODUCT.QUANTITY);
```

The effect of including a function call in the target-list of a READ statement is for the function to be evaluated and the result to be displayed on the user terminal. For example:

```
– READ COUNT (PRODUCT);
> COUNT
> 50
```

The effect of including a function call in the target-list of a SET statement is for the function to be evaluated and the result to be left in the system with the currency named in the SET-statement referring to it. Thus:

```
– SET P TO COUNT (PRODUCT)
– READ P;
> P
> COUNT
> 50
```

Calling Functions as part of a Predicate

Functions may be used in a predicate, providing the result of the function has the mode required by the predicate. For example, using the Purchasing System, we would like to find the name of the customer who has the order with the largest number of items. This could be written as follows:

```
– SET P TO ORDERFROM SUCHTHAT ORDERFROM.QUANTITY
  = MAX(ORDERFROM.QUANTITY);
– READ CUSTOMER.NAME SUCHTHAT CUSTOMER.CODE = P.
  CUSTOMERCODE
```

or alternatively:

- READ CUSTOMER.NAME SUCHTHAT CUSTOMER.CODE = ORDERFROM.CUSTOMERCODE AND ORDERFROM.QUANTITY = MAX (ORDERFROM.QUANTITY);

13.3 Unnormalized Input/Output

So far the specification of CSL has only described means whereby information is presented to RDBMS and output is produced by RDBMS in the form of complete tables of values. However, when using the system on a day by day basis it has been found that more flexible input/output facilities are required, and such facilities may be provided by means of input/output functions. This section briefly describes a generalized input/output function GLUMP which may be used as part of one of the CREATE, DESTROY, UPDATE, and WRITE statements to handle information input and as part of the READ statement to handle information output. The next section describes how CSL may be extended by calling specialist user-written input/output functions.

Glumped Output

For output, GLUMP acts on specific attributes which are identified by the end-user, and the effect of using it is to print changes to the attribute values only. Lack of an attribute value in the output implies that the value remains unchanged from the value in the previous entity. Attribute values to be 'glumped' in this way are identified by using a clause of the form = A where A is an attribute name, and output is triggered by using the symbol '<>'. Figure 13.2 illustrates the use of the function GLUMP: the left-hand side of the diagram is that of a normal READ statement, while the right-hand side is a statement involving the function GLUMP.

```
— READ PRODUCT.(CODE,PRICE);
> PRODUCT
> CODE        PRICE
> 1           0.05
> 2           0.05
> 3           10.00
> 4           10.00
> 5           16.00
```

```
— READ GLUMP (PRODUCT. (CODE,PRICE));
— =PRICE <>
> PRODUCT
> CODE        PRICE
> 1           0.05
> 2
> 3           10.00
> 4
> 5           16.00
```

Figure 13.2 Glumped output

Glumped Input

Using GLUMP for input is similar to using it for output, except that in this case the user has to assign a value to each 'glumped' attribute by using a clause of the

```
— CREATE PRODUCT.(CODE,PRICE);
> PRODUCT
> CODE        PRICE
> 1           0.05
> 2           0.05
> 3           10.00
> 4           10.00
> 5           10.00
> ;
```

```
— READ GLUMP (PRODUCT.(CODE,PRICE));
> = PRICE 0.05
> CODE
> 1
> 2
> = PRICE 10.00
> 3
> 4
> = PRICE 16.00
> 5
> ;
```

Figure 13.3 Glumped input

form '= X Y' where X is an attribute and Y its value. In this case the symbol '< >' is used to request a proforma heading. (Its use is not mandatory.)

Figure 13.3 contains two examples which produce the same effect and represent the use of glumped input.

13.4 Calling User-Written Functions

The Software Environment allows a user to describe new software to RDBMS, and in particular it allows him to describe new functions. Such a function is described by giving it a name and a list of formal parameters, where each formal parameter may take the form of an entity set name or a domain name. When the user calls such a function then he has to ensure that the entity sets and attributes named in the list of actual parameters correspond to the types listed in the formal parameters or can be coerced to those types.

14

The Language Statements

Chapter 11 described the CSL as it is used to handle complete entity sets; this chapter contains a full description of the basic language statements.

14.1 The SET Statement and Currencies

The effect of the SET statement is to set up the named currency to point to the entity set defined by the target-list, predicate, and order-expression-list. The parameters to the SET statement have to observe the following rules and have the following effects.

The Currency-name

When defining a currency, the user can choose any name he wishes providing his choice does not clash with any one of the words reserved by the language. The following interaction is invalid for this reason:

```
  – SET FOR TO SALES;
$             ↑
$
$ ERROR TYPE 200: RESERVED WORD: TO BEING USED AS A
$ CURRENCY NAME
```

If the user chooses a currency name which corresponds to an entity set name where the entity set is currently in use, then the system will fail the request. However, it is permissible to use a currency name which corresponds to an entity set name which is not in use; this then prevents the user from accessing that set as all uses of that name refer to the currency and not the set. The use of this facility is shown in the following example where Statement 2 results in the user accessing a set which is called PRODUCT but contains attributes of PRODUCTCODE, CUSTOMERCODE, ORDERNO etc. The effect of Statement 3 is to deset the currency, and thereby allow the name PRODUCT to return to its original use.

1. – SET PRODUCT TO ORDERFROM;

2. – READ PRODUCT;
   > PRODUCT
   > PRODUCTCODE CUSTOMERCODE ORDERNO etc.
   >

3. – DESET PRODUCT;

In many cases the user may choose to re-use a currency-name. The ensuing effect is implicitly to DESET the currency from the entity set it is referencing, and to perform a SET statement to establish it so that it points at a new set. This is demonstrated in the following sequence of interactions:

1. – LOGIN ATFH, XX3;

2. – SET P TO PRODUCT SUCHTHAT PRODUCT.PRICE > 0.25;

3. – READ P;

   –

   –

12. – SET P TO ORDERTO;

In this sequence of interactions line 2 has the effect of setting currency P to refer to PRODUCT, and line 12 has the effect of implicitly desetting P so that it no longer refers to PRODUCT and sets it to refer to ORDERTO.

The Target-List and Predicate

The entity set which is referenced by the currency named in the SET statement is defined by a target-list and a predicate. The SET statement will accept any valid target-list and predicate. However, the other statements, and particularly CREATE and DESTROY, impose restrictions on the type of entity set on which they can be used. For example, a CREATE statement can only manipulate a set defined by a single-set-target-list and a single-set-predicate. For this reason the user needs to take care to ensure that the currency he is creating is acceptable to all the statements which are to use it.

In the example below the user creates a currency C which identifies a set of products with orders and then attempts to create an entity in this set

– SET C TO PRODUCT.NAME, ORDERFROM.PRODUCTCODE
– SUCHTHAT PRODUCT.CODE *= ORDERFROM.
  PRODUCTCODE;

```
– CREATE C;
$          ↑
$
$ ERROR TYPE 201: CANNOT CREATE USING CURRENCY C
$ WHICH CONTAINS A JOIN
```

The system responds to the CREATE statement with an error message because the currency C has been defined with a target-list and predicate which cannot be processed by a CREATE statement. The restriction is not imposed on the SET statement but on the use of the currency. The reason for the restriction is that in general the join of two entity sets reintroduces the anomalies removed by the normalization process, which is undesirable.

Name Inheritance

When the user establishes a currency to point to an entity set then, as already outlined, the currency inherits the description of the entity set and thus inherits the attribute names. Thus the example:

```
– SET P TO PRODUCT. (NAME, PRICE);
```

has the effect of introducing two new attributes P.NAME and P.PRICE. In this case the inheritance rule is obvious and there is no ambiguity between the names in the entity set referenced via *P*. However, consider the interaction below which asks for all names of PRODUCT and CUSTOMERS where the PRODUCT was delivered to a CUSTOMER after 1/6/74.

```
– SET Q TO PRODUCT.NAME, CUSTOMER.NAME
    SUCHTHAT PRODUCT.CODE *= ORDERFROM.
    PRODUCTCODE
    AND ORDERFROM.CUSTCODE *= CUSTOMER.CODE
    AND ORDERFROM.DELIVERY DATE > 1/6/74;
```

Asking the question was interesting enough, but what are the names inherited by Q? Under the straightforward application of the name inheritance rule they would be Q.NAME and Q. NAME., which is ambiguous. For this reason the rule is modified so that the names can retain the entity set name and thus become:

Q. PRODUCTNAME and Q. CUSTOMERNAME

Should the user find that the application of this rule produces attributes which are not meaningful to him, then he may use an assignment to define his own names.

For example:

- SET Q TO PNAME, CNAME SUCHTHAT PNAME :=
  PRODUCT.NAME, CNAME := CUSTOMER.NAME SUCHTHAT —

creates Q with attributes Q.PNAME and Q.CNAME.

Setting Currencies to Refer to Currencies

It is valid within the language to establish a currency to point to an entity set and to then define another currency to point to the first by naming it in the target-list. For example:

- SET P TO PRODUCT;
- SET P1 TO P;

The effect of the second set statement is to establish a correspondence between P1 and P. The user uses this device when he wishes to create a temporary set referenced by P and then to produce a new temporary set which is referenced by P1 and related to P by one of the relational operators. Thus, in the example below, P refers to a join of PRODUCT and ORDERFROM, and P1 refers to a projection from the result.

- SET P TO PRODUCT, ORDERFROM
  SUCHTHAT PRODUCT.CODE *= ORDERFROM.
  PRODUCTCODE;
- SET P1 TO P.(NAME,CUSTOMERCODE);

Access Rights

When the user issues a SET statement, one of the optional parameters he can submit is a list of access rights. These access rights tell the system how the user intends to access the set identified in the target-list and referred to by the currency.

- SET C FOR (READACCESS, UPDATEACCESS) TO PRODUCT;

In all cases, the access-rights-list appears between the currency-name and the target-list, preceded by FOR. The value of the access rights can be used to define the statements which can be performed on C and, as described in Chapter 11, are used as a basis for establishing interlocks. For this reason, the system performs checks to insure that the access rights are compatible with both the target-list and the predicate.

14.2 The READ Statement

The READ statement can include any valid target-list, predicate, and order-expression-list. Thus it can be used to read all the entities from either a permanent set identified by an entity-set-name or a temporary set identified by either a currency-name or a target-list and predicate.

The effect of the READ statement is to transfer as many entities as possible to the user terminal. If all the entities can be transferred, then the interaction is complete and the terminal will return to command mode. However, if the entity set contains more entities than can be transmitted to the terminal, then the READ statement will output the first buffer full and establish a default currency which will refer to the rest. The terminal again returns to command mode. The rest of the entities can be accessed using 'Within-Set' statements.

Formatting Information

One of the uses of the READ statement is to produce well-organized reports. The output consists of a two-part heading or proforma. The first part contains the entity set name and is produced at the left-hand margin on a line of its own. The second part contains the attribute names which are produced on the line or lines beneath. The proforma heading is followed by the attribute values such that the values of a particular attribute are aligned beneath the appropriate heading. The names used within the proforma and the format of the information values are governed by the entity set description, which has been built up from the Information Environment Schema and the CSL.

Lateral Spacing

The lateral spacing of information across the page is dependent on three factors:

1. the width of the attribute name as defined in the Information Environment Schema;
2. the width of the attribute value as defined in the Information Environment Schema;
3. the total width of the target-list, which means the sum of the maximum of 1. and 2. above.

If the total width of the target-list does not exceed the page width, then the information is output as a rectangular representation of an entity set as shown in the earlier examples. If the width of the target-list exceeds the page width, then the output is folded so that each entity of the entity set is presented on two or more lines. In this situation, conformity between the lines and the control of the folding obeys the following rule. Each attribute name and/or value will occupy 12 print positions with an extra space allowed between each column. This rule will handle all the modes except strings which occupy an integral number of 12 character slots. Should the user require any closer control over his output, then this can be achieved by using output functions (see Chapter 15).

Vertical Spacing

The system provides two facilities for handling vertical spacing. The first is a page heading capability which allows long listings to be separated into pages with a new heading at the top of each page; the second is a capability to insert blank lines after every *n* entities. These features can be activated by the nonstandard statement FORMAT.

14.3 The UPDATE Statement

The UPDATE statement can be used to alter any entity or group of entities providing the alteration does not affect the values of candidate key attributes. The system will accept an UPDATE statement which has a target-list, a predicate, and an order-expression-list. The target-list must identify a single set either by an entity-set-name or a currency-name. Furthermore, the target-list must contain at least the candidate key attributes of the set. If the target-list contains a currency-name then the access rights associated with that currency must include UPDATEACCESS. The predicate associated with an UPDATE statement must be a single-set-predicate. The order-expression-list, if present, defines the order of the entities which are to be submitted via the UPDATE statement.

The system processes an UPDATE statement by evaluating the combined target-list and predicate and outputting a proforma description of the entity set which is to be updated. The user then fills this proforma with the necessary values. These values are accepted by the system, providing they are each individually valid, and the system contains a valid value for the attributes which make up the candidate key. When inputting attribute values, an attribute may be assigned a value of 'unassigned' or 'default' by giving it a value equivalent to a joker character which takes the form of ? or ! respectively. In either case the appropriate value of the domain which is associated with the attribute and defined in the Information Environment is assigned to the attribute. The use of this facility is illustrated in the following example:

```
– UPDATE ORDERFROM;
>ORDERFROM
>PRODUCTCODE    CUSTOMERCODE    ORDERNO
>ORDERDATE      DELIVERYDATE    QUANTITY
– 60     1793     1007     10/4/74     ?     4
– 64     1793     1005     10/4/74     ?     !
– ;
```

where both input lines set DELIVERYDATE to unassigned and the second input line sets QUANTITY to a default value.

In the case where a user updates the projection of an entity set, for example,

UPDATE ORDERFROM. (PRODUCTCODE, CUSTOMERCODE, ORDERNO);

then all the other attributes in the entity set (e.g. ORDERDATE, DELIVERYDATE, and QUANTITY) retain their original values.

An UPDATE statement will fail if any value is found to be invalid, which includes the case where the user assigns to an attribute a default value without having previously defined such a value in the Information Environment. It will also fail if the user fails to identify an existing entity. Finally, if the UPDATE statement contains an order-expression-list, then the statement will fail if the user submits an entity which is not within the defined order.

14.4 The CREATE Statement

The CREATE statement allows a user to add new entities to an existing entity set. The statement will only accept a target-list which names a single entity set and a single-set-predicate. The single entity set may be identified by either an entity-set-name or a currency name. In the case where the set is identified by a currency-name then the access-rights associated with that currency should include CREATEACCESS.

The system processes a CREATE statement by evaluating the combined target-list and predicate and, as in the case of the UPDATE statement, outputs a proforma description of the entity set which the user is addressing. This proforma description must contain the candidate key attributes plus one or more non-key attributes, and failure to name these attributes will lead to an error message and the terminal returning to command mode.

Once the system has output the proforma the user can submit the entities. As with the UPDATE statement, entities may be submitted in any order, except in the case where the CREATE statement contains an order-expression-list. In this case the system checks that the entities are presented in the stated order and the interaction will cease if the system finds an entity which is out of order. As entities are submitted, the system checks that they satisfy the following:

1. Each of the attribute/domains conforms to the validation checks given in the Information Environment Schema.
2. The system does not already contain the given entity.
3. Each complete entity conforms to the dependency checks given in the Information Environment.
4. Each of the complete entities conforms to the predicate associated with the entity set and defined in the Information Environment.

If any of these checks fail then the entity is not accepted for inclusion in the Information Environment and the terminal returns to command mode.

Should the target-list of a CREATE statement identify the projection of an entity set, then the system will check to ensure that the user has satisfied the minimum requirement of identifying all the candidate key attributes. Attributes which are not listed in the target-list and therefore not assigned user-supplied values are automatically set to the appropriate unassigned value.

14.5 The DESTROY Statement

The DESTROY statement will accept a target-list which may only name a single entity set, and a single-set-predicate. The single entity set in the target-list may be identified by either an entity-set-name or a currency-name. If it is identified by a currency-name then the access-rights associated with the currency should include DESTROYACCESS.

The system processes a DESTROY statement by evaluating the combined target-list and predicate and, as in the case of the UPDATE statement, outputs a proforma description of the entity set which the user is addressing. This proforma description must contain the candidate key attributes, and failure to name these attributes will result in an error message and the terminal returning to command mode. Once the system has produced the proforma the user can submit values for the entities which are to be deleted. As with the UPDATE statement, entities may be submitted in any order, except in the case where the DESTROY statement contains an order-expression-list. In this case the system checks that the entities are presented in the stated order, and produces an error message if the order condition is not satisifed. As each entity value is submitted, then providing the following checks are satisfied, the data base entity will be destroyed. The checks which need to be satisfied before an entity will be deleted are:

1. The system contains an entity which exactly matches the values given by the user.
2. Its destruction does not invalidate the predicate associated with the entity set and defined in the Information Environment.
3. Its destruction does not invalidate any of the dependency checks defined in the Information Environment.

If any of these checks fail then the entity will not be destroyed and the terminal returns to command mode with an error message.

14.6 The WRITE Statement

The WRITE statement allows the user to submit information to an entity set without concerning himself as to whether he is creating a new entity or updating an existing entity. A valid WRITE statement must contain a single-set-target-list which can identify an entity set by name or by a currency-name. If it identifies a set via a currency name then the access rights associated with that currency must include either UPDATEACCESS and CREATEACCESS or WRITEACCESS. The single-set-predicate and order-expression-list have exactly the same effect as those associated with a CREATE statement.

The system processes a WRITE statement by evaluating the combined target-list and predicate and, as in the case of an UPDATE statement, outputs a proforma description of the entity set which the user is addressing. This proforma description must contain the candidate key attributes. However, the proforma may contain no more than the candidate key attributes. Once the system has output the proforma the user can submit the entities. Once an entity is complete, the system checks to see if it exists. If the entity exists then the system updates the existing entity with the new values, otherwise it creates a new entity.

14.7 The COPY Statement

In its full form a COPY statement takes the form:

> COPY target-list-1 FOR access-right FROM target-list-2 SUCHTHAT predicate

where:

- target-list-1 defines the entity set which is to receive the entities
- access-right identifies the way in which the entities are to be moved from the entity set identified in target-list-2 to the entity set identified in target list-1 and must take a value of one of WRITEACCESS, UPDATEACCESS, or CREATEACCESS
- target-list 2 defines the entity set which is to supply the entities
- predicate defines the conditions which need to be satisfied by the entities as they are extracted from target-list-2

The conditions governing the use of the target-lists and predicates are best described as follows. Target-list-1 must be a single-set-target-list and, no matter what value is assigned to the access-right, it must identify all the candidate key attributes of the target entity set. However, if the access-right is set to CREATEACCESS or WRITEACCESS then there is no need for the user to specify more than the candidate key attributes, while if the access-right is set to UPDATEACCESS the user is obliged to identify one or more non-candidate key attributes.

The only rule governing target-list-2 is that when each of the attributes identified in the two target-lists is taken in turn then they must be defined over the same domain. This condition is demonstrated in the following example which copies all product codes listed in the entity set ORDERFROM into another entity set TODAYSPRODUCTS which has attribute/domains of CODE/CODE, NAME/NAME, and PRICE/STERLING.

```
– COPY TODAYSPRODUCT.CODE FOR CREATEACCESS FROM
  ORDERFROM.PRODUCTCODE;
```

The rules governing the predicate are fairly straightforward. All entity sets and attributes identified in the predicate must be related to entity sets and attributes identified in target-list-2. The application of this rule is shown by the following example which adds values for product-names and prices to the entity set TODAYSPRODUCT. Providing the price of the product listed in PRODUCT is less than £100, then the product-name for TODAYSPRODUCT is taken directly from PRODUCT while the price of TODAYSPRODUCT is 10% higher than the price quoted in PRODUCT. For products which have a price greater than or equal to £100, the product-name and price is set undefined.

```
– COPY TODAYSPRODUCT.(CODE, NAME, PRICE)
  FOR UPDATEACCESS
  FROM PRODUCT. (CODE, NAME), VALUE
  SUCHTHAT PRODUCT.PRICE < 100,
          VALUE := PRODUCT.PRICE * 110/100;
```

There are no facilities for a user to define the order in which the entities are to be copied from one entity set to another. From a user's point of view the system can be relied upon to optimize the ordering of entities.

Once the system has performed the checks identified above, the copy is performed as a single operation which is either successfully completed or terminates with an error and leaves the entity sets in their original state.

14.8 Error Messages

The system makes a large number of checks throughout the processing of an interaction. Where errors in either the user's request or in some part of the system prevent the successful execution of an interaction, then the system produces an error diagnostic.

There are seven types of error diagnostic:

1. *Syntax errors:* these arise when the user's command fails to comply with the rules of CSL.
2. *Semantic errors:* these arise from inconsistencies in the user command; for example using an attribute name in an order-expression-list when it is not defined in the target-list.

3. *Resource usage errors:* these arise when a user's request requires more of the system resources than the user has been allocated or resources which are temporarily not available (e.g. an entity set being used by another user or being maintained by systems operations staff).

4. *Data errors:* these arise when the user submits information which is either inconsistent or invalid.

5. *Recoverable system errors:* these arise when the system actually fails but retains control sufficiently to recover and continue with the job; in this case the current interaction is abandoned.

6. *Irrecoverable system errors:* these arise when the system fails but retains control sufficiently to tidy up and close down all current user jobs.

7. *System crashes:* these arise when the system fails completely.

The system reports errors by producing an error message which repeats the command and/or information and indicates the error with an ↑ under the offending character or word; this is then followed by an error message. These error messages consist of a fault number followed by a suitable diagnostic. The mapping between fault numbers and diagnostics is under the control of the system's operating staff, thus allowing some flexibility in the actual diagnostic messages. A full error report would look like this:

```
→ READ MEN;
$ READ MEN;
$      ↑
$
$ ERROR TYPE 35 : ENTITY SET : MEN NOT KNOWN
```

15

The External Environment

The External Environment is provided to maintain a permanent representation of the information needs of the end-users of an Information System. Such information needs may be represented by using views, macros, and user-written own-code input/output functions. All these rely heavily on the use of CSL, which explains why they are described in this part of the book.

Basically, a view is best thought of as a derived entity set which is part of the External Environment and is mapped on to the entity sets of the Information Environment by using CSL-style targets and predicates. A macro provides a means whereby a user may give a macro name to any part of a CSL statement and then call it from within another CSL statement. A user-written input/output function is similar to any other function in so far as it alters the legible representation of an entity set. It is supported by a unit of user-written code which is defined using the Software Environment. Hence it can be seen that the facilities of the External Environment provide a means whereby a user may redefine the entity sets, the CSL, and the representation of the information used by an Information System in order to mirror his own views of that system. The rest of this chapter describes these facilities.

15.1 Views

At its simplest, a view takes the same form as an entity set in so far as it is a tabular structure which exists permanently in the External Environment, and furthermore may be accessed by CSL statements. However, a view is described by using CSL-style target-lists and predicates which define how that view is derived from the Information Environment. For example, the interaction below creates a view of the Purchasing System which is known as BIGORDERS and contains all the orders for more than 1000 items.

```
– CREATE VIEW;
> VIEW
> NAME          TARGETLIST     PREDICATE
– BIGORDERS   'ORDERFROM'   'ORDERFROM.QUANTITY > 1000'
– ;
```

The effect of this interaction is to create a view which takes the same form as an entity set in so far as it has a name, contains attributes and entities, and may be accessed via the normal CSL statements. This is shown in the following examples:

```
– READ BIGORDERS;
> BIGORDERS
> PRODUCTCODE  CUSTOMERCODE ORDERNO ORDERDATE
> DELIVERYDATE QUANTITY
> etc.
– CREATE BIGORDERS
> BIGORDERS
> PRODUCTCODE  CUSTOMERCODE ORDERNO ORDERDATE
> DELIVERYDATE QUANTITY
> 1          20          2010              01/10/76          ! 10
> ;
```

These examples show that once a user has created a view, then the name of the view is in effect the name given to a new entity set, the attributes of which have names which are inherited via the normal name inheritance rules from the entity sets identified in the target-list. Should a user wish to override these name inheritance rules, then he may do so by putting the new names as result-names in the target-list and adding the necessary assignment statements to the predicate. The use of this facility is shown in the following interaction, which defines a view SALE which has exactly the same form as ORDERFROM but renames the attributes PCODE, CCODE, ONO, ODATE, DDATE, and QUANT.

```
– CREATE VIEW;
> VIEW
> NAME              TARGETLIST              PREDICATE
> SALE              'PCODE, CCODE, ONO, ODATE, DDATE, QUANT'
>                   'PCODE: = ORDERFROM. PRODUCTCODE,
>                    CCODE: = ORDERFROM.CUSTOMERCODE,
>                    ONO:   = ORDERFROM.ORDERNO,
>                   ODATE:  = ORDERFROM.ORDERDATE,
>                    DDATE: = ORDERFROM.DELIVERYDATE,
>                    QUANT: = ORDERFROM.QUANTITY'
> ;
```

15.2 Macros

In its simplest form, a macro provides the user with a facility whereby he can establish a correspondence between a name and a set of characters. Thus when the name is used in a CSL statement it is replaced by the characters.

For example: the Purchasing System is used every day to find the names of Products with an order for more than 100 items which would normally require a CSL statement of the form:

(1) – READ PRODUCT. NAME SUCHTHAT PRODUCT.CODE = ORDERFROM PRODUCTCODE AND ORDERFROM.QUANTITY>100;

Now, to make life easier, this could be replaced by a macro called DAILYSALES which is defined as:

PRODUCT. NAME SUCHTHAT PRODUCT.CODE = ORDERFROM. PRODUCTCODE AND ORDERFROM.QUANTITY>100;

and using it, the user would write:

(2) READ DAILYSALES;

In this case the system would substitute the text of the macro for DAILYSALES and execute statement (1) above.

The system allows the user to define his own macros by giving him access to the entity set MACRO, two attributes of which are MNAME and MTEXT which define the name and text of the macro respectively. Thus the user would define DAILYSALES by writing:

```
– CREATE MACRO. (MNAME, MTEXT);
> MACROS
> MNAME         MTEXT
> DAILYSALES    "PRODUCT.NAME SUCHTHAT PRODUCT.CODE =
                 ORDERFROM.PRODUCTCODE AND ORDERFROM.
                 QUANTITY>100"
```

Macros with Parameters

In addition to the facilities for manipulating simple CSL strings, the system allows users to define macros with parameters. When the user defines such a macro then each parameter is referred to by the character @ followed by a nonzero positive number where '@*N*' is called a *formal* parameter of the macro; for example, @2 is the 2nd formal parameter.

An example of such a macro could be defined to manipulate DAILY SALES greater than any value specified as a parameter to the macro, in which case the macro would be defined by:

```
– CREATE MACRO   (MNAME, MTEXT);
> MACROS
> MNAME          MTEXT
> DAILYSALES     "PRODUCT. NAME SUCHTHAT PRODUCT.CODE =
                  ORDERFROM.PRODUCTCODE AND
                  ORDERFROM.QUANTITY > @1"
```

As it may be either impracticable or undesirable for an end-user to read through a macro definition to understand the significance of a parameter, the system provides facilities for holding a parameter description using the attribute MACRO.MPARAM. Using this facility the full description of DAILY SALES would read:

```
–CREATE MACRO    (MNAME, MPARAM, MTEXT);
>MACRO
>MNAME           MPARAM                   MTEXT
>DAILYSALES      "NO OF PRODUCTS SOLD"    "PRODUCT.NAME etc"
>;
```

Given this macro, then an end-user would call it by using the CSL statement

```
– READ DAILYSALES (100):
```

where '100' is said to be an actual parameter of the macro. Given a macro with several parameters then the actual parameters are separated by commas. If an actual parameter is not an identifier or an unsigned number then it should be written in quotes.

Macros Called from Within Macros

Once the user has defined a macro then he can call it from within the text of some new macro. In this situation the system will, during the expansion of the macro, check for other macro names and if one is found, then this second macro is expanded and its text added to the command. For example:

```
– CREATE MACRO   (MNAME, MTEXT);
>MACRO
>MNAME           MTEXT
>DSQUANTIFIER    "SUCHTHAT PRODUCT.CODE = ORDERFROM.
>                  PRODUCTCODE AND ORDERFROM.
>                  QUANTITY>100"
>DAILY SALES     "PRODUCT.NAME DSQUANTIFIER"
>;
– READ DAILYSALES;
```

In this example, the first interaction is used to create two macros, so that the second macro calls the first. The third interaction then calls the upper of the two macros and thus produces the desired effect.

In addition to calling one macro from another it is possible to pass parameters between macros, with the restriction that no actual parameter to a macro can contain a formal parameter. The example below illustrates these capabilities:

```
– CREATE MACRO.  (MNAME, MTEXT);
>MACRO
>MNAME           MTEXT
>B               "CD@1"
>A               "B(@1F)"
>;
```

where @1 in the definition of A refers to the first actual parameter in the call of the macro A and not macro B. Hence the statement A(E) produces the result CDEF.

Unlike macro names, formal parameters can occur within identifiers or at the end of numbers, e.g. if:

```
>MNAME           MTEXT
>G               "READ ENTITY@1T"
>H               "5@1"
>;
```

then G(SE) is expanded as READ ENTITYSET, and H(12) becomes 512. However, if the macro body contains a string then any @ within the string is not treated as a formal parameter.

15.3 User-Written Input/Output Functions

An input/output function allows a user to vary the form in which information is represented on his terminal, and thus replace the strict tabular output described in Chapter 14 by diagrams, charts, and the like.

Basically, an input/output function is a unit of software which takes an entity set and maps it into the required form on some legible medium. It is described to the system by using the facilities of the Software Environment and therefore may be defined to access either a specific entity set or some more general structure such as any entity set with a single attribute/domain of type integer. A typical example of such an input/output function is the standard function TREES described in Chapter 9. The trees illustrated in Chapter 9 would be activated by interactions of the form:

```
– READ TREES (UNIT);
– READ TREES (UNIT) SUCHTHAT UNIT.GROUP = 1;
```

where the first of these interactions will produce, within the confines of the output media, a tree representing all the units in the entity set UNITS, while the second will only handle the units in Group 1.

16

The Algorithmic Control Sub-Languages

16.1 Introduction

The Control Sub-Languages are a family of languages aimed at enabling users on terminals and programmers writing programs to access information held in an Information System. With this in mind the family could extend to containing one or two interactive dialects plus a sub-language extension for each of the major programming languages such as COBOL, FORTRAN, or PASCAL. In the event, the implementation of these interfaces is best achieved by defining one standard interface which is supported by RDBMS, and a number of pre-processors which map each of the sub-languages' dialects through the standard languages themselves so that at run time they map on to the single standard interface. This standard interface is known as the Algorithmic Control Sub-Language (ACSL).

Needless to say, an interface such as ACSL can also be used as a target for stand-alone interactive systems such as the LEGOL system (see STAMPER 1) which is being developed at the London School of Economics. Figure 16.1 illustrates an arrangement of interfaces and processors to demonstrate this point.

16.2 The Algorithmic Control Sub-Language

This interface has been designed to allow programs written in high-level languages to access a relational data base supported by RDBMS. The interface is based on a simplified form of the Interactive Control Sub-Language. The main changes which have been introduced concern extensions to permit RDBMS to link with the control mechanisms of a high-level language and modifications required to permit data to be passed between an application program and RDBMS.

Interaction with the Information Environment

RDBMS has been designed so that the Information Environment acts as a target for users on terminals, and for this reason all the attribute/domains are described

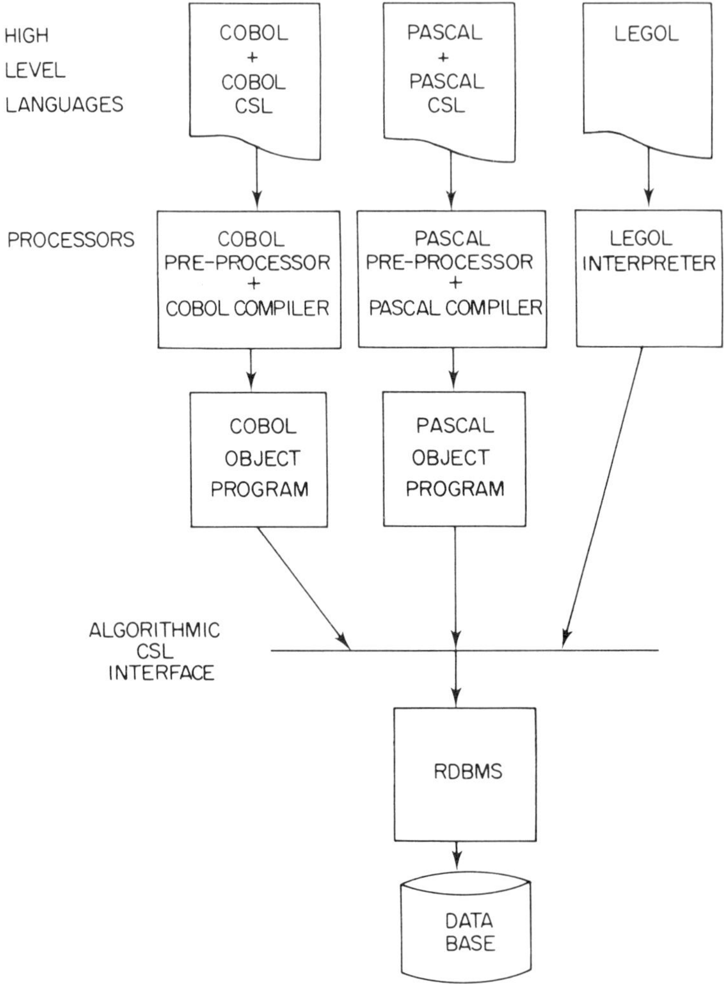

Figure 16.1 The Algorithmic Control Sub-Languages

in their legible form. Such an interface is not well suited for use with the ACSL interface, where information has to be handled in its encoded form. There are basically two solutions to this problem: one solution is to allow users of ACSL interface to interact directly with the Encoded Environment. This is certainly possible, but it has the grave disadvantage that it deprives system designers of the possibility of exploiting the flexibility provided by the information-dependent mappings; furthermore, using the Encoded Environment undermines the integrity and privacy constraints provided by the Information Environment. The other approach, which has been adopted in the system, is to ensure that ACSL users interact with the Information Environment, but to vary the environment definition so that all the attribute/domains take their encoded form. Such an approach ensures that no user undermines the integrity and privacy constraints and maintains a compatible level of interaction for all the Control Sub-Languages.

The Control Mechanisms

As with the Interactive CSL, ACSL operates in command and data mode. However, ACSL does not support an error mode; error responses are returned across the user interface via a user-defined 'Response' parameter which may then be interrogated from within the user program. Such a response parameter takes values which clearly distinguish between the successful execution of an ACSL statement, and exception and error conditions. The example below shows an ACSL statement returning an error response. This and all future examples in this section are written in an enhanced version of the Algol-like language, CORAL 66.

```
'SET' P 'TO' PRODUCT.CODE: RESPONSE;
'IF' RESPONSE = SUCCESS 'THEN'
'BEGIN'
.
.
.
etc.
```

The Basic Statements

The basic statements of the Interactive CSL which have been exploited to form a basis for ACSL are the following:

1. the SET statement,
2. the DESET statement,
3. the SELECT statements (i.e. SELECT, SELECT & READ, SELECT & CREATE, SELECT & DESTROY, SELECT & UPDATE, and SELECT & WRITE).

Given these statements, then their description is exactly the same as the description given in the earlier chapters of this Part. The SET statement gives a user access to all the normal CSL facilities including a target-list, a predicate, an order-expression-list, and where appropriate arithmetic expressions and calls on functions. It also gives him access to the macros and views of the External Environment. The successful execution of this SET statement will result in the creation of a currency which is then named in the target-list of the statements that follow. Figure 16.2 shows the skeleton of a program which reads and prints out the entity set PRODUCT and is therefore called List Products.

```
1.  'PROGRAM' LIST PRODUCTS ('LOCATION' 'INTEGER' RESPONSE);
2.  'BEGIN'
3.  'INTEGER' I; CURRENCY P;
4.  I: = 0
5.  'SET' P 'TO' PRODUCT: RESPONSE;
6.  'IF' RESPONSE = SUCCESS 'THEN'
7.  'BEGIN'
8.  'SREAD' 1 'FROM' P 'STARTING' 0: RESPONSE;
9.  'FOR' I: = I + 1 'WHILE' RESPONSE = SUCCESS 'DO'
10. 'BEGIN'
11.
12.     Print out contents of entity read from P
13.
14. 'SREAD' 1 'FROM' P: RESPONSE;
15. 'END'; (READ & PRINT LOOP)
16. 'DESET' P; RESPONSE;
17. 'END'; (SET)
18. 'END'; (PROGRAM READ PRODUCT)
```

Figure 16.2 The Program: List Products, written in CORAL 66. Note: on lines 15, 17, and 18, the texts in brackets after the semi-colon are comments

Handling Data Values

So far in the description of the ACSL interface no mention has been made of the mechanisms required to pass data values back and forth across the interface. Basically, the interface is designed so that for each of the attribute/domains which appear in the target-list of a SET statement the user has to define a buffer (i.e. address and mode) to contain the appropriate value. The list of such values are passed across the interface by means of a BINDING statement. Such a statement is issued after a SET statement and must identify the currency and attributes which it establishes. In this situation, attributes are identified by name on the assumption that the normal CSL name inheritance rules have been applied. Each attribute name is followed by its associate mode and address parameters. The example in Figure 16.3 illustrates the use of the complete interface.

More Complex Requirements

So far the examples used to describe the ACSL interface have used fairly simple requirements. However, the interface has been structured so that more complex requirements can be satisfied by using the target-list, predicate, and order-expression-list clauses associated with a SET statement.

For example, to change the program in Figure 16.3 to read all the products with a price greater than a £1000 would require the statement on line 8 to be replaced by:

```
'SET' P 'TO' PRODUCT 'SUCHTHAT' PRODUCT.CODE > 1000 :
RESPONSE;
```

```
'PROGRAM' LIST PRODUCTS ('LOCATION' 'INTEGER' RESPONSE);
'BEGIN'
'INTEGER' I; 'CURRENCY P';
'INTEGER' ACODE;
'BYTE' 'ARRAY' ANAME (0: 20);
'FLOATING' APRICE;
I: = 0;
'SET' P 'TO' PRODUCT: RESPONSE;
'IF' RESPONSE = SUCCESS 'THEN'
'BEGIN'
'BINDING' P 'AS' CODE (INTEGER, 'LOC' (ACODE)),
                 NAME (STRING, 'LOC' (ANAME)),
                 PRICE (REAL, 'LOC' (APRICE)):
                 RESPONSE;
'IF' RESPONSE = SUCCESS 'THEN'
'BEGIN'
'SREAD' 1 'FROM' P 'STARTING' 0: RESPONSE;
'FOR' I: = I + 1 'WHILE' RESPONSE = SUCCESS 'DO'
'BEGIN'
PRINT (ACODE, 6,0);
WRITE TEXT (ANAME); (PRINT OUT CONTENTS OF ENTITY)
PRINT (APRICE, 6,2);
'SREAD' 1 'FROM' P: RESPONSE;
'END'; (READ & PRINT LOOP)
'END'; (BINDING)
'DESET' P: RESPONSE;
'END'; (SET)
'END'; (PROGRAM READ PRODUCT)
```

Figure 16.3 The complete program

If further to this it is required to have the entities visible in P ordered on product name then naturally the SET statement would include an order-expression-list as follows:

```
'SET' P 'TO' PRODUCT 'SUCHTHAT' PRODUCT.CODE > 1000
    'WITHORDER' NAME 'UP' : RESPONSE;
```

Using this technique then a user of the ACSL interface can call functions, invoke arithmetic expressions and assignments, and perform joins.

16.3 A Control Sub-Language for COBOL

Chapter 4 stressed the point that the production of a CSL for an Algorithmic Language such as COBOL would naturally lead to some extensions and modifications to that language. It also emphasized that care should be taken to ensure that the addition of a CSL to a language does not unbalance it by duplicating its basic facilities and thus changing the nature of the language.

In 1973, a subgroup of the Advanced Programming Group of the British Computer Society chaired by Professor P. King produced a rendering of Codd's Data Sub-Language Alpha in COBOL syntax (see DEE1). This work represents one of the few attempts to effect a marriage between a relational sub-language and

COBOL, and consequently this COBOL CSL has borrowed some of its concepts.

The actual task of describing a COBOL CSL is primarily a question of deciding on a correspondence between the constructs of the COBOL language as described in a language description (see ICL 5) and the constructs of the Algorithmic CSL described earlier in this section.

In practice there are several areas of correspondence. One area of correspondence concerns the COBOL Data Division where there is an obvious parallel between the definition of the files and records in conventional COBOL and the entity sets, views, and currencies available in ACSL in so far as they serve the purpose of describing the data to be used by the rest of the program. Another area of correspondence concerns the COBOL Procedure Division where there is a parallel between the COBOL data manipulation statements such as Read, Delete, and Write and the ACSL statements Select & Read, Select & Destroy, and Select & Create. One area where there is no direct correspondence between the two languages concerns the COBOL Open and ACSL Set statements. Here the designer is faced with a choice of either modifying the Open statement to encompass the facilities associated with the Set statement or introducing a new statement.

The first option changes the Open statement almost beyond recognition and thus may confuse the normal COBOL programmer. The second option avoids this and for this reason is the one adopted in this system.

The rest of this section briefly describes the modifications which are required to the Data and Procedure Divisions, and then describes the new Set statement.

The COBOL Data Division

Users of COBOL rely on being able to refer to files and records, and for this reason describe them in the File section of the Data Division. It is thus natural for users of COBOL CSL to expect to refer to name data objects such as entity sets, attributes, and views, all of which exist in the Information and External Environments of an Information System by using a similar mechanism. Such users will also expect to be able to manipulate information passed to them from within an RDBMS system by referring to named currencies and other local variables. In order to satisfy these requirements COBOL CSL adds two new sections to the standard COBOL Data Division. These sections are:

1. *A Relational Environment section:* which defines the entity sets and views which are going to be referred to by the rest of the program together with their associated attribute names.
2. *A Local Environment section:* which identifies the currencies which are to be used by the rest of the program, together with a description of their associated attribute names and domain types.

The use of these two new sections is illustrated in Figure 16.4, which shows

```
          IDENTIFICATION DIVISION.
          PROGRAM-ID. LIST PRODUCTS
          AUTHOR. ATFH.

          ENVIRONMENT DIVISION.
          CONFIGURATION SECTION.
          SOURCE  – COMPUTER.ATLAS 1.
          OBJECT  – COMPUTER.ATLAS 1.

          INPUT–OUTPUT SECTION.
          FILE-CONTROL.

             SELECT PRINT-FILE ASSIGN TO CR-1.

          DATA DIVISION.
          FILE SECTION.
          FD PRINT-FILE.
             LABEL RECORDS ARE OMITTED,
             DATA RECORD IS PRINT-LINE.
          01 PRINT-LINE PIC X (128).

*         RELATIONAL ENVIRONMENT SECTION.
*            ENTITY-SET NAME IS PRODUCT.
*               ATTRIBUTES ARE CODE, NAME, PRICE.

*         LOCAL ENVIRONMENT SECTION.
*            CURRENCY NAME IS P
*               ATTRIBUTE CODE PIC 9 (6).
*               ATTRIBUTE ANAME PIC X (20).
*               ATTRIBUTE APRICE PIC 9999V99.

          PROCEDURE DIVISION.
```

Figure 16.4 The declarations for the program List Products written in COBOL CSL. Note: An asterisk on the left indicates a COBOL CSL statement

declarations required for a rendering in COBOL of the program LIST PRODUCTS (see Figure 16.3).

The COBOL Procedure Division

The standard COBOL definition describes six imperative input/output statements: namely, Open, Close, Write, Delete, Rewrite, and Read. The ACSL interface contains seven imperative statements: namely, Set, Deset, Select & Create, Select & Destroy, Select & Update, Select & Write, and Select & Read; and it comes as no surprise to find that it is possible to establish a correspondence between the two sets. With the exception of the Open and Set Statements which are described in the next section, Figure 16.5 shows that there is a direct correspondence between them.

The COBOL CSL Set Statement

The approach which has been adopted to handle the Open and Set statements is

ACSL STATEMENT	STANDARD COBOL STATEMENT	FORM OF COBOL ACSL STATEMENT
Select & Read	Read	READ currency-name ATEND imperative statement
Select & Create	Write	WRITE currency-name
Select & Destroy	Delete	DELETE currency-name
Select & Update	Rewrite	REWRITE currency-name
Deset	Close	CLOSE currency-name

Figure 16.5 Representing ACSL statements in COBOL CSL

to retain the Open statement in its existing form and to introduce a Set statement as an extension to the language. Thus a user of COBOL CSL creates currencies by using a Set statement which identifies a currency-name, a target-list, and an optional predicate and order-expression-list. The full form of the Set statement may be illustrated as follows

SET currency-name TO target-list
    WHERE predicate WITHORDER order-expression-list

Having identified this statement, it immediately becomes apparent that many of the clauses available within an ACSL Set statement may be represented in a COBOL Set statement by using traditional COBOL constructs. Furthermore, it also becomes apparent that in order to preserve the COBOL concepts some of the ACSL Set facilities are best discarded so as not to disturb the traditions of COBOL. The clauses in ACSL which need to be discussed in order to complete the description of the COBOL Set statement are:

1. Currency/attribute relationship
2. Selection expressions
3. Join expressions
4. Arithmetic expressions
5. Assignments.

These seem to be the five key areas in the description of the Set statement; consequently the rest of this section briefly describes them and then gives some examples of their use.

Within ACSL the currency/attribute relationship is typically represented by clauses of the form:

entity-set-name . (attribute-name*,)

Within COBOL CSL it would seem that these relationships are best represented by clauses of the form: attribute-name OF entity-set-name, attribute-name OF view-name, and [attribute-name*,] OF entity-set-name which in practice leads to constructs of the form CODE OF PRODUCT and CODE, PRICE OF PRODUCT.

COBOL relation clauses allow programmers to write expressions of the form:

```
X > Y
X1 > Y1 AND X2 = Y2
X1+X3 > Y1 AND X1*X2 < Y2
```

As the expressions are exactly the same as the comparisons used within ACSL it is obviously possible and desirable to use the traditional COBOL syntax. Furthermore, this syntax can be extended to represent ACSL join clauses by the use of an additional key word JOIN.

Thus the ACSL clause

```
SALE.PRODUCT CODE *= PRODUCT.CODE
```

may be represented in COBOL CSL by

```
PRODUCTCODE OF SALE JOIN = CODE OF PRODUCT
```

COBOL, being a fairly old language, uses the Add, Subtract, Multiply, and Divide statements not only to effect the desired arithmetic operation but also to assign the results to a given variable. As there is obviously very little in common between these statements and the ACSL arithmetic expressions and assignment clauses, it would seem appropriate that there are no facilities in COBOL CSL which map onto the ACSL equivalents. However, just as COBOL allows a user to combine an arithmetic expression with a relation expression, so, as already indicated, such clauses are valid in COBOL CSL.

Unfortunately, the approach described above removes from COBOL CSL one very useful facility, namely that of using assignments to allow users to rename attributes.

For this reason a COBOL CSL predicate will allow a renaming clause which takes the form:

```
RENAME CODE OF PRODUCT AS RESULT 1
```

Given these facilities then Figure 16.6 contains the complete Procedure Division in COBOL CSL for the program List Products.

```
    PROCEDURE DIVISION.
    PARA-1. OPEN OUTPUT PRINT-FILE.
    PARA-2.

*           SET P TO PRODUCT.

    PARA-3.

*           READ P AT END GO PARA-4.
            MOVE  ACODE OF P INTO PRINT-LINE.
            MOVE ANAME OF P INTO PRINT-LINE.
            MOVE APRICE OF P INTO PRINT-LINE.
            WRITE PRINT-LINE AFTER ADVANCING 1 LINES.
            GO PARA-3.

    PARA-4.

            CLOSE PRINT-LINE.
*           CLOSE P.
            STOP RUN.
```

Figure 16.6 The Procedure Division for the program List Products

17

The Multi-Level Schema

17.1 Introduction

The Multi-Level Schema is used by the designer of an Information System to describe his system to RDBMS. As described in Part A there are two possible approaches to formulating the description of the Multi-Level Schema. One approach, which is the approach which has been adopted with System R (see ASTRAHAN 2), is to extend the end-user language, in this case CSL. The other approach is to treat the problem of describing an Information System as an Information System problem and to use entity sets. This second approach is the one which has been adopted with RDBMS, and consequently it comes as no surprise to find that the Multi-Level Schema was designed using the Design Methodology and implemented as a succession of Information Environments. Each of these

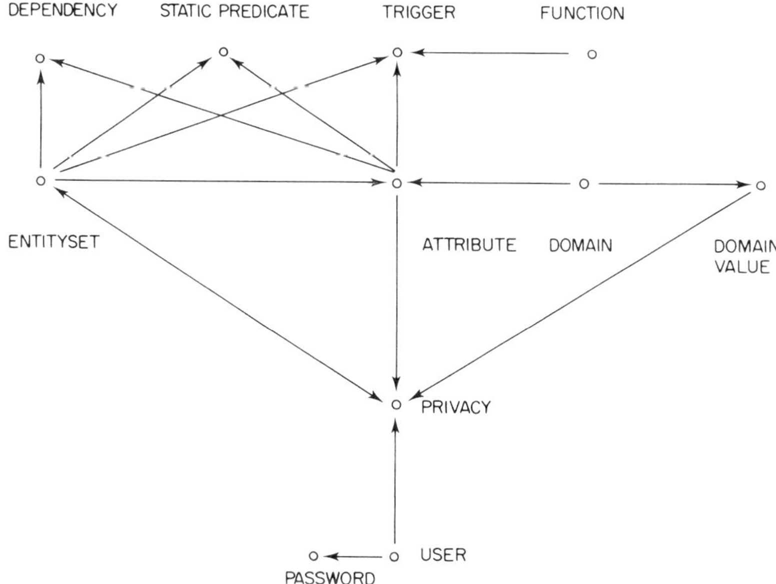

Figure 17.1 Dependency diagram of Meta-Schema for Information Environment schema

Information Environments contain a number of entity sets described with attributes, domains, domain values, dependencies, and static predicates.

One of the difficulties of describing these Information Environments is that they contain a total of 30 entity sets, and thus the complete and detailed description is rather lengthy and would be out of place in this chapter. The approach which has been adopted in the rest of this chapter is to describe briefly the Multi-Level Schema and to complete the work by providing an annotated description of the Multi-Level Schema for the Purchasing System.

17.2 The Multi-Level Schema as an Information System

As explained above, each of the Environments of the Multi-Level Schema is itself described as an Information Environment by using a Meta-Schema. As this Meta-Schema is rather lengthy, this section merely provides a detailed description of the Meta-Schema for the Information Environment Schema and then provides brief summaries of the Meta-Schema for the other Environments.

The Meta-Schema for the Information Environment Schema has been divided into three parts. Figure 17.1 contains a view of the Information Environment Schema in the form of a dependency diagram. Figure 17.2 describes the attributes and domains supported by each of the entity sets identified in the Dependency Diagram, while Figure 17.3 contains a detailed description of the domains. In Figure 17.2, the underlines identify candidate key attributes.

These three diagrams effectively complete the description of the Meta-Schema for the Information Environment. Figure 17.4 contains a brief summary of the entity sets and attributes to support the other environments, while Figure 17.5 contains a dependency diagram which may be used to link them.

Picture/DOM Picture

This has been implemented as two integer attributes L1/DOML and L2/DOML, the values of the integers being dependent on the LMODE setting of the associated domain. The valid values are:

LMODE	Integer L1	Integer L2	Explanation
Integer	*n*	0	*n* defines the number of digits together with the sign.
Real	*n*	*m*	*n* and *m* define the number of digits before and after the decimal point respectively.
String Name	min	max	min and max define the minimum and maximum number of digits in the name or string.
Date	8	8	

ENTITY SET	ATTRIBUTE	DOMAIN	COMMENTS
ENTITY SET	NAME DESCRIPTION	DOM NAME DOM DESCRIPTION	This represents an entity set
DOMAIN	NAME LMODE CARDINALITY VALIDCHECK PICTURE	DOM NAME DOM LMODE DOM CARD DOM V CHECKS DOM PICTURE	This represents a domain which defines a set of data values
ATTRIBUTE	ENTITY SET NAME ATTRIBUTE NAME DOMAIN NAME CANDIDATE KEY	DOM NAME DOM NAME DOM NAME DOM CAND	This represents an attribute of an entity set, which is defined over a domain
DOMAIN VALUE	DOMAIN VALUE USE VALUE	DOM NAME DOM USE DOM ANY	This defines a particular domain value and its use in handling domain validity checks
DEPENDENCY	ENTITY SET 1 ATTRIBUTE 1 ENTITY SET 2 ATTRIBUTE 2	DOM NAME DOM NAME DOM NAME DOM NAME	This represents a dependency between two pairs of entity set/ attributes
STATIC PREDICATE	ENTITY SET ACCESS PREDICATE	DOM NAME DOM ACCESS RIGHTS DOM CSL	This represents a static predicate supporting an entity set
TRIGGER	ENTITY SET ACCESS FUNCTION NAME PREDICATE	DOM NAME DOM ACCESS RIGHTS DOM NAME DOM CSL	This represents a trigger
USER	NAME CODE ADDRESS BUDGET	DOM NAME DOM USER CODE DOM ADDRESS DOM BUDGET	This represents a User
PRIVACY	USER NAME ENTITY SET ATTRIBUTE VALUES ACCESS USER STATUS	DOM NAME DOM NAME DOM NAME DOM CSL DOM ACCESS RIGHTS DOM USER STATUS	This represents a privacy condition
PASSWORD	USER NAME PASSWORD	DOM NAME DOM NAME	This represents a user's password

Figure 17.2 The entity sets, attributes, and domains of the Meta-Schema for the Information Environment

DOMAIN NAME	LMODE	VALIDITY CHECKS	COMMENTS
DOM ACCESS RIGHTS	Name	One or more of 'READACCESS, CREATEACCESS, WRITEACCESS, DESTROYACCESS, UPDATEACCESS' separated by spaces	This describes an access right
DOM ADDRESS	String	None	This describes a user's address
DOM ANY	Any	None	This defines any domain value
DOM BUDGET	Integer	–	This describes a user budget
DOM CAND	Name	One of "CAND, NONCAND"	This describes a candiate key flag
DOM CARD	Integer	+ve integer	The cardinality of a domain
DOM CSL	CSL string	None	A valid CSL string
DOM LMODE	Name	One of 'INTEGER, REAL, NAME, STRING, DATE'	
DOM NAME	Name	Name	
DOM DESCRIPTION	String	None	
DOM OWNER STATUS	String	One of 'OWNER, USER'	
DOM USE	Name	One of 'LB, UB SET, DEFAULT, UNASSIGNED'	LB = Lower Bound UB = Upper Bound
DOM USER CODE	Name	None	–
DOM VCHECKS	Name	One of 'NONE, RANGE, NRANGES, SET, PROC'	PROC implies user written procedure

Figure 17.3 Domain definitions

ENVIRONMENT	ENTITY SET	ATTRIBUTES
OBJECT ENVIRONMENT	OBJECT	NAME, DESCRIPTION, TYPE, CLASS
	OBJECT DEPENDS	OBJECT1, OBJECT2
	INFORMATION	NAME, DESCRIPTION, MODE CORRESPONDING, LMODE, CARDINALITY, VALIDCHECK, VALUE DESCRIPTION
	OBJECT INFO	OBJECT, INFO, RELATIONSHIP
INFORMATION ENVIRONMENT	ENTITYSET	NAME, DESCRIPTION
	DOMAIN	NAME, LMODE, CARDINALITY, VALIDCHECK, PICTURE
	ATTRIBUTE	ESNAME, ANAME, DNAME, CANDIDATE
	DOMAINVALUE	DNAME, USE, VALUE
	DEPENDENCY	ESNAME1, ANAME1, ESNAME2, ANAME2
	STATICPREDICATE	ESNAME, ACCESS, PREDICATE
	TRIGGER	ESNAME, ACCESS, FUNCTION, PREDICATE
	USER	NAME, CODE, ADDRESS, BUDGET
	PRIVACY	USER, ESNAME, ANAME, VALUES, ACCESS, USERSTATUS
	PASSWORD	NAME, PASSWORD
EXTERNAL ENVIRONMENT	VIEW	NAME, TARGETLIST, PREDICATE, DESCRIPTION
	MACRO	MNAME, MTEXT, MDESCRIPTION
ENCODED ENVIRONMENT	ENCODEDENTITYSET	NAME, DESCRIPTION
	ENCODED DOMAIN	NAME, EMODE
	ENCODED ATTRIBUTE	EESNAME, EANAME, EDNAME, ACCESSKEY, START, LENGTH
	DOMAINMAP	DNAME, EDNAME, DEMAPTYPE
	DOMAINMAPCRITERIA	DNAME, DVALUE, EVALUE
	SETMAP	ESNAME, EESNAME, MAPTYPE
	SETMAPCRITERIA	ESNAME, ANAME, EESNAME, EANAME, CRITERIA
STORED ENVIRONMENT	STORED ENTITY SET	NAME, DESCRIPTION, OSDESCRIPTION
	STORED DOMAIN	NAME, SMODE
	STORED ATTRIBUTE	SESNAME, SANAME, SDNAME, START, LENGTH
	SDOMAINMAP	EDNAME, SDNAME, SDMAPTYPE
	MAPPING	SET1, SET2, MAPPING
SOFTWARE ENVIRONMENT	CALLS	GROUP, REF, PHASE, NAME, CALL
	FUNCTION	NAME, TYPE, UNIT
	FUNCTION PARAM	FUNCTNAME, PARAMROLE, PARAMNAME, PARAMDOMAIN
	DATAOBJECT	GROUP, REF, PHASE, NAME, DESCRIPTION, DECLARED
	UNIT	GROUP, REF, PHASE, LEVEL, NAME, UNITTYPE, NARRATIVE, LANGUAGE, SOURCE, OBJECT
	UNITUNIT	UGROUP, UREF, LGROUP, LREF, PHASE, RELATIONSHIP
	USES	UGROUP, UREF, UPHASE, UNAME, PARAMTYPE, DATATYPE, DATAIDENT, PHASE, ACCESS
	RESPONSIBILITY	UGROUP, UREF, UPHASE, USER, STARTDATE, ENDDATE

Figure 17.4 Summary of the Multi-Level schema

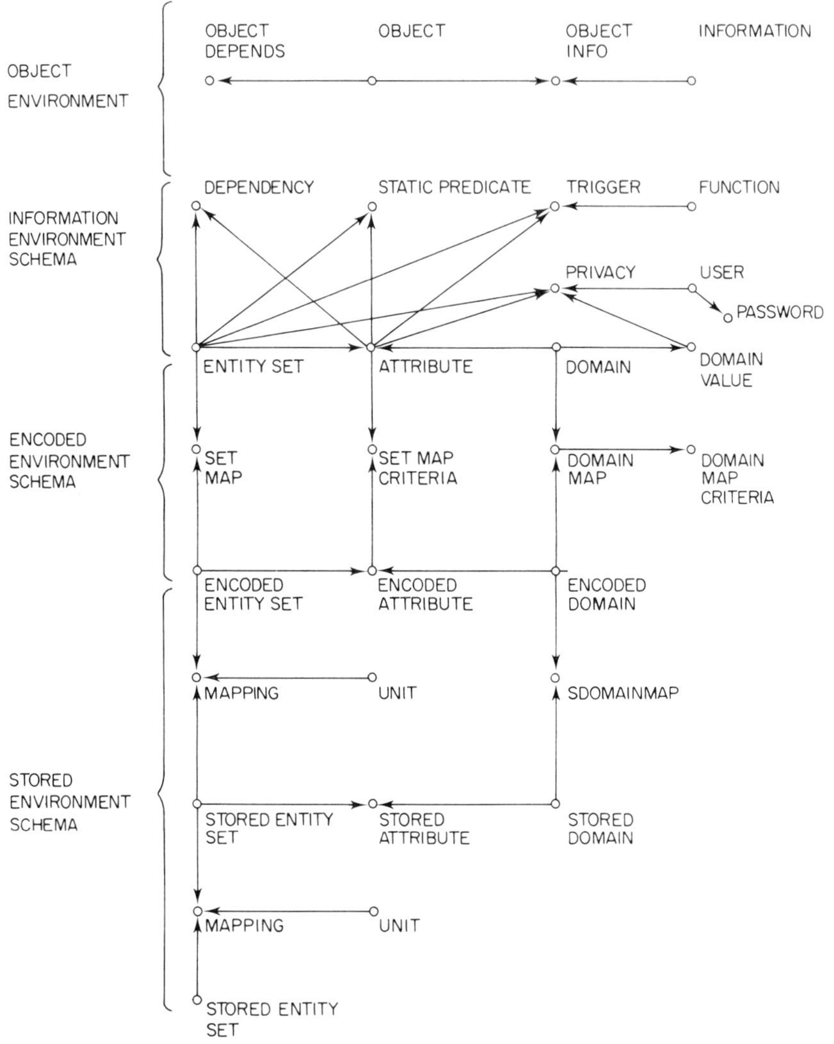

Figure 17.5 Dependency diagram of the Multi-Level schema

17.3 Using the Multi-Level Schema

This section contains an annotated copy of a job run on a terminal using Interactive CSL to implement the entity set Product of the Purchasing System described in Part A. A revision of Sections 6.8 and 7.6 will show that the entity set Product is implemented via a direct encoding of both the domains and the set, and furthermore the resulting encoded entity set may be supported using a data-dependent mapping of type sequential. Chapter 3 briefly described how the Multi-Level Schema incorporates defaults which may be used for direct mappings, and in this example the use of such defaults have removed the need for explicitly describing an Encoded Environment. For this reason the complete description may be achieved by using the Information and Stored Environment schemas alone.

With this in mind the following is an annotated copy of the terminal log. The texts beginning and ending in ≠ are comments and may appear anywhere in an interaction.

```
> THIS IS THE RELATIONAL DATA BASE MANAGEMENT SYSTEM
> RUNNING AT THE ATLAS LABORATORY AT 09:00:00 ON 28/2/78

> RDBMS READY
- LOGIN MOP1, ESSK;
                                        # INFORMATION ENVIRONMENT #
> RDMBS READY
- CREATE ENTITYSET;
> ENTITYSET
> NAME       DESCRIPTION
- PRODUCT    "DESCRIBES THE COMPANY'S PRODUCTS"
- ;

> RDBMS READY
- CREATE DOMAIN;
> DOMAIN
> NAME        LMODE     CARDINALITY    VALIDCHECK   L1    L2
- DOMNAME     STRING    1000           RANGE        6     0
- DOMNAME     STRING    1000           NONE         1     20
- DOMPRICE    REAL      1000           RANGE        4     2
- ;
> RDBMS READY
- CREATE DOMAINVALUE;              # THESE ARE THE VALUES USED
                                     IN THE VALIDATION CHECKS
                                     FOR DOMAINS #
> DOMAINVALUE
> DNAME       USE           VALUE
- DOMCODE     LOWERBOUND    0
- DOMPRICE    LOWERBOUND    0.00
- DOMPRICE    UPPERBOUND    1000.00
- ;

> RDBMS READY
- CREATE ATTRIBUTE
> ATTRIBUTE
> ESNAME      ANAME     DNAME       CANDIDATE
- PRODUCT     CODE      DOMCODE     CAND
- PRODUCT     NAME      DOMNAME     NONCAND
```

```
– PRODUCT     PRICE       DOMPRICE    NONCAND
– ;
                                      # THE ENCODED ENVIRONMENT
                                        IS DEFAULTED OUT #
                                      # STORED ENVIRONMENT #
> RDBMS READY
– CREATE STOREDENTITYSET.NAME;
> STOREDENTITYSET
> NAME
– PRODDATA
– ;

> RDBMS READY
– CREATE MAPPING;
> MAPPING
> SET1             SET2    MAPPING
– PRODUCT PRODDATA  DEFAULTDIRECT    # THE DEFAULT MAPPING #
– PRODDATA     OS   SEQUENTIAL       # MAPPING TO THE
                                       OPERATING SYSTEM
                                       I.E. OS #
– ;

> RDBMS READY
– LOGOUT;
> STOP
```

Part D

RDBMS

18

The Objectives of RDBMS

All engineered systems are evolved from the systems which predate them; consequently, in order to understand the design objectives of RDBMS, it is necessary to identify those developments which have influenced it. The developments span a wide spectrum of different aspects of informatics which include language design, operating system design, the development of file handling techniques, abstract modelling, and software engineering techniques. The rest of this chapter reviews these developments and then states the design objectives of RDBMS as a logical progression from them.

18.1 Languages

From the point of view of language design the origins of RDBMS may be traced to those early languages which led to the definition of ALGOL 60 (see ALGOL 1). Much of the emphasis in those early days was to provide a representation of first order predicate calculus within a programming language. In the event these attempts led to the definition of the ALGOL 60 boolean clause which contains a complete set of logic operators. However, many future language designers have considered that the ALGOL 60 boolean operators were too powerful, because they have been excluded from later languages such as CORAL 66 (see WOODWARD 2), ALGOL 68 (see WIJNGAARDEN 1 and LINDSEY 1), and PASCAL (see WIRTH 1).

In the 1970s interest in predicate logic was revived by the work of logicians such as Kowalski and data base theoreticians such as Codd. Kowalski (see KOWALSKI 1) recognized that, using predicate calculus as a programming language, it was possible to write programs which could produce proven results; furthermore, the design of languages based on predicate calculus such as REL and the development of improved theorem provers have produced some impressive results.

This work has been paralleled by developments in the design of traditional programming languages. Dijkstra (see DIJKSTRA 2) recognized that it was possible to define a language which clearly defined boolean clauses or guards which must be satisfied before an alogrithm could be performed. His designs have re-incorporated many of the concepts of predicate calculus into a programming language and have led to a greater understanding of those concepts.

Finally, in 1971, Dr E. F. Codd described a language: Data Sub-Language Alpha (see CODD 2), which was based on first order predicate calculus and designed to access a relational data base. This language arose from a need to provide the user of a relational data base with a flexible and powerful language which could be shown to produce consistent results, so again this basic requirement led to the use of predicate calculus.

The languages supported by RDBMS must be regarded as a development of Data Sub-Language Alpha; however, many of the ideas developed by both the logicians such as Kowalski, and the Language designers such as Dijkstra, have also been influential.

18.2 Operating Systems

The descriptions of the Multics Operating System (see CORBATO 1) and ICL's George III Operating Systems (see ICL 1) are significant in the development of RDBMS because they describe systems which maintain a catalogue of system users, together with details of the files they own and the files and hardware devices they use. Furthermore, these systems support facilities to back-up and recover both the catalogue and the files described therein. Finally, the systems were designed for interactive use, and thus in many ways they must be seen as direct fore-runners of the interactive information system of the type described in Chapter 1.

The design and implementation of a large modern operating system such as ICL's 2900 VME/B (see ICL 2 and 3) has gone a stage further than the Multics System. VME/B is a general purpose operating system which supports batch, interactive, and transaction processing facilities and runs on the larger 2900 machines. The paper HUTT1 shows that the system was designed as an Information System by representing the system resources such as jobs, files, and discs as if they existed in a data base. The system also demonstrates the relationship between the description of a resource such as a disc and the resource itself.

The design of operating systems such as VME/B shows that a large operating system is an Information System designed to control a computer system. Consequently, the development of operating systems has been a necessary step towards the development of the generalized data base management system. Furthermore, many of the techniques evolved in the development of operating systems, such as lock management and deadly embrace detection, are fundamental to the development of data base management systems.

Data and Information

These operating systems developments have made a significant contribution to the understanding of the difference between data and information. For many years, the data processing community has toyed with the philosophical distinction to be drawn between data and information, and for the most part people still do not distinguish between the two terms. However, when dealing with a software system, it is necessary and possible to distinguish between them.

The first important fact is that data and information are not the same thing; however, the two are highly interrelated. For example, consider the case of a Personnel file of man records, which contains details of men working at a factory. The Personnel file, which is organized as an indexed sequential file, is read and written by application programs in the Personnel suite. From the point of view of the Personnel suite of programs, each man record is treated as information because it is validated and manipulated in a way which implies intelligence of its contents. From the point of view of the indexed sequential file manager, the man records are treated as data, as the file manager has no knowledge or interest in the contents of the record.

From this it may be recognized that it is possible to distinguish between data and information. However, the distinction may be made only from the point of view of a unit of code. It may also be recognized that information at one level in the system is held as data at lower levels in the system.

18.3 Access Methods

When discs were first added to a computer system many application programmers found that they had to write programs which were complicated by the fact that they had to issue instructions, often in the form of hardware command chains, to a disc controller. The release of the ISAM access methods (see IBM 3) must be seen as a step towards reducing the complexity of these application programs by providing a higher level and thus simpler interface to a disc device. This simplification was produced by representing a disc file as an indexed record structure. However, since then there have been many other representations such as Binary-Trees (see BAYER 1 and 2), chain lists, and pointer structures (see KNUTH 1), each of which embody algorithms with different performance characteristics. This work culminated in the development of the generalized data base management system which usually embodied a number of algorithms under a single high-level interface. A typical example of this type of system is IBM's Information Management System (IMS) (see IBM 4).

At the time when work started on RDBMS the development of this type of system culminated in the proposals of the Codasyl Data Base Task Group (see CODASYL 1), which provides a single high-level interface to a number of algorithms which employ inter-record pointers and pointer-arrays, which in turn use common facilities for data base backup, recovery, and concurrency control.

18.4 Abstract Models

Mathematical modelling is one of the most important tools available to the modern scientists; consequently it comes as no surprise to find that abstract modelling is being exploited in a number of areas of system design. The significant models which have contributed to RDBMS are models of data and models of system and application programs.

Models of Data

The first and probably best understood model of data is that used by the Codasyl Data Base Task Group which defines a data base as containing records held in areas and linked by sets (hereafter known as Cosets (see NIJSSENS 1)). However, a model which is of greater significance to RDBMS is the Relational Data Model identified by Codd in 1970 (see CODD1,2,3,4,5,6, and 7). This model was conceptually simpler than the Codasyl model, and furthermore it had a fairly sound design methodology which led to data bases easier to understand than those designed by other means, while it also linked fairly naturally with the languages identified in Section 18.1. There have been many modifications and changes to the Relational Data Model, and periodically an attempt is made to consolidate the definition. The consolidation published in 1976 may be found in CHAMBERLIN 1.

Following the definition of the Relational Data Model, the working conferences sponsored by IFIP TC2 have produced many other data models which have been designed to encompass new problems. Finally, in 1973, ANSI established the ANSI/X3/SPARC Data Base Study Group which produced proposals (see ANSI SPARC 1 and ANSI SPARC 2) which used yet another abstract model to model a data base system. Much of the work is contemporary with the development of RDBMS and it has obviously influenced the design of the data models used within the system.

Models of Information Systems

One of the earliest users of abstract modelling is Langefors (see LANGEFORS 1), who for many years has been recommending that the best way of designing an Information System is to design an abstract model of the system and then transform that model into a working computer system; otherwise, all too frequently, computer-oriented problems cloud the initial design of an Information, and this can lead to an unsuccessful system. Langefors proposed that the use of an abstract model in the initial design stages of the system, followed by a cookbook approach to realizing that model, seemed to offer a good chance of producing a successful system.

Following Langefors a number of groups (see TEICHROEW 1, SNOWDEN 1, and PEARSON 1) have been using abstract models to represent both application programs and operating systems, and, by 1973, several systems had been designed using methods which incorporated hierarchical or tree structures. The groups have all found that systems produced in this way were easier to understand, produce, and maintain than systems produced by less formal methods.

18.5 Engineering Techniques

From the previous sections it is apparent that any system which draws upon such a wide spectrum of interests must necessarily incorporate a fairly wide spectrum of engineering techniques, and this is undoubtedly the case. The techniques which seem to be of significance to this type of system are:

1. *Compiling techniques:* which are used to realize the language processor required by the system. Such techniques are dependent on the use of formal grammars, such as LL1 grammars (see GREIS 1) and syntax analyser generators (see SIMPSON 1).
2. *Optimizing techniques:* which are used to map a user request expressed in an applied predicate calculus into the many calls used to drive an underlying data base, and to produce the simulators and data base optimizers so necessary to this class of system.
3. *Conceptual machine concepts:* which are used to realize the software used to maintain and manage a particular set of information and/or resources using a specific group of mapping algorithms. Such machines were first identified by Dijkstra (see DIJKSTRA 1) and later developed by Brinch Hansen to produce Task Orient Systems (see BRINCH HANSEN 1) and by Hutt *et al.* to produce Data Oriented Systems (see HUTT 1).
4. *Binding techniques:* which influence the system in many ways. Firstly, these techniques allow the system to enhance itself by loading and entering new code modules as and when they are required, and, equally, allow vital disposing of unwanted and unused code. Secondly, these techniques handle the problems of binding application programs to the underlying data base management system.

18.6 The Objectives

The primary objective behind designing the Relational Data Base Management System was to build a system which would support an Information System of the type identified in Chapter 1, would come into service late in the 1970s, and would still be viable in the mid-1980s.

In order to achieve this objective it seemed that the system should incorporate a combination of features which individually had been identified as being useful, but which in combination could result in a very powerful system. Consequently, realizing the primary objective was separated into the task of realizing the following secondary objectives.

1. Identify a set of abstract models which could be used to describe the many facets of an Information System.
2. To build a data base management system based on the Relational Data Model which could be used to provide end-users and system designers with com-

prehensive facilities for manipulating the information relevant to their allotted roles.

3. To define a design methodology which integrated the abstract models identified in 1 with the data descriptions required by 2. This was felt to be vital because one of the problems with the Codasyl DBTG proposals was that they presented a Data Description Language and felt the prospective implementor with the often costly task of finding out how to use it.

4. To design and implement a single family of languages based on first order predicate calculus so that end-users, system designers, and operations staff can all interact with the relational data base in the same way. This approach has meant that all users have a minimum of details to learn before they can use the system. Their abilities after that point depend entirely on their understanding of the data base itself rather than the knowledge of further languages.

5. To use the new and as yet largely untried techniques for structuring data base software to see if they really resulted in a cost effective system.

Given these objectives then it is worthwhile reviewing them to confirm that they produce a viable system.

A brief look at the current usage of many commercial systems suggests that many systems which came alive in 1967 and were still running in 1975, which means that an 8 year life span is not too long from a user's point of view. Furthermore, the fact that the Relational Data Model incorporates a high degree of data independence and can be supported using intelligent disc controllers and specialist micro-programmed algorithms seems to suggest that such a system could survive several new and radical changes in hardware.

An attempt to realize a series of abstract models and to integrate them into the Data Base Schema facilities is recognized to be a shot in the dark; however, it is meant to prevent chief accountants, clerks, and others from having to understand any of the complexities of the actual computer system. This is a laudable aim and in this case the implementation awaits further trials. The use of abstract models in the definition of software is much safer, and could be regarded as an attempt to bring good practices out of the laboratory and into the real world. However, it has a more practical side. One of the problems of the CODASYL own-code procedures is that they are implementor-defined and operate as if by magic; the use of an abstract model helps to overcome the need for some of this magic.

19

An Overview of the RDBMS Software

This chapter provides a complete overview of all the RDBMS software and places particular emphasis on those system components which are to be discussed in the chapter which follows.

The design of the RDBMS software has been recorded in a Software Environment of the type described in Chapter 9 and can thus be described using a hierarchical tree. The top three levels of this tree are illustrated in Figure 19.1. This Software Environment tree has been ordered so that the lower numbered groups are nearer to the hardware than those with high numbers. Thus the Basic Services Group (Group 1) is lower in the system structure than the CSL Pre-Processors (Group 9). Within a group, the numbering is reversed so that the higher numbered sub-group is lower in the system. These conventions have been adopted because the tree is normally represented in a two-dimensional form. The rest of this section contains a description of the first two levels of the system.

19.0 RDBMS

While it is being used, the RDBMS Software consists of a number of autonomous processes with communication links between them. These processors are:

1. *A Primary Processor:* this contains the bulk of the system software. In the implementation for ICL 1900 series of computers the Primary Processor supports all the active users of a particular data base, while in the implementation for ICL 2900 series of computers there is a separate instance of the Primary Processor for each active user.

2. *A number of demons:* demons are small processes which carry out specific tasks within the system. Typical demons are the Communications Demon, which is responsible for maintaining the communications network of interactive terminals, and the Sort Demon, which is responsible for receiving an encoded entity set and sorting it into a given order.

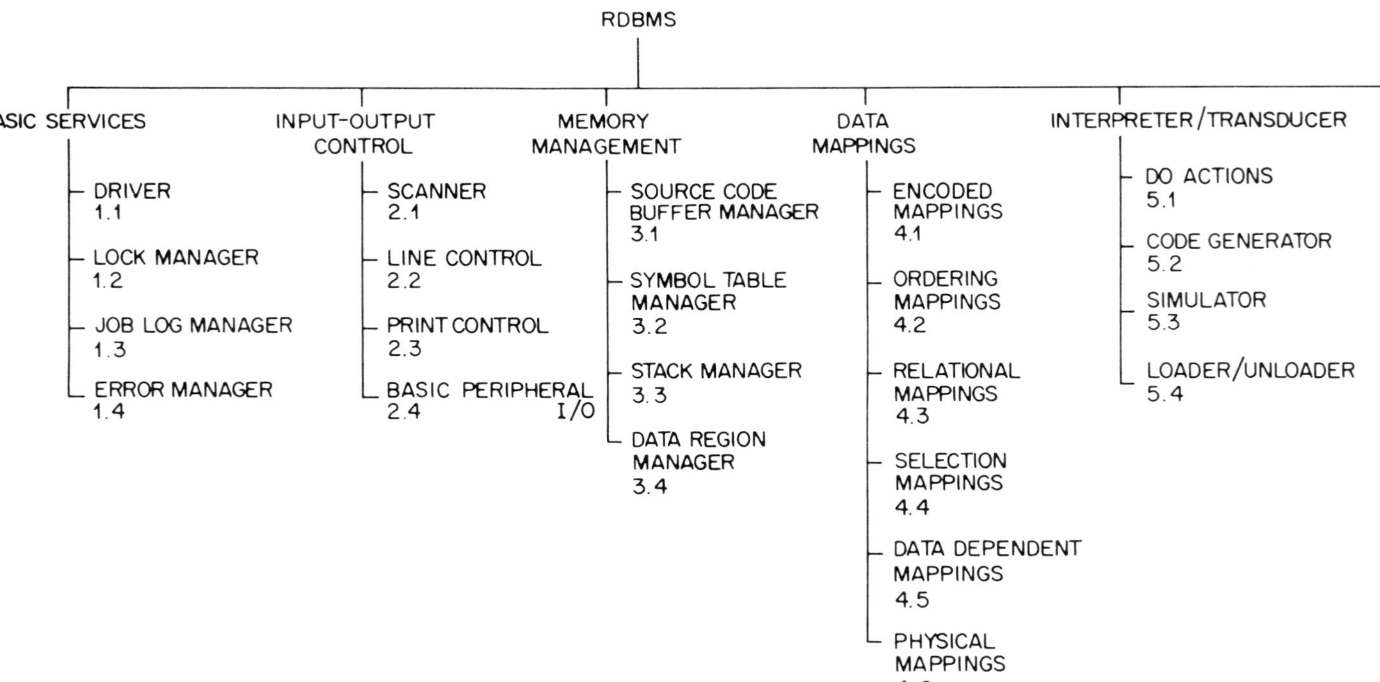

Figure 19.1(a) The Software Environment for RDBMS—Part 1

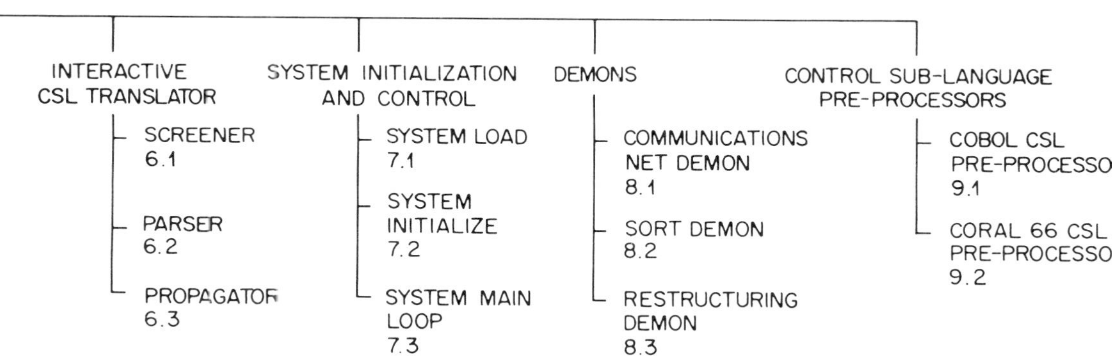

Figure 19.1(b) The Software Environment for RDBMS—Part 2

3. *Subsidiary Processors:* the CSL allows end-users to invoke functions. Some of these functions make only moderate use of the CPU and are thus processed directly by the Primary Processor; however, those functions which involve large quantities of software are relegated to a Subsidiary Processor and left to operate in an autonomous manner.

4. *Language Pre-Processors:* when an Algorithmic Language is enhanced by the addition of a CSL, it is necessary to provide a Pre-Processor to map this extension into conventional language statements. The Pre-Processors operate on the source statements of the Algorithmic Language, prior to it being input to a conventional Algorithmic Language Compiler.

Figure 19.2 illustrates the relationship between these Processors.

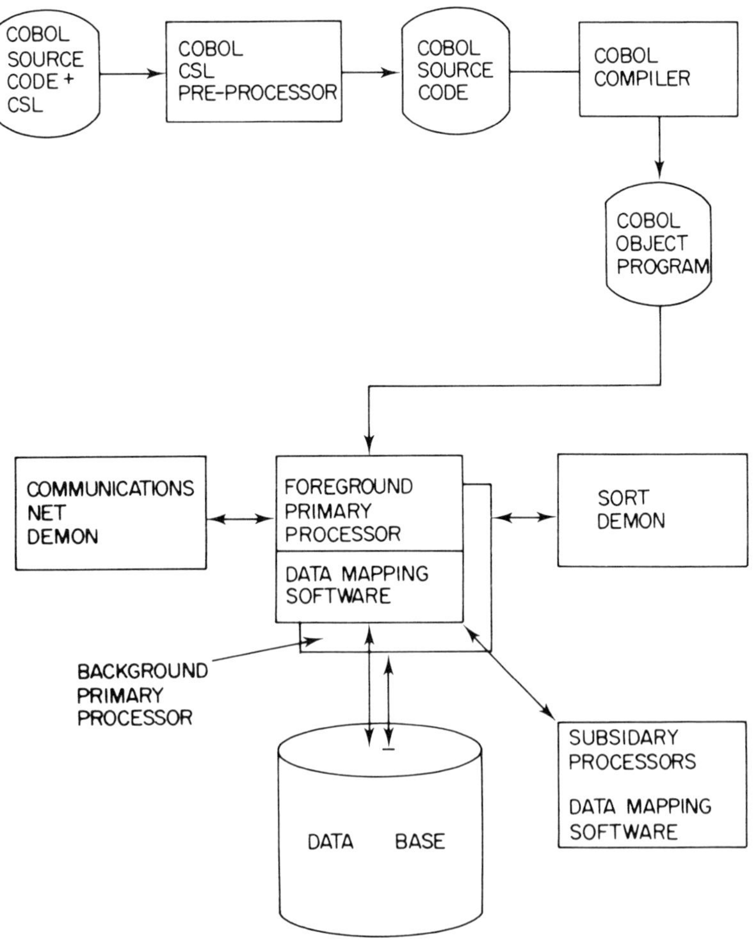

Figure 19.2 The RDBMS Processors

Communication between the Primary Processor, the Demons, and the Subsidiary Processors is dependent on the underlying operating system. The 1900 series implementations of RDBMS running under the George 3 Operating system achieves this communication by using the Job Control Language and the 'With-in Machine Communication' facilities. The 2900 implementation of RDBMS running under VME/B achieves this communication by using shared segments and the interrupt mechanisms.

Foreground and Background Primary Processors

The Primary Processor is responsible for taking each user request for information from the data base and producing the necessary results with the least inconvenience to that user. This necessarily demands that the Primary Processor optimizes each individual request, but there are requests which are too expensive to process in this way and these may have to be abandoned. It may happen that several users require a response to the same request and, although each request is too expensive to process individually, the cost of processing them is not too high when they are considered as a group. RDBMS recognizes this fact by providing two versions of the Primary Processor. One version, the Foreground Primary Processor, optimizes each individual request and rejects requests which are too expensive to handle; the other version, the Background Primary Processor, optimizes groups of similar or related requests which have been passed to it by the Foreground Primary Processor.

In essence the Foreground Primary Processor operates in a normal interactive environment while the Background Primary Processor carries out the same functions but operates in something like a batch environment. This use of two processors ensures that the system generates the required information at a cost and in a time scale which is commensurate with a reasonable use of user budgets and computer resources. Communication between the Foreground and Background Primary Processors is via shared files which may be thought of as part of the data base.

Note: In some early releases of RDBMS, the Foreground Primary Processor will be made available as a single processor system and will support a single multi-access terminal.

19.1 Basic Services

This group contains all those facilities which are operating-system dependent. In particular, it contains units for Inter-Process Communication, Error Control, and Error Monitoring. These facilities are usually provided as standard by the underlying operating system; however, as no two operating systems provide exactly the same facilities, the units in this group cover up these differences and thus provide the rest of the RDBMS software with a standard operating system interface. This group also contains units to handle lock management and deadly-embrace detection. These have been assigned to this group because it is vital that 'record' locking should become a standard feature of all operating systems, and identifying a separate deadly-embrace detection mechanism may speed this necessary enhancement.

19.2 Input/Output Control

This group is responsible for all input and output on visible media and it thus provides interfaces to allow other system units to access interactive terminals and slow peripherals. For output the group provides facilities for formatting pages and screens of information and for outputting red tape information such as page headings. For input the group controls the input of both Interactive Control Sub-Language statements and information. This control is exercised via a single scanner which is shared by both the CSL Lexical Analyser (Unit 6.1) and the Encoding Mappings (Unit 4.1).

19.3 Memory Management

This group contains a number of conceptual machines, each supporting one of the data structures used within the system. These data structures are:

1. *The Symbol Table:* which is used to maintain a statement of the Multi-Level Schema in a form which can be used by the rest of the system.
2. *The Data Region or Heap:* which is used to hold partial results and other data used during the operation of the system.
3. *A number of stacks and buffers.*

There is a separate conceptual machine to support each of these data structures. Each machine supports a language, the Internal Data Manipulation Language, which allows all the other systems components to access and manipulate the contents of the structure for which it is responsible. This language is described in HUTT 2 and HUTT 4.

19.4 Data Mappings

This group contains all the data handling and manipulation software used within the system. The software has been structured so that each major relational operator and storage algorithm is supported by a separate conceptual machine known as a *Data Mapping*. Each Data Mapping is responsible for supporting a set of data objects which may be an entity set, an encoded entity set, or a stored entity set, and it does so by using some lower level set of data objects.

Within a system such as RDBMS, there is a large number of Data Mappings capable of a wide spectrum of different transformations, and for this reason the mappings have been ordered. The order is dependent on the set of data objects supported by each mapping and the algorithms involved, thus the highest level mappings are concerned with encoding entity sets to encoded entity sets, while the lowest level mappings are concerned with maintaining stored entity sets.

Processing a CSL statement normally requires the use of several Data Mappings, the choice being dependent on the complexity of the request and the data definition submitted via the Multi-Level Schema. With this in mind, the request is processed by selecting the relevant Data Mappings and linking them together. Such a structure is known as a *Currency Hierarchy* and is best considered as a hierarchical tree where each of the nodes represents a Data Mapping and each of the arcs represents a linkage between them. Once a Currency Hierarchy has been created then it can be called in the same way as one would call a procedure and by its action will produce the necessary result. Chapter 20 contains a detailed description of Data Mappings and the Currency Hierarchies used to activate them.

19.5 The Interpreter/Transducer

The Interpreter/Transducer is responsible for building Currency Hierarchies and for interpreting CSL statements. When it is called, it receives a CSL statement in the form of a fully validated and flattened Semantic Tree which contains operators and operands and defines the order in which they are to be executed. The Interpreter/Transducer processes the tree and, depending on the operators, either interprets it directly or uses it to build a Currency Hierarchy.

Building a Currency Hierarchy involves a number of steps:

1. Identifying the stored entity sets and from them identifying the Data-Dependent Mappings which are to be used at the lowest levels of the Hierarchy.
2. Taking the operators of the CSL statement and from them identifying the relevant Data Mappings required to fill the middle of the Hierarchy. The operands for these operators provide the linkages to the Data-Dependent Mappings identified in 1. above and the parameters for these Mappings to use.
3. Taking the Target List with its descriptors and deciding on the Data Mappings required for processing Arithmetic Expressions, Functions, and Domain Encoding.

Given that this successfully builds a Currency Hierarchy, then the Interpreter makes calls to load and initialize it, and finally to execute it.

19.6 The Interactive CSL Translator

The Interactive CSL serves two purposes; on the one hand it allows end-users to interact with an Information System, while on the other it allows system designers and operations staff to access the Multi-Level Schema and thus define and tune the system. This use of the Interactive CSL as a System Control Language has meant that the Interactive CSL Translator has a special position in the software architecture: it is the only language processor to be maintained within the Primary Processor.

When in use, the Interactive CSL Translator receives language statements from user terminals and translates them into the Semantic Tree required by the Interpreter/Transducer. The code of the Translator may be separated into three parts:

1. *Screener:* which receives a stream of tokens from the Scanner (2.1) and using the Symbol Table translates them into a stream of Symbols.
2. *Parser:* which uses the Syntactic Definition of the Interactive CSL to validate the stream of Symbols and outputs a Conceptual Parse Tree.
3. *Propagator:* which takes the Conceptual Parse Tree and performs a number of transformations which finally produce the Flattened Semantic Tree required by the Interpreter/Transducer. These transformations include the following:
    1. *Semantic Checks:* which ensure that the CSL statement complies with the semantics of the language.
    2. *Transforming the predicate* (should one exist) into Prenex Normal Form.
    3. *Applying Default CSL:* these are defaults which have been submitted to the system via either other CSL statements, the Multi-Level Schema or the Meta-Definition.
    4. *Equivalencing:* which is concerned with mapping semantically equivalent sub-trees into a single common form.
    5. *2nd level translation:* which is concerned with mapping the predicate from the Information Environment into the Encoded Environment.
    6. *Ameliorations:* which have the effect of changing the position of operators so as to improve the efficiency of the resulting Currency Hierarchy.
    7. *Flattening the Tree:* which produces the Semantic Tree required by the Interpreter/Transducer.

A more detailed discussion of these tasks may be found in Chapter 18.

19.7 System Initialization and Control

Many data base management systems have an architecture which separates the software into two distinct parts: one is responsible for compiling the data description and data manipulation languages into some internal data structure and the other is responsible for using the information from these tables to direct the Data Mapping software. This system is slightly different in so far as these two parts have been linked together to form a single data base processor. This amalgamation has led to a lot of shared system components which in turn has led to the use of a Meta-Definition for parameterizing the different parts of the system. The Meta-Definition of RDBMS contains the following:

1. The syntactic definition of the Interactive Control Sub-Language.
2. The language defaults which are to be applied to this particular Information System.
3. The definitions of the entity sets which make up the Multi-Level Schema.
4. The mapping of the Multi-Level Schema on to the underlying operating system.

The use of the Meta-Definition enhances the system in two ways. Firstly, it ensures that many system units can be used to support both the Multi-Level Schema and the Information System, which naturally leads to a reduction in the number of units. Secondly, it provides a mechanism whereby the designers of a particular Information System can tune and enhance the system to meet their particular needs and requirements.

System Initialization and Control is responsible for processing the Meta-Definition and for controlling the overall action of the system.

19.8 Demons

A demon is a unit of software which runs as an autonomous process and carries out a specific system function. Communication between a demon and the Primary Processor relies on the use of operating system facilities such as shared segments and interrupt mechanisms. Within RDBMS there are three demons:

1. *The Communications Demon:* which is responsible for maintaining the communications network and for relaying messages from the network to the Primary Processor.
2. *The Sort Demon:* which is responsible for sorting large stored entity sets.
3. *Restructuring Demon:* which is responsible for restructuring large areas of the data base.

Within any system there is always a question as to whether simple tasks should be allocated to demons which operate out of line or be dealt with by in-line code. Within RDBMS it has been felt that there is much to be gained from using separate autonomous processors; however, the reason for separation is different for each demon. The Communications Demon has been made autonomous because this decision improves the overall reliability of the system. For example, on the 1900, a fault in a Primary Processor will lead to a complete system collapse with problems for all the end-users and the provision of an autonomous Communications Demon ensures that end-users can be informed of the trouble and can to some extent be insulated from it. Similarly, on both 1900 and 2900 systems, the use of a Communications Demon prevents a fault in the communications network from knocking out the Primary Processor. The Sort Demon has been made autonomous because a sort requires larger areas of work space than can reasonably be provided by the Data Region, and has CPU utilization characteristics which are totally unlike the Primary Processor; for these reasons alone, it warrants separate treatment. Similar criteria have led to the creation of the Restructuring Demon.

19.9 The Language Pre-processors

Each algorithmic language which has been enhanced by a Control Sub-Language has to have a Pre-Processor to map the CSL into a form which is acceptable to the algorithmic language compiler. (This does not suggest that it is not possible to incorporate the CSL Pre-Processor with the algorithmic language compiler: it merely suggests that it should be possible to add a CSL enhancement to a language in spite of the compiler writers.)

In simple terms, the Pre-Processor takes the application program written in an algorithmic language plus CSL and produces a new application program written solely in the algorithmic language. Thus the action of the Pre-Processor is to take a set of CSL statements and replace them by:

1. *A list of syntactic elements (Tokens):* each of which describes the parts of the Information Environment which the application program is going to manipulate.
2. *One or more Parse Trees:* which describe the operations which are to be performed on the Information Environment.

These are presented as pre-set arrays in the algorithmic language. This approach leaves the binding between the application program and RDBMS to be done at run-time, which allows the system designer to redefine and reorganize the data base without considering the application programs. At run-time, the binding between the application program and RDBMS requires the list of syntactic tokens to be checked against the Symbol Table; thereafter the Parse Trees can be fed directly into the Propagator part of the CSL Translator.

20

Architectural Features

The previous chapter described, at a fairly high level of abstraction, the totality of the RDBMS software. As this book is primarily concerned with giving insight into the design decisions and methodologies used to implement these design decisions, there is little or no benefit to be gained in continuing down the path of step-wise refinement in order to study the system. The approach which has been adopted is to identify three main areas which seem to be of interest to designers of data management systems and to study them in more detail. These areas are:

1. The design of the data mapping software used within the system.
2. The compiler architecture used within the system.
3. The optimizations performed within the system while processing CSL statements.

Each of the following sections describes one of these areas of interest.

20.1 Data Mappings

Extracting data from a data base in order to process a request for information requires the use of a large number of small algorithms. Some of these algorithms are responsible for validating domain values, others are responsible for set-encoding, while others still are responsible for maintaining stored entity sets. Much of this software comes with the basic system, but with a system of this type it must be possible for system designers to incorporate their own algorithms and thus replace and enhance the basic software. The requirement to control and organize these mappings naturally leads to a requirement for a coherent architecture. Such an architecture may be produced using only two concepts, namely that of a Data Mapping and that of a Currency Hierarchy which consists of a succession of Data Mappings linked together at run time.

A Data Mapping

A Data Mapping embodies a very simple concept which is best described as follows.

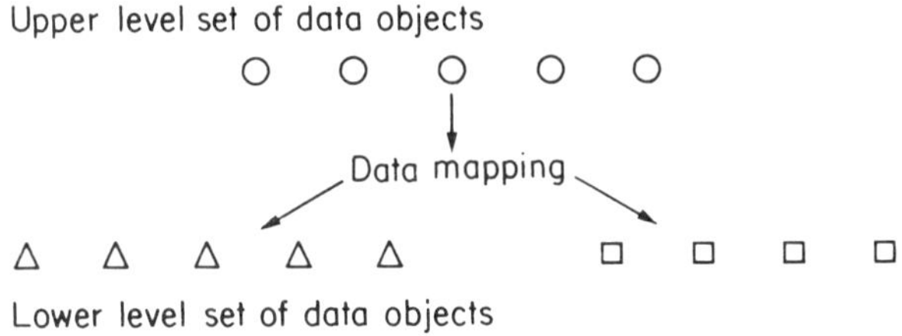

Figure 20.1 A data mapping

The user of a Data Mapping sees a set of data objects where the term set is used in the mathematical sense, and where a data object may be any identifiable unit of data such as a block, a record, or an entity in an entity set. This set is called the upper level set and the Data Mapping is responsible for supporting this upper level set by mapping it on to one or more other sets which may be called the lower level sets. This may be shown diagrammatically in Figure 20.1.

Naturally each Data Mapping may embody several basic data handling algorithms, but within this architecture a Data Mapping is the smallest indivisible unit of system modularity. It is also necessary to recognize that each set of data objects has associated with it a Data Mapping which defines how the set is to be derived or created from the lower level set of data objects.

Binding Data Mappings

As a Data Mapping is basically a collection of one or more algorithms, it must be able to have an existence which is distinct from any particular set of data objects. With this in mind it is possible to identify a spectrum of binding for a particular Data Mapping, and the following sections show that a Data Mapping can exist in three possible states:

1. *A Data Mapping:* which is the name used to describe it when seen as a collection of algorithms.
2. *A Static Data Mapping:* which is the name used to describe a Data Mapping which has been associated with a particular set of data objects.
3. *A Dynamic Data Mapping:* which is the name given to a static Data Mapping which has been activated and thus added to a Currency Hierarchy.

Obviously, it may be possible to identify Data Mappings in some other state such as 'being added to a Currency Hierarchy but not activated', but at present there is little to say about a mapping in this state. Figure 20.2 illustrates the three states of a Data Mapping, while the following sections provide a detailed description of these states.

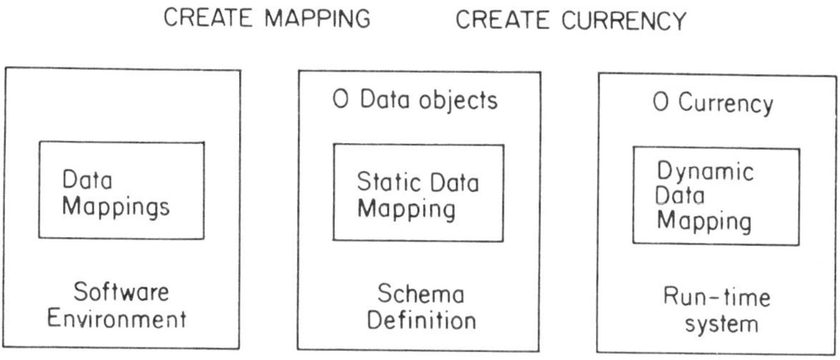

Figure 20.2 States of a data mapping

Data Mapping

The term Data Mapping is used to describe a group of algorithms which handle data. The executable body of these algorithms may be held as object code in a software library. Thus a typical Data Mapping is the B Tree algorithms published by Bayer (see BAYER 1).

Static Data Mapping

When a system designer defines a particular data object such as an entity set, an encoded entity set, or a stored entity set, then his definition is not complete until he has defined a Data Mapping to support it. Within the RDBMS Multi-Level Schema this requires the designer to issue statements of the form:

CREATE SETMAP; or CREATE MAPPING;

Depending on the environment in which the designer is working, such a statement has the effect of associating a Data Mapping with a particular instance of a data object, and the result of this association is a Static Data Mapping.

It should be recognized that a Data Mapping is associated with a data object type while a Static Data Mapping is associated with a single data object instance.

Dynamic Data Mapping

When a user accesses a set of data objects he does so by creating a pointer or currency which refers to that set. When creating this currency, the user is allowed to provide a local description which is associated with the currency and defines criteria which members of the set must satisfy in order to be visible via the currency. Typically this local description allows the user to subset the set members and to reorder them. Needless to say the effect of creating a currency which refers to a particular set of objects is to load the Static Data Mapping associated with the set, and to initialize it with the local description; the end result is a Dynamic Data Mapping.

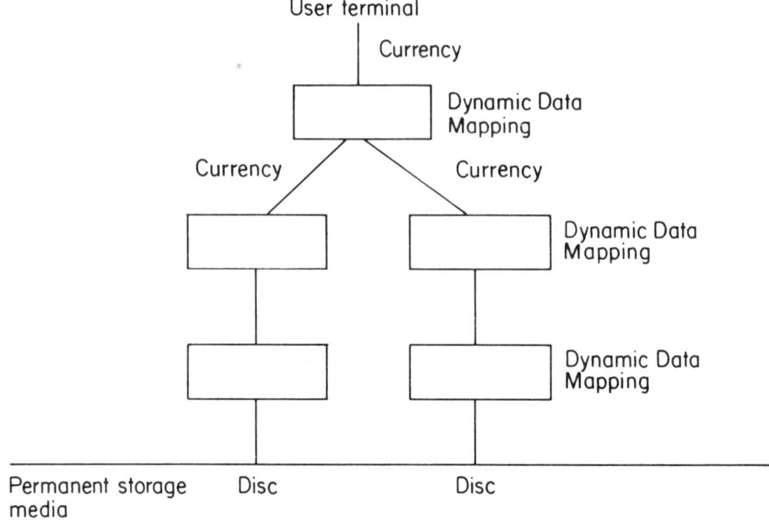

Figure 20.3 A currency hierarchy

Currency Hierarchies

A Currency Hierarchy is a hierarchical tree in which each node identifies a Dynamic Data Mapping and each of the arcs identifies a currency which links two Dynamic Data Mappings. A Currency Hierarchy is always constructed dynamically in response to a user's request for information and establishes a linkage from the user to the discs containing the necessary basic data. When creating a Currency Hierarchy, cognizance is given to algorithms at the application program level and all the data handling subsystem levels, and to the operating system level. Once a Currency Hierarchy has been created, it can be treated as a single conceptual machine which gives the specific result required by the end-user.

The construction and execution of Currency Hierarchies is fundamental to this type of system, and consequently it is worth giving some examples of the hierarchies which are required to process a number of different user requests. These examples are based on a relational data base containing two entity sets, one of which maintains details of products, and the other of which maintains details of orders for products from customers. The entity sets are mapped into three encoded entity sets which in turn are mapped into three stored entity sets. Figure 20.4 describes the schema used by this system.

Example 1 Read Details of Products

CSL – READ PRODUCT;

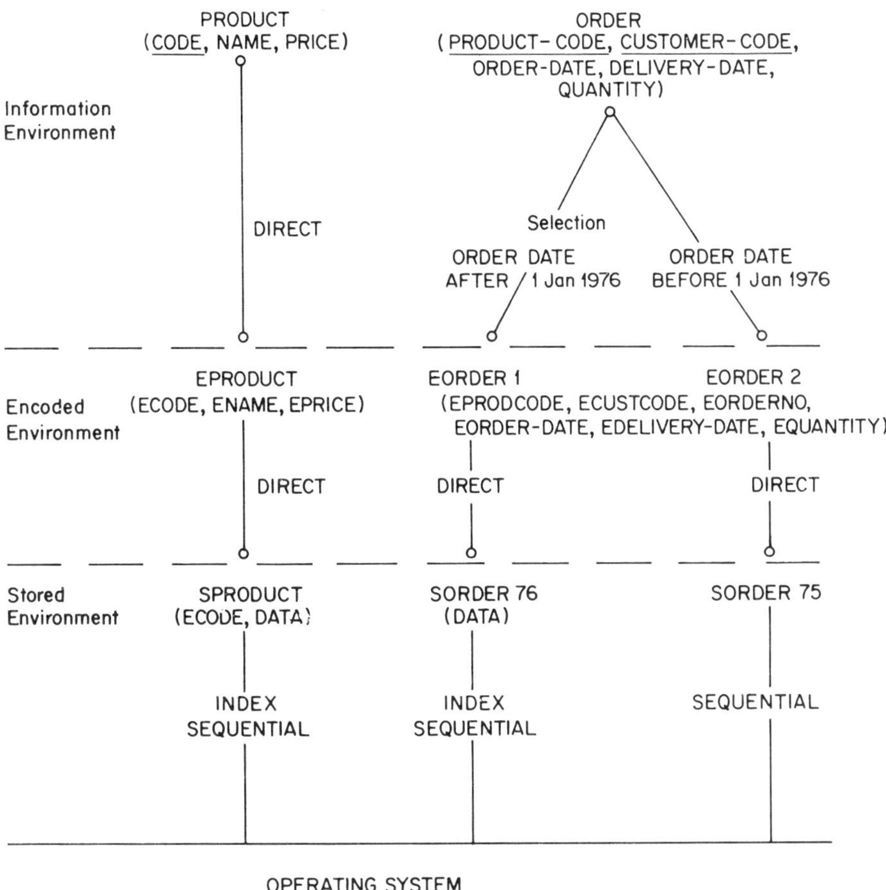

Figure 20.4 A sample of a mapping established by System designers when creating the entity sets Product and Order

This is processed by using a Currency Hierarchy which contains two Dynamic Data Mappings, namely:

1. *Interface handler:* which is responsible for domain encoding and output page formatting.
2. *Index sequential:* which is used to generate entities in the set Eproduct.

Example 2 Read all the unique Product Prices

CSL – READ PRODUCT PRICE;

This can only be processed by using a Currency Hierarchy which contains four Dynamic Mappings, namely:

1. *Interface handler:* which is responsible for domain encoding and output page formatting.
2. *Projection:* which is responsible for deriving unique values of Price from Product.
3. *Order:* which is used to sort values of Price from Product so that projection can maintain uniqueness.
4. *Index sequential:* which serves the same purpose as in Example 1.

Example 3 Read details of those Products which have a price over £20 and for which there is an Order to be delivered in the period to June and September 1977.

```
CSL – READ PRODUCT SUCHTHAT PRODUCT.PRICE>20 AND
      PRODUCT.CODE = ORDERFROM.PRODUCTCODE AND
      ORDERFROM.DELIVERYDATE > 1/6/77
      AND ORDERFROM.DELIVERYDATE < 31/9/77;
```

This enquiry can only be processed using a Currency Hierarchy which contains five Dynamic Data Mappings, namely:

1. *Interface handler:* which is responsible for domain encoding and page formatting.
2. *Restriction:* which selects those Products with a Code which matches Product Code in Order and checks the delivery dates.
3. *Selection:* which selects Products with a Price over £20.
4. *Index sequential:* which supports Product.
5. *Index Sequential:* which supports Eorder1.

The Currency Hierarchy containing these Dynamic Mappings is illustrated in Figure 20.5.

From these examples it can be seen that the construction and execution of Currency Hierarchies is fundamental to the problem of building cost-effective Information Systems. However, a reader must recognize that the efficiency of the Information System is directly dependent on the rate of execution of its Currency Hierarchies, which in turn reflects the algorithms in the individual Data Mappings.

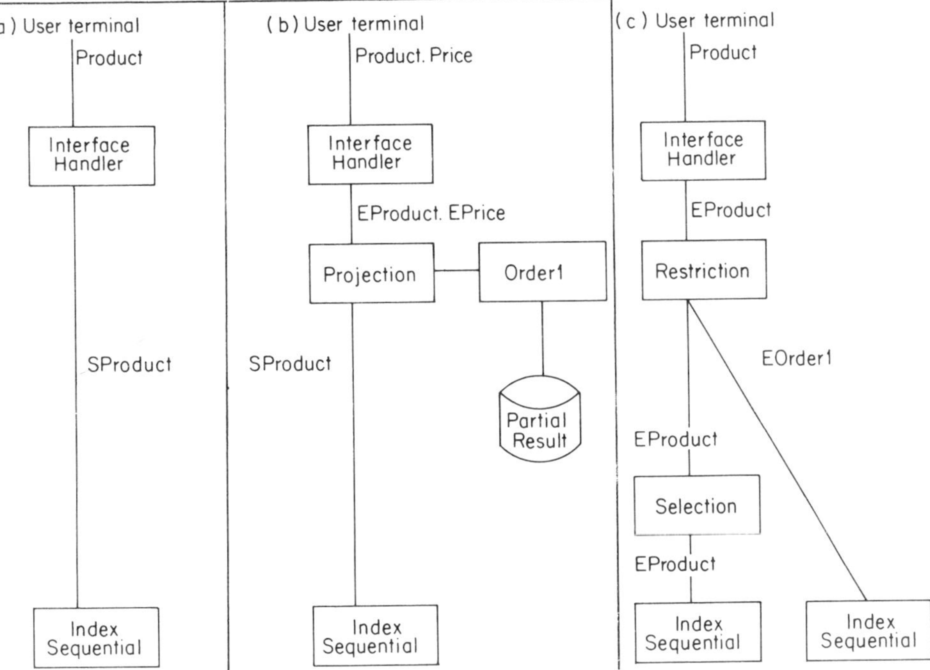

Figure 20.5

Realizing Mappings

Each of the Data Mappings described above is symmetrical in the sense that each mapping supports a complete set of actions which parallel the CSL statements (read, destroy, create, etc.). One implication of this is that a mapping such as 'join' will support the normal operator join for the read action, and the operator projection for the actions destroy, create, update, and write. This symmetry has also been used to sub-divide Data Mappings into eight groups, which emphasizes the fact that mappings within a group may share similar subroutines. These groups are:

1. *Encoding Mappings:* which are responsible for domain encoding and thus for mapping information between an entity set with attributes and an entity set with encoded attributes. It is also responsible for page-formatting and providing other red-tape information on outputs and inputs.

2. *Information-Dependent Mappings:* which are responsible for processing CSL arithmetic expressions, and CSL functions. These mappings all map one upper level entity set with encoded attributes into one or more lower level sets.

3. *Ordering Mappings:* which are responsible for ordering either entity sets with encoded attributes or encoded entity sets.

4. *Relational Mappings:* which are responsible for the relational operators permutation, projection, and join.
5. *Selection Mappings:* which are responsible for handling the relational operators: selection, restriction, union, intersection, and difference.
6. *Multi-Level Schema translator:* which is responsible for mapping the Multi-Level Schema into the Symbol Table.
7. *Data-Dependent Mappings:* which support a stored entity set.
8. *Physical Mappings:* which support the block access methods.

Several of these mappings embody algorithms which are published in the literature. Particular attention is drawn to the following: Selection (see GUDES 1), Sort (see HOARE 1), Join (see TODD 1), and Data-Dependent Mappings (see 1900 Housekeeping System, ICL3).

20.2 A Compiler Model for RDBMS

From the previous section it can be seen that RDBMS is like a compiler in so far as it takes a succession of CSL statements and translates each of them into a form which can be used to create and/or call a Currency Hierarchy. For this reason, the initial software design was based on one of the many compiler models which were then available. Several models were considered as possible choices and some attention was given to those of Hopgood (see HOPGOOD 1) and Gries (see GRIES 1); however, the model which was eventually chosen was that of Waite (see GOOS 1). This model was first introduced on the EEC Advanced Course on Compiler Construction in 1974/75. As this compiler model has had a fundamental effect on the structure or RDBMS, the next section is devoted to discussing it, while the following section describes the compiler model which was actually used within RDBMS.

A Basic Model Compiler for use Within RDBMS

The Waite compiler model separates the compilation process into 4 parts which are sub-divided further into 7 major stages. Figure 20.6 illustrates these stages, which may be described as follows:

Scanner

This is responsible for viewing a language statement as a stream of characters and for using some in-built rules to represent the statement as a stream of tokens where a token has the form of a string and may represent a variable, an operator, or a literal.

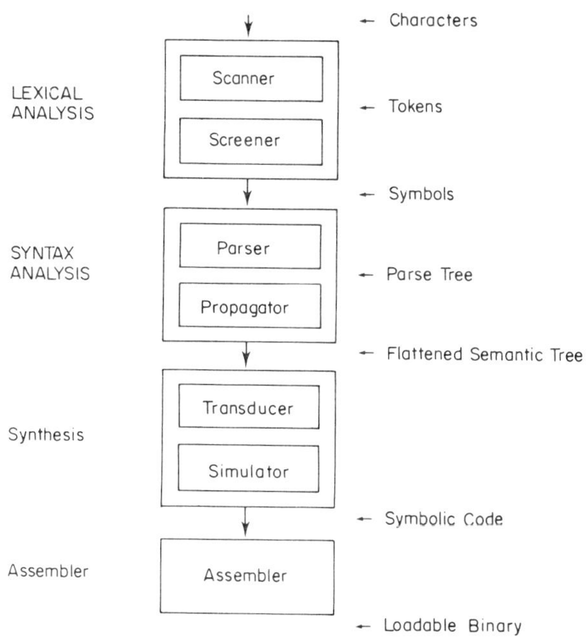

Figure 20.6 The Waite Compiler model

Screener

This views a language statement as a stream of tokens and uses information held in the Symbol Table to map these tokens into the operator names of the language, the variable names used in the program, and literal values. The output from the Screener is a language statement in the form of a stream of symbols, each of which refers to an entry in the Symbol Table.

Parser

The Parser receives a language statement in the form of a stream of symbols and makes syntactic checks by using one of the standard parsing techniques. The output from the Parser is a Parse Tree, which may be entirely conceptual in so far as it is generated as a series of sub-trees and is never realized in its entirety.

Propagator

The Propagator receives the Parse Tree in some convenient form such as a series of triples, each of which contains an operator with two operands, and performs three distinct operations.

1. It uses the type information from the Symbol Table to carry out semantic checks.

2. It may have a standardizer function, which is responsible for working round the Parse Tree and for mapping together semantically equivalent sub-trees.
3. It flattens the tree and orders it so as to define the order in which it is to be executed.

The output from the Propagator is a Flattened Semantic Tree.

Note: In many cases the Propagator merely consists of the semantic routines which are a feature of all compiler models.

Transducer

The Transducer may be thought of as a push-down automaton which receives as input the Flattened Semantic Tree and encodes the limited information available in the tree to produce a sequence of commands, each with its associate operands.

Simulator

The Simulator maintains a definition of the operating environment of the program and, by interpreting each command output by the Transducer, generates code suitable to carry it out. It also simulates the effect of that code in terms of the operating environment and thus maintains up-to-date details of register usage and stack status.

Assembler

This receives the code generated by the Simulator and maps it into a form which can be presented to the Loader. The Loader has a fundamental role to play in the task of compilation but is not considered to be part of the compiler.

The Actual Compiler Model used with RDBMS

The previous section outlined a conceptual model for a compiler which processed an algorithmic language by transforming it into loadable binary. It may have been possible to build RDBMS using this complete compilation process; however, the design of the Data Mappings described earlier suggested that the system would be better constructed as a Translator/Interpreter. Such an approach would require that the Transducer, the Simulator, and the Assembler of the compiler model be replaced by an Interpreter which directly processed the Semantic Tree. It was however found that the use of Currency Hierarchies and the Data Mappings described in the previous chapter favoured a half and half situation where the Semantic Tree output by the Propagator was input to a Transducer/Interpreter.

In this case, part of the Semantic Tree was interpreted directly while the other part was used by the Transducer to generate code for a Currency Hierarchy. Figure 20.7 illustrates the complete architecture of the system. The Scanner,

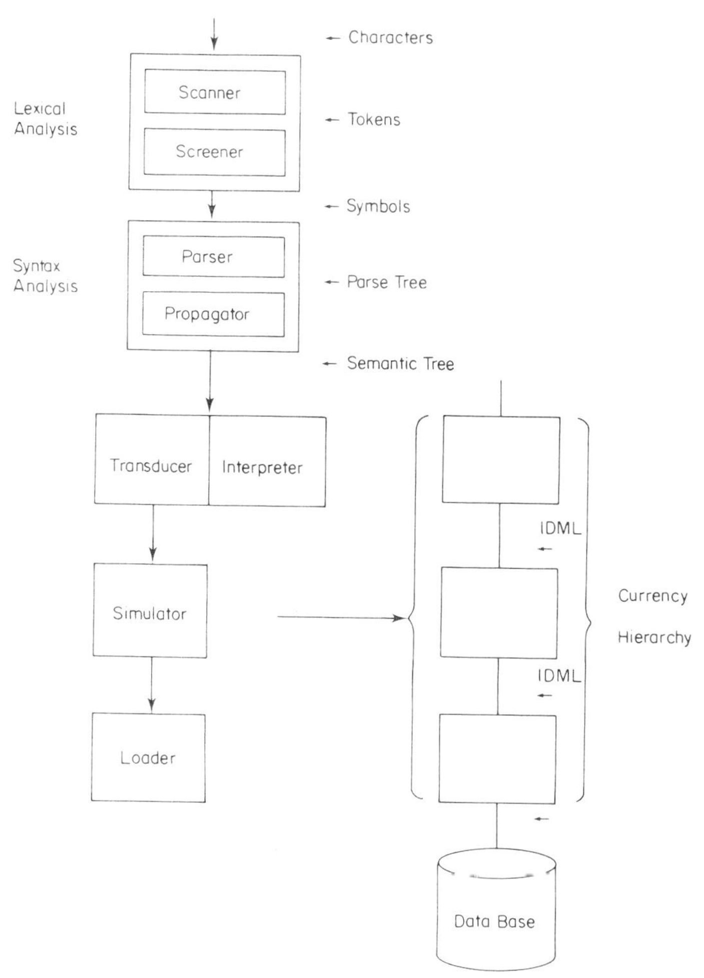

Figure 20.7 The RDBMS System model

Screener, and Parser serve exactly the same roles as those in the compiler model but thereafter the model is different. The rest of this section discusses these differences.

Propagator

The Propagator in the RDBMS model receives the Parse Tree in the form of a series of n-tuples and performs three distinct operations:

1. It uses the type information from the Symbol Table to perform semantic checks.

2. It performs a number of standard optimizations on the tree in order to improve its run-time efficiency. These optimizations are discussed at greater length in the next section.
3. It flattens the tree and orders it so as to define the order in which it is to be presented to the Transducer/Interpreter.

Transducer/Interpreter

This is a Push-Down Automaton which processes the Semantic Tree as a single stream of n-tuples, each of which defines an operator and its operands. Depending on the operator, some of these n-tuples are interpreted directly while others are used to generate part of a Currency Hierarchy. It has been found that the design of CSL allows a clear separation between the operators which are to be interpreted and those which are to be used by the code generators. This separation is not altogether fortuitous, and the paper SAMSO 1 contains a detailed explanation of the techniques used to ensure that there is no ambiguity between the two classes.

Those operators which are interpreted result in direct calls on:

1. Part of the Interpreter.
2. The top level of an already activated Currency Hierarchy.
3. The top level of a Currency Hierarchy which is completely defined but not yet loaded.

In the first two cases, the action of the system is necessarily straightforward, while in the last case, the system loads and activates the Currency Hierarchy and then enters it in the normal way.

Those operators and operands which are used to construct a Currency Hierarchy are used to identify:

1. Mappings which are to be used to act on particular sets of data objects which have been created as part of the action of the Currency Hierarchy.
2. *Stored entity sets:* which need to be accessed in order to respond to the request together with their associate Static Mappings.
3. *Dynamic Predicates:* which are to be fed into the Mappings identified as a result of 1. and 2. above.

The Simulator

The Simulator is responsible for maintaining the status of a Currency Hierarchy as it is being built; consequently it maintains details of the sets of data objects required and produced by each of the currencies and ensures that they map together smoothly. The Simulator is also responsible for ensuring that the system exploits some of the storage-dependent aspects of the data base.

The Loader/Unloader

The Loader is responsible for loading a pre-defined Currency Hierarchy. This requires finding the lowest level currencies and initializing them first. The higher currencies are then initialized, in their turn, until the complete structure has been initialized. This process of initializing from the bottom ensures that every Dynamic Mapping knows that its lower level currencies are already initialized, thus permitting it the freedom to use the data from these currencies to create partial results.

The Unloader is responsible for unloading a Currency Hierarchy and starts at the top of the Hierarchy and moves downwards, de-initializing each of the currencies in turn. De-initializing from the top down ensures that any Dynamic Mapping which is holding a partial result can return the data to the data base through its underlying currencies.

20.3 Optimization and Transformation of a Single CSL Statement

So far this book has discussed CSL from the point of view of formulating relational expressions, and has considered the necessary software required to process these expressions. However, it is already apparent that there are a number of added complexities, which may be summarized as follows:

1. Using CSL it is possible to formulate two enquiries which produce the same result but use vastly different computer resources to process them.
2. In the Information Environment Schema the system designers can define integrity and privacy constraints which are best processed by adding information to an incoming CSL statement.
3. In the Encoded Environment Schema the system designers can encode the same information in more than one encoded entity set, in which case the system needs to choose the most appropriate encoded entity set. This choice is dependent on the incoming CSL statement and the cost of using the underlying stored entity set.

Given this state of affairs, then the system needs to provide facilities which can make modifications and additions to an incoming CSL statement in order to ensure that it can be processed as cheaply as possible. These transformations are discussed under the heading of Optimization and Transformation of a single CSL statement.

Given a CSL statement, then the system needs to perform a number of transformations, the outcome of which is the Flattened Semantic Tree required by the Transducer/Interpreter. These transformations may be identified as follows:

1. *Applying defaults:* which adds default CSL parameters to the incoming CSL statement. These are default parameter values which have been submitted previously via the System Meta-Definition, the Multi-Level Schema and other CSL statements.
2. *Transforming the Predicate into Prenex Normal Form:* which ensures that all the quantifiers precede the propositions within the predicate.
3. *Equivalencing:* which ensures that statements which have a different syntactic form but the same meaning are mapped into a single form.
4. *Second Level Translation:* which is concerned with mapping the predicate from the Information Environment into the Encoded Environment.
5. *Ameliorations:* which have the effect of changing the position of operations so as to improve the efficiency of the resulting Currency Hierarchy.
6. *Flattening the Tree:* which produces the input for the Transducer/Interpreter.

The following sections briefly discuss these transformations.

Applying Default CSL

One of the design objectives of CSL was that a user with a simple requirement should only need to use a few simple CSL statements. This is obviously a very desirable design objective for an interactive language, but it naturally implies that in general the system needs to add extra default information to the statement. In fact, extra information is added to a CSL statement to handle the following:

1. Predefined and unstated CSL clauses.
2. Details of privacy constraints.
3. Details of dependencies and static predicates.

These can be described as follows:

Predefined and unstated CSL clauses One example of the addition of CSL clauses to a CSL statement may be seen in the following interaction:

```
– SET P FOR READACCESS TO PRODUCT ST ...,
– READ P;
```

When processing the SET statement, the system may optionally create and load the Currency Hierarchy associated with P, or it may retain the parameters for use later. If the first option is chosen then READ P results in a call to the already created Currency Hierarchy, but if the second option is chosen, then details of the SET statement are substituted for P in the READ statement and are then used to create the Currency Hierarchy. This is an example of the substitution of an existing clause by a predefined clause. An example of adding an unstated clause is the addition of COUNT to a READ statement to ensure that the output from the statement does not exceed the capacity of the user's terminal.

Privacy constraints The Information Environment Schema allows the system designer to define that access to a particular data object (an entity set or attribute) is protected by a privacy constraint. If an end-user then submits a CSL statement which accesses a data object X which is subject to a privacy constraint, then privacy clauses are added to the predicate. An example of this concerns the implementation of the constraint that user X is only allowed read access to those entities in the entity set PRODUCT where CODE lies in the range 10 to 50. Such a constraint is implemented by taking a user's request.

– READ PRODUCT;

and adding to it the clause:

SUCHTHAT 10 ⩽ CODE AND CODE ⩽ 50.

Dependencies and static predicates The Information Environment allows the system designer to define dependencies between entity sets. If an end-user submits a CSL statement which accesses an entity set which is party to a dependency, then dependency clauses are added to the predicate. For example, the CSL statement:

– CREATE ORDERFROM;

is enhanced by the following predicate:

SUCHTHAT ORDERFROM.PRODUCTCODE = PRODUCT.CODE
AND ORDERFROM.CUSTOMERCODE = CUSTOMER.CODE

Dependency clauses are also added to DESTROY, UPDATE, and WRITE statements. A similar mechanism is used to implement static predicates.

Transforming the Predicate to Prenex Normal Form

As described in Chapter 13, predicates may be written so that quantifiers are embedded within the propositions; the first step to processing a CSL predicate with embedded quantifiers is to transform it to Prenex Normal Form. The six equations for solving this problem may be found in KORFHAGE 1. The chief difficulty is that of ensuring that the binding of the variables remains the same before and after the application of the six equations.

Equivalencing

Equivalencing is the task of ensuring that statements which have a different form but the same meaning are mapped into a single form. Typical examples of equivalencing are the disposal of NOT statements, and the disposal of unnecessary joins. The following examples illustrate these transformations:

– READ PRODUCT SUCHTHAT NOT (PRODUCT.CODE > '0033');

which transforms to

– READ PRODUCT SUCHTHAT PRODUCT.CODE ⩽ '0033';

and

– READ PRODUCT SUCHTHAT PRODUCT.CODE *= ORDERFROM.
PRODUCTCODE
AND ORDERFROM.DELIVERYDATE = 26/8/76;

which transforms to

– READ PRODUCT SUCHTHAT PRODUCT.CODE = ORDERFROM.
PRODUCTCODE
AND ORDERFROM.DELIVERYDATE = 26/8/76;

The Second Level Translations

The Information-Dependent Mappings of the Encoded Environment provide a means whereby a system designer can match the CSL request patterns with the encoded entity sets. Obviously, there is no problem in processing a CSL statement which maps directly to a single encoded entity set. However, in those cases where a CSL statement names an entity set which maps to more than one encoded entity set, then a problem can arise. Basically, this problem is concerned with identifying the sets which are required and the order in which they are to be accessed. Dearnley (see DEARNLEY 1 and 2) and Ghosh (see GHOSH 1) have defined a number of criteria for choosing the necessary sets. Dearnley bases his proposals on the fact that the cost is dependent on the number of blocks (stored entities) which would need to be accessed to carry out the request, while Ghosh uses an approach which uses the cardinality of the attributes and the number of encoded entities involved. Of these algorithms, the Dearnley algorithm seems to give a more realistic estimate of the actual costs involved in processing the request.

Ameliorations

When a Currency Hierarchy is first created, the placing of particular operations such as selections, joins, and projections is dependent on the incoming CSL statement and the various defaults which have been added to it. Once the Second Level Translations have been made, then the lower levels of the Currency Hierarchy are clearly identified and any additional relational operators required to exploit the Information-Dependent Mappings are added to the tree.

An Amelioration is the term given to the task of either removing from the tree an operator which is redundant or moving a specific operator to a specific part of the tree. Hall, in his paper (see HALL 1), has described specific ameliorations concerned with moving selections as low down the tree as possible. Another amelioration which needs to be considered is that of moving an ordering to a point where the number of encoded entities is at a minimum and unavoidable. In general, order operates as high in a hierarchy as possible, and if possible on a small partial result, such as produced by a projection.

The Order of the Transformations

One of the major problems with this type of system is that of finding the exact order in which to apply these transformations. At present, it looks as if the order given at the beginning of this section is more or less correct, and this has been verified by the pilot system for simple examples and by hand worked examples of more complex cases, though more work is required.

The Cost of a CSL Statement

In Chapter 12, it was shown that a CSL statement could only be rejected if it costs too much to process. For this reason it is necessary to establish the rules for costing a CSL statement. These rules are: firstly, translating a CSL statement into a Flattened Semantic Tree and producing a cost estimate is free. This estimate is established at the same time as the Flattened Semantic Tree and is then compared with the user's budgets to see if the statement can be completed. Secondly, from the users' point of view, the cost of processing a CSL statement is defined as being the cost estimate irrespective of the actual cost incurred. Thirdly, the cost estimate is an estimate of the cost of the computer resources required to process the Currency Hierarchy which is called by the CSL statement. Given this position, then the vital computer resources to which costs are actually applied are: the number of block transfers from the underlying Operating System, and CPU time used within the Currency Hierarchy, and the size of any partial results.

One of the difficulties of estimating costs is that there is little information which can be used as a sound basis for this work. Starting from the CSL and Information Environment the following is known:

1. The defaults controlling the number of entities visible via a particular interaction.
2. The cardinality of both the domains and the encoded domains.

3. The numbers of stored entities within a particular stored entity set.
4. The number of blocks in a particular primitive file.
5. A cost estimate for the CPU time required for one call of a particular mapping.
6. An accurate estimate of the working storage required by a Data-Dependent mapping.

Given this information, then it is possible to take a Currency Hierarchy and using a fairly crude formula establish estimates for block transfers, CPU time, and the partial results.

21

Assessment and Conclusion

21.1 Introduction

An assessment of the work described in this book would normally be separated into assessments of the work described in the three main parts. Unfortunately, this approach would not necessarily reflect the fact that many others are working on this type of system and, consequently, any assessment must, to some extent, take their interests into consideration.

Ever since the publication of the 1971 Codasyl Report (see CODASYL 1), it has been recognized that the development of generalized data base management systems is to a large extent governed by the development of the interfaces supported by those systems, and for the last few years there have been a number of conferences and working parties established to study this work. The three main working parties have been the Codasyl Data Description Language Committee (DDLC), the ANSI/X3/SPARC Data Base Study Group, and the IFIP TC2 Working Group on Data Base Systems. The first two groups in this list have from time to time produced reports (see CODASYL 2, ANSI SPARC 1, and ANSI SPARC 2), while the third has held a number of working conferences the proceedings of which cover the broad spectrum of data base work. For this reason some part of the assessment of RDBMS must be addressed to these interests.

The other main area of interest is the question of whether relational systems are usable. In the years which have elapsed since Codd first formalized the relational data model, a large number of implementations have been produced. The earliest systems such as STDS (see CHILDS 1) and MACAIMS (see GOLDSTEIN 1 and STRNAD 1) were largely experimental systems; however, some later systems such as PRTV (see TODD 2) have been used, while more recent implementations such as INGRES (see MCDONALD 1) are now widely used to implement moderate sized data bases to satisfy the data needs of either individuals or small groups of co-workers. Finally, IBM have released the specification of SYSTEM R (see ASTRAHAN 1), which may well be capable of providing a replacement of IBM's IMS system (see IBM 4).

From this it can be seen that the relational data model may provide a basis for a number of generalized data base systems which together will satisfy the broad spectrum of future information system needs. For this reason it is necessary first to assess this specification in order to identify any shortcomings which may prevent it becoming usable as a product, and then to identify possible implementations of specific products.

With this in mind, an assessment of this work has been subdivided into five main parts. These parts are:

1. The Design Methodology as a design process, which is an assessment written in lay terms and highlights the specific needs of the users of such a methodology.
2. A comparison between the Design Methodology and the work of the CODASYL DDLC and the ANSI SPARC working group on data base systems.
3. An appraisal of the Multi-Level Schema as a satisfactory mechanism for describing an Information System.
4. An assessment of the Control Sub-Languages as an interface suitable for driving RDBMS.
5. A discussion of the products which may be realized from this specification.

The chapter, being the last in the book, concludes with some comments on possible future expectations in the development of relational data base management systems.

21.2 The Design Methodology as a Design Process

An assessment of any engineering process requires some criteria for measuring the quality of the output from the process and resources consumed by the process. One possible list of criteria is:

1. *The Quality of the Output:* measured in terms of its durability, its appearance, and its performance.
2. *The resources required by the process:* measured in terms of the raw materials consumed by the process and the time required to carry out the process.
3. *The skill of the operators who perform the process:* measured in terms of diplomas and/or years of training and practice.
4. *The reject rate of the process:* measured in terms of spoilt work and scrap.

This is not a minimal list of criteria for assessing the Design Methodology but it provides a firm basis for the following discussion.

The Quality of the Output

One of the fundamental problems of creating Information Systems is that, although the high level design of a system can be produced in a relatively short time, the complete operational system can only be developed via a succession of phased releases. The result of any phased release must be a stable system which, once in use, does not require a succession of amendments and modifications to keep it alive. The Design Methodology recognizes these two facts by providing a clear separation between the Object Environment, which reflects the real world as it is, and the Information Environment, which defines the field of perception of the Information System. The stability of an Information System is dependent on the stability of the Information Environment and the use of entity sets which are linked by dependencies, governed by predicates, and incorporate stable time constraints, goes some way to ensuring that this Environment is stable.

The fact that the usage constraints of a particular Information Environment are used to develop the Encoded Environment again assists in the objective of keeping the Information Environment stable because it recognizes that for a given Information Environment there are many different possible Encoded Environments. This tolerance is further increased by using the Software Environment.

All these levels of flexibility ensure that a system designer using the Design Methodology will produce an Information System which is both durable and cost effective.

The Cost of the Methodology

The cost of producing an Information System may be subdivided into the cost of the high level design (systems analysis), the cost of the low level design, and the cost of writing and testing the software system. The use of the Design Methodology alleviates some of these costs because it ensures that effort is not wasted on achieving unnecessary goals. The use of the Multi-Level Schema may in fact save costs because one of the costly aspects of the low level design is understanding the connectivity of the system. The Software Environment Schema can only be used to generate software providing it contains a full definition of the connectivity of the system; it is also in a form which can be accessed and summarized using CSL, thus providing an easy method of understanding system connectivity.

The Experience of the System Users

The design of an Information System requires contributions from all the system users, who are a vast group of people from widely different backgrounds. The design requires the insight of the end-user, the skills of the system's analyst, the tenacity of the programmer, and the cooperation of the computer operator, which raises the question how are they to work together? One solution is to teach everybody about computers, and then force them to produce a single definition.

This is now recognized as being unnecessarily restricting and the Design Methodology recognizes this by providing a number of abstract models, each oriented towards a specific group of users. This ensures that an Information System based on the Methodology benefits from the applied skills of all the system users, and furthermore, the Design Methodology makes no excessive demands on the skills of its users.

The Reject Rate

An Information System is not successful if it either fails to reflect the real world or performs badly, and in both cases the lack of success may be attributable to an error in judgement on the part of the system designer. If it is recognized that the purpose of the Design Methodology is to guard against these errors in judgement, then an unsuccessful system must surely reflect badly on the Design Methodology.

From this evaluation it seems that the Design Methodology provides a group of system users with a method for designing a stable Information System which can be tuned to give an acceptable performance.

21.3 A Comparison between the Multi-Level Schema and the Proposals of Codasyl and ANSI SPARC

The Codasyl Proposals

The original 1973 Codasyl DBTG Report proposed that an Information System can be described using three main levels of description. These levels are the Schema Data Description Language, which is used to describe a data base, the Sub-Schema Data Description Language, which is used to describe that part of the data base which is visible to a group of application programs, and COBOL, which is used to describe the application programs. Since 1973, the Codasyl Data Description Language Committee have separated all those aspects which are concerned with the physical storage and layout of data from the Schema Data Description Language to form a further level of description, namely the Data Media Control Language. This now gives the four-level schema illustrated in Figure 21.1.

From this figure it may be seen that COBOL code is used in two places: firstly to write application level programs, and secondly to write user-own code procedures which are called from within the Schema DDL. The figure also shows that the fundamental difference between the Codasyl and the RDBMS proposals is that the Codasyl proposals are aimed at providing data base support for application programs, while RDBMS is aimed at directly supporting end-users. This difference is sufficient to require the extra upper levels of schema supported by RDBMS.

The other main difference between the facilities described in the Codasyl proposals and those provided with RDBMS concerns the question of data base

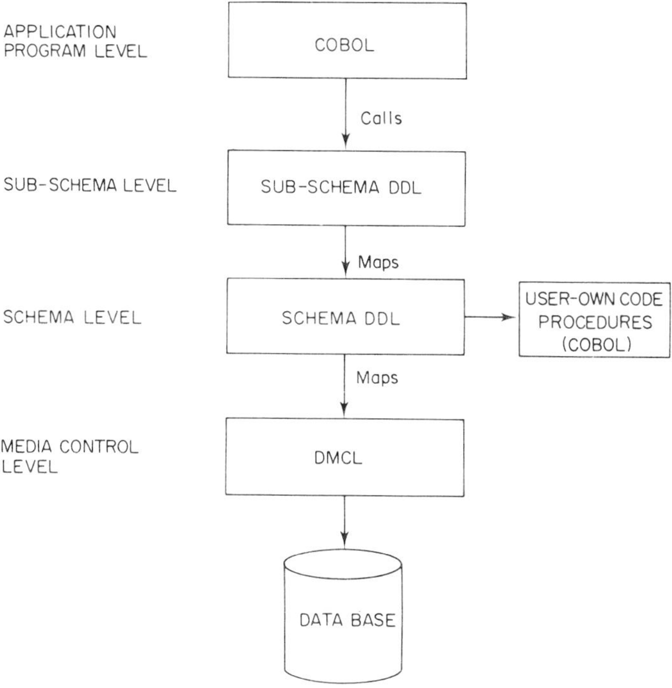

Figure 21.1 The Codasyl schema proposals

optimization. The Codasyl proposals make a basic assumption that data base optimization is best carried out by the system designers, and for this reason both the Data Description and Data Manipulation Languages are defined at a very low level. The design of RDBMS is based on the assumption that through lack of accurate information at design time a system designer is not able to optimize either the structure of the data base or the schedule of jobs using that data base, and for this reason it was better to handle the optimization problem within RDBMS itself.

One advantage of this approach can be seen by considering a simple example. Given an Information System which has been implemented in parallel using both a Codasyl system and RDBMS, then suppose the case arises where a system designer wishes to change a record/entity set and hold it as two projections in two records/encoded entity sets. Within the 1973 Codasyl proposals, this can only be achieved by changing the Schema, Sub-schema definitions, and the application program code, while within RDBMS the change can be accomplished without modifying the application program. At present, Codasyl is enhancing the capabilities described in their proposal; however, it may be some time before they can encompass the ability to permit the system to optimize its own storage structures.

The ANSI/X3/SPARC Data Base Study Group

The ANSI/X3/SPARC Study Group on data base management systems was set up by the American National Standards Institute to review existing and proposed data base systems and to develop proposals for those areas which appear suitable for standardization. At an early date the Study Group recognized that there was no possibility of standardizing the components of a data base management system, and therefore devoted their efforts to discussing the interfaces between components. The Study Group has produced an Interim Report (ANSI SPARC 1) and a Final Report (ANSI SPARC 2) which defines their findings and recommendations.

Basically, these reports discuss the scope of a data base management system, and provide a framework for describing the component parts of such a system and the interfaces between them. As seen from the earlier sections of this chapter, there is no clear distinction to be made between the data base management system and the underlying operating system, and to some extent the choice is dependent on the packaging of the eventual end product. In fact, the scope of a data base management system as described in the report does not vary markedly from that assumed in this book. The report describes a data base management system by a canonical schemata which requires 42 interfaces to separate the various system components from each other and the human roles associated with the system.

Any comparison between the ANSI SPARC work and RDBMS must necessarily compare the interfaces provided by the two systems. ANSI SPARC has proposed that the main data definition interface should support three schemas, namely the Conceptual Schema, the Internal Schema, and the External Schema and, in essence, there is a fairly straightforward correlation between these schemas and those provided by RDBMS.

1. The Conceptual Schema provides a definition of an Information System as understood by the Enterprise. The schema includes a definition of conceptual objects, their properties, and the relationships between them. It also includes details of the operations permitted on the objects, and consistency, integrity, security, recovery, and administrative matters. Seen in this light the conceptual schema is an exact parallel of the Information Environment. In the Interim Report, the Conceptual Schema was also required to serve the purpose of describing the Enterprise. Fortunately, this has been abandoned because, as shown in Part B, this task is best delegated to a separate level of description; in RDBMS, the Object Environment.

2. The External Schema defines the information as seen by users by the Information System. RDBMS has provided an External Environment to satisfy this requirement; however, within RDBMS recognition has been given to the fact that if users understand the conceptual view of data then they should be able to interact at that level. This is typical of the differences which occur when a comparison is made between a conceptual study of a data base management system and a live implementation.

3. The Internal Schema defines the implementation of the data base defined in the Conceptual Schema, and is therefore comparable with the RDBMS Encoded and Stored Environments. The ANSI SPARC Report does not dwell on the problems of defining optional and efficient storage structures and consequently the RDBMS implementation must be seen as a practical implementation of the proposals.

Further to the definition of these three interfaces it is worthwhile considering some of the other interfaces identified in the report. From the point of view of end-users the Report carefully identifies four separate interfaces, one each for specifying Reports, Enquiries, Updates, and Parametric Interfaces. On the other hand, given some improvement to the report generating facilities of CSL, RDBMS only provides one single interface to satisfy these user needs. Again this emphasizes the fact that whereas the Report is aimed at analysing the functional capability of a data base management system, RDBMS is aimed at satisfying user needs, and thus does not have the same objectives.

Depending on the eventual fate of the ANSI SPARC Report, there may be some benefit in taking each of its interfaces and identifying either a comparable RDBMS interface or the reason why no such interface is actually provided.

21.4 The Multi-Level Schema

The Multi-Level Schema is used to describe Information Systems, and consequently it is inevitable that it should be compared with a language such as the Codasyl Schema Data Description Language (DDL). This section compares the strengths and weaknesses of the two approaches.

The strength of the DDL is that the description of a large Information System can be maintained in a compact form which is readily understood by system analysts and programmers. Furthermore, the fact that the information is expressed as a language simplifies the task of writing the complicated conditions which occur inside an Information System. The main weakness of DDL is that there is no place in the language for the large amount of information which is required by system designers in order to understand their system. Several Codasyl users have overcome this deficiency by building a data dictionary system (see ICL 6) to contain this extra information. Another weakness of DDL is that it is difficult to produce summaries of the description. Most Codasyl implementations now provide facilities to interrogate the Object Schema to provide these summaries.

Undoubtedly, the great strength of the Multi-Level Schema is that, subject to privacy constraints, it is available to all system users. Furthermore, since the information from the schema is presented in the same form as all other information, it is readily understandable. The schema for RDBMS exploits this capability in the following ways. Firstly, the schema is defined using a meta-definition, which can be modified by senior system designers in order to extend the schema to incorporate that extra information which is required by system users but not required by RDBMS; secondly, a user can use CSL to manipulate the schema and thus produce summaries of the system description; thirdly, it is easy to compare the schema with the system monitor output which is presented in a similar form.

In the past, the use of schemas has been discouraged because of the difficulty of expressing the semantics governing the schema, and because it was difficult to use a schema to express complex conditions. This book has shown that the first of these problems can be overcome by using the Relational Data Model enhanced with dependencies as described in Chapter 6 as a basis for the schema. It has also shown that the second of these problems can be overcome by embedding clauses of CSL inside attribute values in the schema; certainly an embedded 'Order-Expression-List' is an easy way of allowing designers to define the order of an Encoded Entity Set.

Finally, one point which is worthy of mention is that a schema is much cheaper to support than a language; one group implementing a Codasyl system explained that half the effort used to build their system was devoted to building the DDL Translator. Experience with RDBMS has shown that schemas are relatively cheap to support providing the implementor uses a meta-definition and re-uses as many of the normal system components as possible.

In conclusion, this book has shown that a schema is at least as useful as a language. Furthermore, a schema has many inbuilt advantages over a language.

21.5 The Control Sub-Languages

Part C shows that this family of languages may be seen either as an implementation of Codd's Data Sub-Language Alpha or an extension of that work. CSL may be assessed from two points of view: firstly whether the language is complete, and secondly whether it provides a suitable interface for a usable data base system.

Completeness

In his paper 'Relational Completeness of Data Base Sub-Languages' (see CODD 5) Codd proposed that a language is relationally complete if it has the same level of facility as provided by the relational algebra. He also went on to show that Data Sub-Language Alpha is relationally complete, which raises the question: is CSL relationally complete? Appendix A contains not only a list of relational operators but also a clear statement showing how each of these operators is represented in CSL; it clearly demonstrates that CSL is relationally complete. When Codd designed Data Sub-Language Alpha, his clear intent was to design a language which demonstrated the power of predicate calculus; however, CSL is a language for use on a terminal, and consequently it has been necessary to extend the original design. These extensions include the functions, arithmetic expression, and macros. With these extensions it is possible to identify a new level of completeness — Arithmetic Completeness — which may be described as an ability to perform computations of any degree of complexity based on the arithmetic operations and the concept of functions. A language such as Algol 60 is arithmetically complete because it can be used to describe any level of arithmetic expression; similarly the extensions to CSL make it arithmetically complete.

Is CSL Usable?

In answering this question, it is perhaps most important to understand that CSL is only a Sub-Language which, in order to produce a complete system, needs to be embedded either with a Job Control Language or an Algorithmic Language. For this reason CSL cannot be assessed as a stand-alone user interface. Having said this the rest of this section discusses the effectiveness of CSL as a Sub-Language; the question of its position in a total user interface is discussed in the next section.

Chapter 2 identified that there are three classes of user associated with an Information System based on RDBMS, namely end-users (e.g. information specialists and parametric users), system designers, and system operators; consequently, it is important to recognize the extent to which Interactive CSL will satisfy their total needs.

From the point of view of end-users, CSL as it is currently defined has two main weaknesses.

1. There is a need to output information to and receive information from some source other than the user's terminal. Typically, this should allow output to be directed to a printer or external file, and input to be received from an external file.
2. The system should support a simple report generator which should be capable of producing not only tabular output but simple graphs.

The approach which is being adopted to handle both these problems is to add a separate Presentation clause to each of the Basic CSL Statements, thus resulting in a statement of the form:

Action Target-list Predicate Order-expression-list Presentation

Using the Presentation clause a user is able to direct his output to an external file to define his page format and heading requirements.

The facilities provided for the parametric user may be sufficient because the macros, functions, and views are certainly flexible enough to allow a system designer to build up completely new views of an existing Information System. The proposed report generator facility identified above would only serve to increase the usefulness of these interfaces.

From the point of view of system designers and operators CSL is more or less complete in the facilities it provides. From the point of view of this level of user the only problems which may arise concern the way in which the facilities are packaged.

21.6 RDBMS as a Family of Relational Products

Section 21.1 described how the current relational systems were being used to satisfy a wide spectrum of different types of Information System. For example, PRTV has been used to run a large information system for an international organization, INGRES has been used by a large number of universities and research establishments to run systems for individuals and small groups of co-workers, while System R may become an eventual replacement of IMS. From this it can be seen that the ideal relational product is one which can be used to support small personal data bases and be capable of being upgraded to the point where it will support a large corporate data base. This naturally raises the question: can a system such as RDBMS act as a basis for such a spectrum of products?

The answer to this question lies in product packaging. If the objective is to build a full-blown relational system capable of handling large Information Systems, then the easiest way to package the product is to integrate it with the Operating System and thereby produce a complete user machine capable of carrying out the job. If the objective is to build a completely stand-alone system for use by individuals and small teams, then the best solution is to add to RDBMS all those operating system facilities which are necessary to produce a complete user interface. Typical additions to the user interface are: a more sophisticated user login facility, a built in text editor, help facilities, and some system recovery mechanisms. Once this has been achieved, then, depending on the anticipated technical knowledge of a typical system user, it may be necessary to reduce the complexity of the resulting product by removing some of the schema levels. The Object, Encoded, and Software Environments may not be necessary in a simple-to-use relational product.

It is perhaps worth mentioning that IBM have already recognized the enormous potential of relational systems. In their SYSTEM 38 announced in Autumn 1978, IBM have combined the operating system with a simple relational data base management system, and there is no doubt that with the introduction of cheap micro-processors more systems of this type will undoubtedly appear.

21.7 Finale

When work started on RDBMS in 1973, the relational model of data was only two years old and there were only a few experimental systems which exploited it. One reason was that the relational data model was radically different to more traditional approaches to the data base problem, and, in the first instance, difficult to understand. Another reason was that many research workers and almost all the mainframe manufacturers and software houses were busy developing implementations of the Codasyl proposals. As time went by, the number of experimental systems proliferated but individual workers tended to emphasize different aspects of their architecture. For example, the workers at Peterlee and San Jose wrote at great length about their end-user languages at the expense of other aspects of their work, which made it very difficult to build up the experience required to specify a complete system architecture. The paper on System R (see ASTRAHAN 2), the Ph.D thesis *A Relational Data Base Management System* (see HUTT 3), and the papers on INGRES published at Berkeley in about 1976 finally heralded the period when it was at last possible to provide a statement of a complete architecture for a relational data base management system.

From their first appearance these papers showed that relational data base management systems should in theory provide enough capability to generate a complete Information System.

In and around 1976 a number of relational implementations of Information Systems were built, but most of these early systems suffered from the fact that they were either slower than a traditionally hand coded system, supported very smal quantities of data, or relied on user-written application code to cover up deficiencies.

As a result of these trials, most groups working in this area have been enhancing the capability of their systems in terms of both user facilities and performance, and this work is still progressing.

Lack of performance, and the fact that support for a relational data base management system is best treated as a total system problem, has led many workers to consider hardware solutions to their difficulties. For several years workers at ICL have been building a family of data base processors known as the Content Addressable File Store Devices (CAFS) (see COURLOURIS 1) which look as if they may provide a solution. Further to this, workers at Peterlee have discussed the possibility of using an array processor to support relation operators which may provide a different solution.

There is no doubt that the development of relational systems has reached a point where all the major facilities which need to be provided by such a system are understood. Furthermore, there exists a framework for discussing the system trade-offs which need to be taken into account when producing such a system. However, so far very few systems have actually been built and used to handle real Information Systems.

Seen in this light, this book provides a statement of the design of RDBMS. It describes the main purpose of the system, it describes its facilities, and also gives some indication of how it has been implemented. However, this can only be a description of the current position.

22

Bibliography

ABRIAL 1.
Abrial, J.R.
Data Semantics.
Proc. IFIP TC–2 Working Conference on Data Base Systems, Cargese, Corsica, April 1–5, 1974. North-Holland, 1974.

ACM 1.
Proceedings of ACM-SIGFIDET Workshops on Data Description, Access, and Control are available from ACM Order Dept, 1133 Avenue of the Americas, New York.

ALGOL 1.
Naur, P. *et al.*
Report on the Algorithmic Language ALGOL 60.
Comm. ACM., Vol. 3, No. 5, May 1960.

ANSI 1.
American Institute of Standards.
COBOL Standard.
USAS–X3.23–1968.
ANSI, 1968.

ANSI SPARC 1.
Interim Report ANSI/X3/SPARC Study Group on Data Base Systems.
ANSI, July 1977.

ANSI SPARC 2.
The ANSI/X3/SPARC DBMS Framework.
Report on the Study Group on Data Management Systems, edited by Tsichritzsis, D. and Klug, A.
ANSI, July 1977.

ASTRAHAN 1.
Astrahan, M.M. *et al.*
Concepts of a Data Independent Accessing Model.
Proc. 1972 ACM–SIGFIDET Workshop on Data Description, Access, and Control. See ACM 1.

ASTRAHAN 2.
Astrahan, M.M. *et al.*
System R: Relational Approach to Data Base Management.
ACM Transactions on Data Base Systems, Vol. 1, No. 2, June 1976.
P97–137.

BABB 1.
Babb, E.
Implementing the Join Operator in the Relational Data Base.

RADC Technical Note TN77/3, ICL Research & Development Laboratory, Stevenage, UK, 1977.

BACHMAN 1.
Bachman, C.W.
Data Structure Diagrams.
In: *Data Base,* Vol. 1, No. 2, 1969, Quarterly Newsletter of ACM SIGBDP, P4–10.

BAYER 1.
Bayer, R., McCreighton, E.
Organisation and Maintenance of Large Ordered Indexes.
Acta Informatica, Vol. 1, Fasc. 3, 1972.

BAYER 2.
Bayer, R.
Symmetric Binary B Trees: Data Structure and Maintenance Algorithms.
Acta Informatica, Vol. 1, Fasc. 4, 1972.

BENCI 1.
Benci, E., Bodart, F., Bogaert, H., Cabanes, A.
Concepts for the Design of a Conceptual Schema.
Proc. IFIP Wrking Conference on Modelling in Data Base Management Systems, Freudenstadt Jan. 5–9, 1976, North-Holland, 1976.

BOYCE 1.
Boyce, R.F., Chamberlin, D.D., King III, W.F., Hammer, M.M.
Specifying Queries as Relational Expressions: Square.
Proc. ACM SIGPLAN-SIGIR Interface Meeting, Gaithersburg, Maryland, Nov. 4–6, 1973.

BRINCH HANSEN 1.
Brinch Hansen, P.
Operating System Principles.
Prentice-Hall, 1973.

CHAMBERLIN 1.
Chamberlin, D.D., Boyce, R.F.
Sequel: A Structured English Query Language,
Proc. 1974 ACM–SIGFIDET Workshop on Data Description, Access, and Control. See ACM 1.

CHAMBERLIN 2.
Chamberlin, D.D.
Relational Data Base Systems.
Computing Surveys, Vol. 8, No. 1, March 1976.

CHEN 1.
Chen, P.P.
The Entity-Relationship Model – Towards a Unified View of Data.
Proc. International Conference on Very Large Data Bases, Framingham, Mass., USA, Sept 27–29, 1975.

CHILDS 1.
Childs, D.L.
Description of a Set Theoretical Data Structure.
FJCC., 1968.

CODASYL 1.
CODASYL.
Data Base Task Group Report 1971.
April 1971.
Available from ACM (see ACM 1) or British Computer Society.

CODASYL 2.

CODASYL.
DBTG Subset Specifications.
Oct. 1973.
Available from ACM (see ACM 1) or British Computer Society.

CODD 1.
Codd, E.F.
A Relational Model for Large Shared Data Banks.
Comm. ACM., Vol. 13, No. 6, Jun. 1970, P377–387.

CODD 2.
Codd E.F.
A Data Sub-Language based on the relational Calculus.
Proc. 1971 ACM–SIGFIDET Workshop on Data Description, Access, and Control. See ACM 1.

CODD 3.
Codd, E.F.
Normalised Data Base Structure: A Brief Tutorial.
Proc. 1971 ACM–SIGFIDET Workshop on Data Description, Access, and Control. See ACM 1.

CODD 4.
Codd, E.F.
Further Normalisation of the Data Base Relational Model.
Courant Computer Science Symposium 6, 1972, Data Base Systems, ed. R. Rustin, Prentice-Hall.

CODD 5.
Codd, E.F.
Relational Completeness of Data Base Sub-Languages.
Courant Computer Science Symposium 6, 1972, Data Base Systems, ed. R. Rustin, Prentice-Hall.

CODD 6.
Codd, E.F.
Seven Steps to Rendezvous with the Casual User.
Proc. IFIP TC–2 Working Conference on Data Base Management Systems, Cargese, Corsica, April 1–5, 1974. North-Holland, 1974.

CODD 7.
Codd, E.F.
Recent Investigations in Relational Data Base Systems.
Information Processing 1974, Proc. IFIP Congress, Aug. 5–10, 1974, Sweden. North-Holland, 1974.

CORBATO 1.
Corbato, F.J., Vyssotsky, V.B.
Introduction and Overview of Multics System.
Proc. FJCC., 1975.

COURLOURIS 1.
Courlouris, G.F., Evans, J., Mitchell, M.J.
Towards Content Addressing in Data Bases.
Computer Journal, Vol. 15, No. 2, 1972.

DAHL 1.
Dahl, O. J., Dijkstra, E.W., Hoare, C.A.R.
Structured Programming.
Academic Press, 1972.

DATE 1.
Date, C.J.
An Introduction to Data Base Systems.
Addison-Wesley, 1975.

DEARNLEY 1.
Dearnley, P.A.
A Model of a Self-Organising Data Management System.
Computer Journal, Vol. 17, No. 1, P13–16, 1974.
DEARNLEY 2.
Dearnley, P.A.
The Operation of a Self-organising Data Management System.
Proc. IFIP TC–2 Working Conference on Data Base Management System, Cargese, Corsica, April 1–5, 1974. North-Holland, 1974.
DEE 1.
Dee, E., Hilden, W., King, P.J.H., Taylor, E.
COBOL Extensions to handle a Relational Data Base.
Computer Science Dept., Birkbeck College, London, 1973.
DELOBEL 1.
Delobel, C.
An Abstract Data Model for Designing Information Systems.
Proc. Computer Systems Architecture Course, Alpe d'Huez, Dec., 1972.
DELOBEL 2. See ADIBA 1.
DIJKSTRA 1.
Dijkstra, E.W.
The Structure of the 'THE' Multi-programming System.
Comm. ACM., Vol. 11, No. 5, May 1968, pp.341–346.
DIJKSTRA 2.
Dijkstra, E.W.
A Discipline of Programming.
Prentice-Hall, 1976.
FLORENTIN 1.
Florentin, J.J.
Consistency Auditing of Data Bases.
Computer Science Dept., Birkbeck College, London, 1972.
FLOYD 1.
Floyd, R.W.
Syntactic Analysis and Operator Precedence.
JACM, Vol. 10, July 1963, pp.316–333.
FOX 1.
Fox, A.J., Edwards, P.W.
Implementation of a Syntax Driven Interpreter for Data Base Retrieval.
Computer Journal, 1969.
GHOSH 1.
Ghosh, S.P., Astrahan, M.M.
A Translator Optimiser for obtaining answers to Entity Set Queries from an Arbitrary Access Path Network.
Information Processing 1974, Proc. IFIP Congress, Aug 5–10, 1974, Sweden. North-Holland.
GOLDSTEIN 1.
Goldstein, R.L., Strnad, A.L.
The Macaims Data Base Management System.
Proc. 1971 ACM-SIGFIDET Workshop on Data Description, Access, and Control. See ACM 1.
GOOS 1.
Goos, G., Hartmaris, J.
Compiler Construction.
Lecture Notes in Computer Science 21. Springer Verlag 1974.

GRIES 1.
Gries, D.
Compiler Construction for Digital Computers.
J. Wiley & Sons, New York, 1969.

GRINDLEY 1.
Grindley, K.
Systematics – A New Approach to Systems Analysis.
McGraw-Hill, 1975.

GUDES 1.
Gudes, E., Reiter, A.
On Evaluating Boolean Expressions.
Software Practice and Experience, Vol. 3, 1973, pp.345–350.

HALL 1.
Hall, P.A.V.
Optimisation of a Single Relational Expression in a Relational Data Base Management System.
IBM Scientific Centre Report UKSC 0076, June 1975.

HALL 2.
Hall, P.A.V., Hitchcock, P., Todd, S.J.P.
An Algebra of Relations for Machine Computations.
IBM Scientific Centre Report UKSC 0066, Jan. 1975.

HEATH 1.
Heath, I.J.
Unacceptable File Operations in a Relational Data Base.
Proc. 1971 ACM–SIGFIDET Workshop on Data Description, Access, and Control. See ACM 1.

HOARE 1.
Hoare, C.A.R.
Quicksort.
Computer Journal, Vol. 5, No. 1, 1962, p.10.

HOPGOOD 1.
Hopgood, F.R.A.
Compiling Techniques.
American Elsevier Inc., New York, 1969.

HUTT 1.
Hutt, A.T.F.
A Data Base Approach to System Architecture.
Information Processing 1974, Proc. IFIP Congress, Aug. 5–10, 1974, Sweden.
North-Holland.

HUTT 2.
Hutt, A.T.F.
RDBMS Reference Manual.
Southampton University, 1975.

HUTT 3.
Hutt, A.T.F.
A Relational Data Base Management System.
Doctoral Thesis, Southampton University, 1976.

HUTT 4.
Hutt, A.T.F.
Data Mapping Again.
Software Practice and Experience, Vol. 8, 1978, pp.483–493.

HUTT 5.
Hutt, A.T.F.

A Compiler Model for a Relational Data Base Management System.
Software Practice and Experience, Vol. 9, 1979, pp.157–169.

HUTT 6.
Hutt, A.T.F.
Organising the Description of a Relational Data Base.
Software Practice and Experience, Vol. 9, 1979, pp.361–368.

IBM 1.
APL/360 Primer.
IBM Ref. GH20–0689–2.

IBM 2.
Fortran (H) Compiler Programming Logic Manual.
IBM Ref. 428–6800.

IBM 3.
OS/360 Data Management Services Guide.
IBM Ref. GC26–3746.

IBM 4.
Information Management System/360 Version 2
System/Application Design Guide.
IBM Ref. SH20–0910.

ICL 1.
Operating System George 3 & 4.
Tech. Pub. 4267, International Computers Limited, ICL House, Putney, London SW15, UK, 1971.

ICL 2.
System B Design.
Tech. Pub. 6102, International Computers Limited, ICL House, Putney, London SW15, UK, 1974.

ICL 3.
System B Capabilities.
Tech. Pub. 6113, International Computers Limited, ICL House, Putney, London SW15, UK, 1974.

ICL 4.
1900 House Keeping System.
Tech. Pub. 4207, International Computers Limited, ICL House, Putney, London SW15, UK, 1974.

ICL 5.
COBOL.
Tech. Pub. 4427, International Computers Limited, ICL House, Putney, London SW15, UK, 1976.

ICL 6.
Data Dictionary System.
Tech. Pub. 6504, International Computers Limited, ICL House, Putney, London SW15, UK, 1978.

ICL 7.
IDMS Integrated Database Management System.
International Computers Limited, ICL House, Putney, London SW15, UK, 1976.

KAY 1.
Kay, M.J.
An Assessment of the Codasyl DDL for use with a Relational Subschema.
Proc. IFIP TC–2 Special Working Conference on 'A Technical In-depth Evaluation of the DDL', Namur, Belgium, Jan. 13–17, 1975.

KING 1. See DEE 1.

KLEENE 1.
Kleene, S.C.
An Introduction to Meta Mathematics.
North-Holland, Amsterdam, 1952.
KNUTH 1.
Knuth, D.E.
Art of Computer Programming, Vol. 1 – *Fundamental Algorithms.*
Addison-Wesley Pub. Co., 1968.
KORFHAGE 1.
Korfhage, R.R.
Logic and Algorithms.
John Wiley & Sons, New York & London, 1966.
KOWALSKI 1.
Kowalski, R.
Predicate Logic as a Programming Language.
Information Processing 1974, Proc. IFIP Congress, Aug. 5–10, 1974, Sweden.
North-Holland, 1975.
LANGEFORS 1.
Langefors, B.
Theoretical Analysis of Information Systems.
Student Literature, 1966.
LINDSEY 1.
Lindsey, C.H., Meulen, S.G. van der.
Informal Introduction to Algol 68.
North-Holland, 1971.
MARGARIS 1.
Margaris, A.
First Order Mathematical Logic.
Blaisdell Publishing Co., A Division of Ginn & Co., London, 1967.
MCDONALD 1.
McDonald, N., Stonebraker, M., Wong, E.
Preliminary Design of Ingres – Part 1 Query Language, Data Storage and Access.
Memorandum No. ERL–M435, University of California, Berkeley, USA, April, 1974.
MACGREGOR 1.
MacGregor, D.R., Thompson, R.G., Dawson, W.A.
High Performance Hardware for Data Base Systems.
Systems for Large Data Base Systems. North-Holland, 1977.
MCKEENAN 1.
McKeenan, W.M.
Programming Language Design.
Compiler Construction, Lecture Notes in Computer Science 21. Springer Verlag, 1974, pp.514–524.
MOULIN 1.
Moulin, P., Randon, J., Teboul, M. *et al.*
Conceptual Model as a Data Base Design Tool.
Proc. IFIP TC–2 Working Conference on Modelling in Data Base Systems, Freudenstadt, West Germany, Jan. 5–9, 1976. North-Holland.
NIJSSENS 1.
Nijssens, G.M.
DDL Illustrated with Data Structure Diagrams.
Proc. IFIP TC–2 Working Conference 'A Technical In-depth Evaluation of the

DDL', Namur, Belgium, Jan. 13–17, 1975. North-Holland.
NOTLEY, M.G.
The Peterlee IS/1 System.
IBM UK Scientific Centre Report UKSC–008, March 1972.
PALERMO 1.
Palermo, F.P.
A Data Search Problem.
Fourth International Symposium on Computer and Information Science, Miami Beach, Dec. 14–16, 1972. Academic Press.
PEARSON 1.
Pearson, D.J.
CADES – Computer Aided Design and Evaluation System.
Computer Weekly, Sept. 8, 1973.
PECK 1.
Peck, J.E.L.
Algol 68 Implementation.
Proc. IFIP Working Conference on Algol 68 Implementation, Munich, July 20–24, 1970. North-Holland, 1971.
PIROTTE 1.
Pirotte, A., Woden, P.
A Comprehensive Formal Query Language for a Relational Data Base : FOL.
Report 2743, M.B.L.E. Research Laboratories, Brussels, Belgium, 1974.
ROBINSON 1.
Robinson, J.A.
Mechanising Higher Order Logic.
Machine Intelligence 4, pp.151–170, Edinburgh University Press, 1969.
ROSENBLOOM 1.
Rosenbloom, P.C.
The Elements of Mathematical Logic.
Dover Publications, New York, 1950.
SAMSO 1.
SAMSO Project.
Space Programming Machine Architecture Study, Space and Missile Systems Org., US Air Force Systems Command, Air Force Unit Post Office, Los Angeles, Cal., 30045, June 1972.
SENKO 1.
Senko, M.E., Altman, E.B., Astrahan, M.M., Fender, P.L.
Data Structures and Accessing in Data Base Systems.
IBM Systems Journal, 1973.
SENKO 2.
Senko, M.E.
The DDL in the Context of a Multi-Level Structured Description.
Proc. IFIP TC–2 Special Working Conference 'An In-depth Evaluation of the DDL', Namur, Belgium, Jan. 13–17, 1975. North-Holland.
SENKO 3.
Senko, M.E.
DIAM as a detailed example of the ANSI SPARC Architecture.
Proc. IFIP TC–2 Working Conference on Modelling in Data Base Management Systems, Freudenstadt, West Germany, Jan. 5–9, 1976.
SHARMAN 1.
Sharman, G.C.H.
A New Model of Relational Data Base and High Level Languages.
Technical Report TR.12.136, IBM Hursley Park Laboratory, England, Feb., 1975.

SIMPSON 1.
Simpson, P.
Compact Form of One Track Analyser.
Computer Journal, Vol. 12, pp.223–243, 1969.
SMITH 1.
Smith, M.S., Ghang, P. Y-T.
Optimising the Performance of a Relational Algebra Interface.
Comm. ACM., Vol. 18, No. 10, Oct., 1975.
SNOWDEN 1.
Snowden, R.W.
Interactive use of a Computer in the Preparation of Structured Programs.
Thesis, University of Newcastle, UK, 1974.
STAMPER 1.
Stamper, R.K.
The LEGOL Project – A Survey.
IBM Scientific Report No. 81, IBM Scientific Centre, Peterlee, Co. Durham, 1976.
STOCKER 1.
Stocker, P.M., Dearnley, P.A.
Self-Organising Data Management Systems.
Computer Journal, Vol. 16, No. 2, pp.100–105, 1973.
STRNAD 1.
Strnad, A.L.
The Relational Approach to the Management of Data Bases.
Information Processing 1971, North-Holland, 1972, pp.901–904.
SUNGREN 1.
Sungren, B.
An Infological Approach to Data Bases.
Urnval No. 7, University of Stockholm, 1973.
TEICHROEW 1.
Teichroew, D., Hersey, E.A., Bastarache, M.J.
An Introduction to PSL/PSA.
ISDOS Working Paper No. 86, Dept. of Industrial & Operations Engineering, College of Engineering, University of Michigan, Ann Arbor, USA, March 1974.
TEICHROEW 2.
Teichroew, D., Berg, D.L.R., Hersey, E.A.
An Example of the Use of PSL using Top-down Analysis.
ISDOS Working Paper No. 74, Dept. of Industrial & Operations Engineering, College of Engineering, University of Michigan, Ann Arbor, USA, April 1974.
TITMAN 1.
Titman, P.J.
An Experimental Data Base System using Binary Relations.
Proc. IFIP TC–2 Working Conference on Data Base Management Systems, Cargese, Corsica, April 1–5, 1974. North-Holland, 1975.
TODD 1.
Todd, S.J.P.
Implementation of Join Operator in Relational Data Bases.
Tech. Note TN15, IBM Scientific Centre, Peterlee, Co. Durham, 1975.
TODD 2.
Todd, S.J.P.
PTRV : A Technical Overview.
IBM Scientific Centre Report UKSC 0075, May 1975.

WICHMAN 1.
Wichman, B.A.
Assessment of Five Algol Compilers.
Computer Journal, Vol. 15, No. 1, pp.8–12, 1971.
WIJNGAARDEN 1.
Wijngaarden, A. Van *et al.*
Report on the Algorithmic Language ALGOL 68.
Mathematisch Centrum, Amsterdam, 1969.
WILKES 1.
Wilkes, M.V.
The Outer and Inner Syntax of a Programming Language.
Technical Memorandum No. 67/4, University Mathematical Laboratory, Cambridge, July 1967.
WIRTH 1.
A Programming Language Pascal.
ACTA Informatica, Vol. 1, No. 1, pp.35–63, 1971.
WOODWARD 1.
Woodward, P.M.
ALGOL 68 Users Guide.
HMSO, London, 1974.
WOODWARD 2.
Woodward, P.M., Wetherall, P.M., Gorman, B.
Official Definition of CORAL 66.
HMSO, London, 1970.

Appendix A : The Relational Operators

These are mathematical operators which take as operands one or two entity sets and produce a new entity set. The operators supported by RDBMS are:

1. Permutation
2. Projection
3. Selection
4. Restriction
5. Join
6. Division
7. Union
8. Intersection
9. Difference

These operators may be defined rigorously. However, it is sufficient for our purposes to explain their operation by using examples.

A.1 Permutation

Given a single entity set such as PRODUCT, say, then the permutation operator allows a user to change the ordering of the attributes in the entity set without affecting the contents or ordering of the entities. The diagrams below show the entity set PRODUCT, a permutation of the entity set, and the CSL statement needed to generate that permutation.

PRODUCT

CODE	NAME	PRICE
102	INK	0.24
103	INK	0.24
110	RULER	1.00

A permutation of PRODUCT

PRICE	CODE	NAME
0.24	102	INK
0.24	103	INK
1.00	110	RULER

– READ PRODUCT.(PRICE, CODE, NAME);

A.2 Projection

Given a single entity set such as PRODUCT, say, the projection operator allows a user to define a new entity set which contains a subset of the attributes.

The entities selected for the new entity set are all unique; duplicate rows are automatically suppressed. The diagram below shows the entity set PRODUCT, two projections of the entity set, and CSL statements used to generate them.

PRODUCT

CODE	NAME	PRICE
102	INK	0.24
103	INK	0.24
110	RULER	1.00

First projection

CODE	PRICE
102	0.24
103	0.24
110	1.00

– READ PRODUCT.(CODE, PRICE);

Second Projection

NAME
INK
RULER

– READ PRODUCT,NAME;

A.3 Selection

Given a single entity set such as PRODUCT, say, then the selection operator allows a user to define a new entity set by defining a selector which selects entities from the old entity set. The attributes for the new entity set are exactly the same as those of the original entity set; the entities for the entity set are all those entities of the existing entity set which satisfy the selector.

The diagram below shows the entity set PRODUCT, the effect of the selection operator, and the CSL statement used to generate it.

PRODUCT

CODE	NAME	PRICE
102	INK	0.24
103	INK	0.24
110	RULER	1.00

Selector: PRODUCT.CODE>103

CODE	NAME	PRICE
110	RULER	1.00

–READ PRODUCT SUCHTHAT PRODUCT.CODE>103;

A.4 Restriction

Given two entity sets A and B which each have an attribute defined over the same domain or a compatible domain, then the restriction operator allows the user to create a new entity set which contains a subset of the entities of entity set A providing they satisfy a selection criteria involving entities from entity set B. The diagrams below show how it is possible to create a variant of the entity set PRODUCT providing that values of PRODUCT CODE match values of PRODUCTCODE in the entity set ORDERFROM.

PRODUCT

CODE	NAME	PRICE
102	INK	0.24
103	INK	0.24
110	RULER	1.00

ORDERFROM

PRODUCT CODE	CUSTOMER CODE	QUANTITY
102	1	10
103	1	30
102	2	10

Selector PRODUCT.CODE = ORDERFROM.PRODUCTCODE

CODE	NAME	PRICE
102	INK	0.24
103	INK	0.24

–READ PRODUCT SUCHTHAT PRODUCT.CODE = ORDERFROM.PRODUCTCODE;

A.5 Join

Given two entity sets A and B which each have an attribute which is defined over the same or a compatible domain, then the join operator allows the user to create a new entity set which contains a combination of entities from both the entity sets, the choice of entities being controlled by a selection expression. In simple terms the operator works by linking each entity of A to each entity of B (e.g. producing the Cartesian product of A and B) and then applying the selection expression to the result. The example below shows how it is possible to join together the entity sets PRODUCT and ORDERFROM on the basis that values of PRODUCT CODE in the two entity sets match.

PRODUCT

CODE	NAME	PRICE
102	INK	0.24
103	INK	0.24
110	RULER	1.00

ORDERFROM

PRODUCT CODE	CUSTOMER CODE	QUANTITY
102	1	10
103	1	30
102	2	10

Join condition: PRODUCT.CODE = ORDERFROM.PRODUCTCODE

CODE	NAME	PRICE	PRODUCT CODE	CUSTOMER CODE	QUANTITY
102	INK	0.24	102	1	10
102	INK	0.24	102	2	10
103	INK	0.24	103	1	30

```
–READ PRODUCT,ORDERFROM SUCHTHAT PRODUCT.CODE*=
 ORDERFROM.PRODUCTCODE;
```

A.6 Division

Given a single entity set, then the user may wish to confirm that all the rows in the table satisfy a given condition. The user achieves this by defining a new entity set which if the condition is true will contain exactly the same contents as the original entity set, otherwise it will be empty. The example below shows how it is possible to use division to verify that the entity set PRODUCT satisfies two conditions.

PRODUCT

CODE	NAME	PRICE
102	INK	0.24
103	INK	0.24
110	RULER	1.00

Condition 1: All P ∈ PRODUCT (P.CODE > 100) results in the table containing the same values

```
–READ PRODUCT SUCHTHAT ALL P FROM PRODUCT (P.CODE>100);
```

Condition 2: Some P ∈ PRODUCT (P.CODE < 100) results in an empty table

```
–READ PRODUCT SUCHTHAT SOME P FROM PRODUCT (P.CODE<100);
```

A.7 Union

Given two entity sets which are defined over the same description, then the union operator allows a user to combine the entities of the two entity sets to create a single entity set. Duplicate entities are automatically suppressed. The example below shows the use of this operator.

PRODUCT 1

CODE	NAME
101	INK
103	RULER
104	PENCILS
106	RUBBER

PRODUCT 2

CODE	NAME
100	PENS
101	INK
105	GLUE

PRODUCT

CODE	NAME
100	PENS
101	INK
103	RULER
104	PENCILS
105	GLUE
106	RUBBER

This is achieved by using two statements

```
–COPY PRODUCT FROM PRODUCT1;
–COPY PRODUCT FOR WRITEACCESS FROM PRODUCT2;
```

A.8 Intersection

Given two entity sets which are defined over the same description, then the intersection operator allows a user to create a new entity set which contains all those entities which appear in both sets. The example shows the use of this operation.

PRODUCT 1

CODE	NAME
101	INK
103	RULER
104	PENCILS
106	RUBBERS

PRODUCT 2

CODE	NAME
100	PENS
101	INK
105	GLUE

PRODUCT

CODE	NAME
101	INK

```
–COPY PRODUCT FROM PRODUCT1 SUCHTHAT
        PRODUCT1.CODE = PRODUCT2.CODE
```

A.9 Difference

Given two entity sets which are defined over the same description, the difference operator allows a user to create a new entity set which contains all those entities which appear in one of the sets but not both. The example shows the use of this operator.

PRODUCT 1

CODE	NAME
101	INK
103	RULER
104	PENCILS
106	RUBBERS

PRODUCT 2

CODE	NAME
100	PENS
101	INK
105	GLUE

PRODUCT

CODE	NAME
100	PENS
103	RULER
104	PENCILS
105	GLUE
106	RUBBERS

This requires the use of two statements

```
–COPY PRODUCT FROM PRODUCT1 SUCHTHAT
        PRODUCT1.CODE<>PRODUCT2.CODE;

–COPY PRODUCT FROM PRODUCT2 SUCHTHAT
        PRODUCT2.CODE<>PRODUCT1.CODE;
```

Index